Buddhist

Buddhist Reflections

by

Lama Anagarika Govinda

Translated by
Maurice Walshe

SAMUEL WEISER, INC.
York Beach, Maine

First published in 1991 by
Samuel Weiser, Inc.
Box 612
York Beach, Maine 03910

Library of Congress Cataloging-In-Publication Data

Govinda, Anagarika Brahmacari.
    [Buddistische Reflexionen. English]
    Buddhist reflections : the significance of the teachings and
methods of Buddhism for the West / Lama Anagarika Govinda
(Anangavajra Khamsun Wangchuk); translated by Maurice
Walshe.
        p.   cm.
    Translation of: Buddistische Reflexionen.
    1. Buddhism—Doctriens. I. Title.
BQ4165.G68   1991
294.3'42—dc20   90-40864
                                                CIP

ISBN 0-87728-714-7
MV

Text illustrations are brush drawings by Lama Anagarika Govinda
after old Tibetan stone drawings. © 1991 Lama Anagarika
Govinda.

Cover art is a painting entitled "Unfolding Mirrors,"
© 1991 Rob Schouten. Used by kind permission of the artist.

Typeset in 11 point Goudy.
Printed in the United States of America

Contents

———

Part One
The World and Its Interpretation

Part Two
The Inward Path

Part Three
Art as Creative Meditation

Part Four
The Meeting of East and West

Acknowledgments

———

The author wishes to thank all his pupils and friends in the Buddhist Religious Community Ārya Maitreya Maṇḍala, whose help made the publication of the German edition of this book possible—in particular Sumatikīrti-Suvarṇavajra, who undertook the main burden of work, and Dr. Hans and Hedwig Lauckner for their careful checking and help with proofreading. Special thanks to Anila Li Gotami Govinda for photographing my drawings.

Translator's Note

———

I am most grateful to the Ven. Advayavajra, Head of the Arya Maitreya Mandala, for kindly reading through my translation, suggesting some improvements, and supplying some references, as did Sister Vajramala of that order in Germany. In a few cases, the English originals of quotations could not be traced, and I have retranslated Lama Govinda's German version into English. Strangely enough, this applied to the few passages quoted from that prolific writer, Alan Watts, which even the knowledgeable John Snelling could not find for me—but my gratitude to him is none the less for trying.

Preface

There is a Tibetan prophecy attributed to the great Indian sage and guru Padmasambhava: "When the iron bird flies, the *Dharma* (the Buddhist teaching) will go to the west." It was mainly through European scholars that, about the end of the last and the beginning of the present century, the West came to learn about the teachings the Buddha (the Awakened One), the man who proclaimed his gospel of liberation from suffering and of the highest enlightenment, two thousand five hundred years ago.

This message was conveyed without the sword. It was laid before us for our critical judgment with the Buddha's invitation: "Come and see!" And now, without the aid of any loud missionary propaganda, Buddhism has taken root in the West, has found many youthful enthusiasts, and has become a factor in our intellectual life that can no longer be ignored. One man—from the stillness of his hermitage in the foothills of the Himālayas—who has become one of the leading Buddhist personalities in the West is Lama Anagarika Govinda. He is a recognized Buddhist scholar, interpreter and spiritual teacher, and his works—which are continually in print in German, English, French, Italian, Spanish, Portuguese, Swedish, Dutch and Japanese editions—have reached many millions of readers.

Having been raised in a European cultural background, he was—as he wrote at the age of 21 in 1919—at first an enthusiastic follower of Christianity; but soon, after wrestling intensively with the God-concept, he turned away from Christianity and found the type of religious experience that was congenial to him in Buddhism. His scientific methodology was formed by European universities, where he studied philosophy, architecture and, later, archaeology. His education was further enriched by language studies (in addition to European languages, he studied Pali, then Sanskrit, Tibetan, and the rudiments of Chinese) and also by painting.

As an active member of the Buddhist movement in the '20s (principally in Germany and Italy), in 1928 he went to Sri Lanka and joined the European monastic community there under the Ven. Nyānatiloka Thera under the name of Brahmacāri Govinda. A year later he took ordination in Burma as an Anagārika. Finally, in 1931, he met with the great Tibetan teacher Tomo Geshe Rimpoche in Darjeeling, and this meeting was to be decisive for his later life.

The Anāgarika, whose thinking had previously been entirely conditioned by the culture of Europe, now opened up fully to the Asian way of thinking that surrounded him. He registered its differentness, absorbed it and made it his own; then, in the course of many years of assimilation, he completed that integration of thinking and feeling that has now made him such a great interpreter for the occidental Buddhism of today.

He spent more than thirty years in Ceylon, Burma, Sikkim, Tibet and India—as student, scholar, university teacher, painter and hermit—before returning to the West where he initiated a course of lecturing activity that was to lead him right round the world. The essays, lectures and conversations included in this book give some understanding to the range of Lama Govinda's creative activity and influence. They are aimed at different audiences, addressing each according to its capacities, always opening up fresh perspectives. The result is a gradually unfolding survey of Buddhism for the present age, one not caught up in the dogmatic disputes of the schools.

This book is distinguished not only by its convincing scholarship, the author's narrative skill, and the brilliant synopses that derive from the wisdom of a life fulfilled and rich in activity and contemplation alike—it is above all the compassionate understanding and the responsible humanity that appeal so directly to us—even when the author shows himself opposed to all dogmatically fixed positions, some hallowed by long tradition.

—Advayavajra

Introduction
The Buddha's Message for the World
of Today and Tomorrow

W hen the Buddha, after his enlightenment, entered the Deer Park at Benares, he was just a solitary wanderer— a pilgrim like thousands of others who daily visited the holy city. He had been deserted by his friends and given up by his family. No one knew of his great victory, there was no visible sign to convince the world. And even if it had been possible to impress those about him by signs and wonders, the Buddha would have been the last to use such means. And yet, this solitary pilgrim brought into the world, concealed in his heart, the light of an understanding that was to change the face of one part of the human race.

It is a good thing to bear in mind that those who have proved stronger than the might of kings with their armies, stronger than time and even than death, have also wandered, just like so many of us, alone and deserted in the unpitying desert of *Saṁsāra*.[1] This can give us the

---

[1]*Saṁsāra* is often misleadingly translated as "world of transmigration" or "phenomenal world." But *saṁsāra* is not "world" in the ordinary sense, but the subjectively experienced world of unenlightened beings. *Nirvāṇa* as the opposite of *saṁsāra* is therefore neither a place nor a metaphysical principle, but the state of experience of one who is fully enlightened and who recognizes the world, without passion, for what it really is. Thus,

assurance that we, too, bear the seed of enlightenment within us, and that it depends on our efforts alone whether we bring it to germination and allow its fruits to develop. This faith in our own indwelling powers is the only faith that the Buddha asks of us. The Buddha's first words after his enlightenment were:

Apārutā tesam amatassa dvārā;
ye sotavanto, pamuñcantu saddham.

Opened are the doors of the Deathless *(amatassa)*;
Let those who have ears to hear put forth faith.[2]

That the Buddha did not expect to find this "faith" in the easy credulity of the masses is shown by the fact that he made the first proclamation of his teaching to those former companions who had lost their trust in him, and who regarded him with the deepest suspicion. When they saw the Buddha approaching through the Deer Park, they decided neither to greet him nor to make him welcome, but to treat him with contemptuous indifference. But what happened? As the Buddha came nearer, one after the other rose and went toward him. His face showed his great spiritual victory, his eyes revealed the profound brilliance of one who has passed through the mysteries of life and death and overcome; his whole personality radiated bliss, as if the inner light shone through the outer form.

Never did the expression and behavior of a human being reveal a greater sincerity and assurance, born of the wish to proclaim to others this supreme realization, for the benefit of all living beings, than did those of the Buddha in that historic moment. It was this perfect oneness of his whole being that gave his words the power of conviction which

---

nirvāṇa is realized as liberation from greed, hate and delusion, whereby one is simultaneously filled with boundless compassion for all living beings trapped in the cycle of birth and death.

[2]The translation of the last words of this passage, which occurs in several places in the Pali Canon (e.g., *Dīgha Nikāya* 14.3.7) *pamuñcantu saddham*, has been disputed, but that given by Anagarika Govinda is certainly correct. The footnote on page 6 of F.L. Woodward's *Some Sayings of the Buddha*, giving a contrary opinion, is wrong. *Tr.*

was to endure for thousands of years, evoking an echo in us as strong as
if they had only just been spoken. The bliss that the Buddha enjoyed
silently in the solitude of the forests during the weeks that passed after
his enlightenment is contained in his solemn pronouncement to the
five ascetics in the Deer Park:

Lend an ear, o monks!
Deliverance from death has been found.

It is strange how this happy message has been almost forgotten by
Buddhists today, especially by those in the West who have tried to read
pessimism or a life-denying rationalism into the Buddha's teaching. But
this very first utterance of the Buddha's, beginning with such words of
triumph, clearly shows the basic position of his teaching: the idea of a
middle path equidistant from a life of selfish enjoyment or one of self-
torment and misery. Being freed from these extremes, it gives vision to
the eye and clarity to the mind, leading to peace, understanding and
enlightenment.

The requirement to avoid extremes applies to practical life as well
as to that of the mind, and it led to a new way of thinking, in fact to
a new system of logic. From it there were to arise the great philosophies
of Asia, the core of which is the idea of the conditionality of all things.
Rightly understood, these ideas could be of immense value for our world
today. But as yet we are far from an attitude of understanding that would
lead to a living kinship with all that breathes and to the creation of
genuine tolerance.

The fact that tolerance can go hand in hand with utter conviction
has been demonstrated through the practice of the middle way in the
history of Buddhism. And thus I believe that Buddhism is especially
suited to the task of creating peace and harmony in the modern world.

Just as a doctor does not enquire about a patient's religious beliefs,
but only about his sickness, so, too, the Buddha investigates the suffering
of mankind. Having analyzed this, he recognizes the cause and prescribes
the medicine for its cure: the Noble Eightfold Path which leads to

mental health and harmony and, ultimately, to *Nirvāṇa*. The steps of this path are:

1) Perfect View (*sammā diṭṭhi*)
2) Perfect Intention (*sammā sankappa*)
3) Perfect Speech (*sammā vācā*)
4) Perfect Action (*sammā kammanta*)
5) Perfect Livelihood (*sammā ājīva*)
6) Perfect Effort (*sammā vāyāma*)
7) Perfect Mindfulness (*sammā sati*)
8) Perfect Concentration (*sammā samādhi*).

There is nothing on this path which could not be accepted by any individual or any religion. It contains only what is found in all religions and avoids anything that might cause dissension.

In Buddhism there is no "thou shalt. . ." or "thou shalt not. . .," but only "I make a decision," "I promise myself," "I undertake," and "I am prepared to take the consequences." There is no room for sin and damnation. As long as you do not yet have the proper insight into the laws of life and the nature of things, you will behave foolishly and suffer in consequence. This suffering is not a humiliating punishment but the natural outcome, which teaches even more effectively than the commands of an external power.

The Buddha rejects belief in authority. He did not expect his own disciples to elevate his teaching to a dogma or set his personality up as an authority. He once asked Ānanda whether he followed him out of faith and reverence, or because he had understood and realized the teaching (*Dharma*) for himself. When Ānanda replied that he followed the Buddha's teaching because of his own insight, the Buddha expressed his satisfaction, saying that his teaching was only of use to those who did not follow it out of blind faith. The Buddha did not want his pupils merely to believe his words: these should rather form a starting-point for personal decisions and experiences. The greatest knowledge cannot help you unless you have gained it by your own effort. And therefore the showing of the path that leads to the realization of the truth is the teacher's principal task, for enlightenment arises through getting rid of the hindrances which hide the light.

Light is universal, but you must each see it with your own eyes. Buddhism is, as its name implies, the way to enlightenment. And this way was proclaimed—as had never previously occurred in the history of religion—through a teaching that was directed to everyone and not confined by the barriers of caste, race, nation or culture. In place of an arbitrarily ruling god who gave vent to his favor or anger at the beings created by him, or of a blind fate, the Buddha pointed to a rule of law, valid alike for macrocosm and microcosm, which places individual responsibility on human beings, and which—when properly applied—enables you all to develop your latent powers to the full.

This teaching of the Buddha received, in the course of hundreds and thousands of years, specific forms conditioned by the cultural, climatic, and historical situation in the various countries that received the *Dharma*, whether in the countries of south and east Asia or in the Far East. Each one of these tendencies or schools has stressed and assimilated certain essential features of the *Dharma*, without ever making a complete breach from their own original culture.

We in the West can and must learn from these now traditional schools without imitating them. It would be an anachronism it we were simply to take over lock, stock, and barrel the intellectual products of centuries of experiences that were produced under entirely different cultural conditions, just as it would be senseless to accept the results of thought based on experiences we have not ourselves had. In other words, it is not sufficient to identify emotionally with one or another phase of Buddhism. Just as the embryo in the womb repeats the phases of human development in abridged form, so we must repeat the spiritual development inherent in the Buddhist doctrine at all levels of our own existence.

Intuition, the power of empathy, and sympathetic experience must play a large part in this. As long as intuition does not find clear expression, it cannot influence our lives, and runs the risk of being swallowed up in a mist of vague feelings and dreamy imaginings and visions, for the intuitive power cannot work if it is not formed and directed. On the other hand, thoughts, recognitions, or truths that have been developed merely on an intellectual level must find confirmation in experience, must by their immediacy become part of the lived and experienced world of reality, if they are to have the power to transform our lives and reform us in our deepest essence.

People who always dwell in the realm of thought remain the prisoners of their mental constructions, trapped in a net that draws ever tighter around them. On the other hand, those who live in their own more or less vague intuitions (for what is the criterion of a true intuition, what distinguishes it from a mere illusion?) are likewise prisoners of their passing emotions and sensations. People who are able to harmonize thinking and intuition make the best use of both: they have the liberty of an intuition not hemmed in by any conceptual restrictions, and the creative joy of being able to fit together the bricks of intuitive experience to create the mighty structure of an all-embracing world-view—a structure that is continually growing, and whose keystone and crowning glory will be the shining jewel of perfect enlightenment when the building is completed.

This act of assimilation of the Buddha-Dharma is a creative process which leads to a re-creation. If Buddhism is to take root in the West, we must play our part in the further development of the *Dharma*, thus infusing it with fresh blood and life. The doctrine of the Buddha is not a belief based religion but one of experience and recognition—an experience which must be born anew in each individual. Furthermore, we must liberate ourselves from the domination of traditional concepts which can easily lead to dogmatic ossification. Another danger we must guard against is that of being misled by resemblances to various formulations of Kant, Schopenhauer or St. Francis of Assisi, of Meister Eckhart and the Christian mystics, modern existentialists, or modern science and psychology, and throwing everything into the melting-pot of an all-embracing "comparative religion" that basically believes in everything and nothing, calling this tolerance. We can respect any form of spiritual expression—whether we personally accept it or not—as one manifestation of the multiplicity of life's forms, in the same way as in a garden we can admire the variety of the plants on display without basing our judgment on personal preferences. Thus our minds will remain alert and open, ready to accept any manifestation, but at the same time we are able to distinguish the genuine from the artificially created.

Accordingly we should avoid joining in the currently fashionable syncretism which, for instance, equates *Nirvāṇa* with "eternal bliss" in order to prove that "all religions are really the same." We should also guard against the idea of the "holy one" as a man who has perfected himself so as to be no more capable of development, petrified in his perfection and having shaken off all humanity and—filled with omniscience—incapable of any human emotion, except perhaps a vague compassion for the crowd of fools surrounding him. A "holy one" incapable of further development is spiritually dead, as is everything that cuts itself off from the law of the living flux and flow, of the possibility of living transformation.

The "holy one" as we understand him, is one who has become whole, who has given up all limitations and prejudices and has become perfectly open and transparent and thus capable of accepting even the unimaginable. He is a human being open to all experience and therefore receptive to that which has not yet been experienced. Put another way, he is someone who is no longer opposed to change, transformation and mutation, and is thus in possession of the fullness of life. And if late Buddhist schools ascribe omniscience to the Buddha, we should not accept something merely because of the alleged historicity of this assertion, which conflicts with everything else that is stated in the classical texts about the Buddha's personality. For an omniscient Buddha would be a being devoid of all capacity for experience or empathy.

The Buddha was undoubtedly a man far ahead of his time but who, in order to make himself understood, had to express himself in terms of his time. He was a man who retained his liveliness of mind and was capable of clearly seeing all the problems of his time. But every age has its own problems, and the Buddha did not claim to be able to solve problems that had not arisen. On the other hand, he was no mere collector of intellectual knowledge, the piling-up of which can never make one into a cultured person, since we can only speak of true culture when what one knows has been experienced and what one has experienced has shaped one's life.

If the Buddha gave a special and central role in his teaching to ignorance (*avidyā*), we must always remember that this ignorance (or nescience) does not mean a lack of factual information, but rather the *ignoring* of our inner experience, the non-recognition of our own nature, occasioned by our postulation of a separate and unchanging ego.

This ego-concept—which deludes us with the idea of an eternal, eternally self-identical ego, self or soul—is continually deduced from the experience of the centralization of every living process. But if we observe life or nature, we find that it is really a matter of the focusing of the momentarily arising contents of consciousness—in other words, a *process* of continuous change.

The more our consciousness occupies itself with thoughts based on mere conceptual abstractions, the less we live in the world of reality, i.e., the world of immediate experience. Concepts can be moved about like the pieces in a chess game, according to the rules of the game that we call logic. But there are various board games all with different sets of rules, and also different systems of logic, each consistent in itself, so that it is not possible to say that one is right or the other wrong.

Therefore, if we work with concepts in order to make ourselves understood, we must always remember to be clear about the experience-contents that underlie them, and take account of these if we don't want to get stuck in the hollow metaphysical speculation that the Buddha always rejected. For this reason we must be especially critical of the terms used in Western languages as equivalents of the traditional Sanskrit or Pali expressions for the explanation of the Buddha-Dharma. Every single concept that we have previously accepted unchecked must be strictly examined. As Buddhists, it is incumbent on us to experience for ourselves what the Buddha taught, and therefore all concepts must again be made into what they once were—fingers pointing the way.

Consider, for example, the Buddhist concept of *anicca* (sanskrit *anitya*), which has always been considered a negative factor, rendered by various expressions as "impermanent." But *anicca* denotes not only impermanence but also arising, fresh beginning, growth. *Nicca* means eternal, permanent, and *a-nicca* is non-eternal, impermanent. Because we have raised the concept of eternity to an ideal—without realizing that we have been misled by a concept created by our abstracting intellect and without anything corresponding to it in reality—we cling to this concept, and interpret all forms of change as transience or annihilation. But change—or rather transformation—is not only annihilation, it is also becoming, birth or rebirth, the transformation into something new. For if old conditions are not removed, nothing new could come to be. If suffering were eternal, there would be no liberation, no overcoming of suffering. And finally, is happiness imaginable without the contrary emotion? Is not eternal bliss a contradiction in terms?

The emotion of happiness is based on change and variety; otherwise we would live in a state of eternal boredom—which is probably the most severe form of suffering. We seek to avoid change by clinging to things and conditions. We are like the miser who sits on his moneybags and starves to death. The fact that things are not eternal should teach us not to clamor for them, but simply to enjoy them while they are there without clinging. It is not impermanence that is the cause of our suffering, but our attachment, our clinging, our thirst (*taṇhā*). In other words, it is not *anicca* that causes us to suffer, but our desire to possess. That is why people retire into solitude and become hermits or *sanyāsins*. They want to liberate themselves from all possessions. Those who succeed seem like saints to us. But they are only saints if their minds have become clear and transparent—not if they believe they have nothing more to learn! Whoever has lost the capacity for growth is dead. For standing still *is* death.

The wise person is not he or she who knows many things, but the one who is always ready to expand that knowledge. Ignorance consists of a mind that is closed and unprepared to take in anything fresh—irrespective of the amount of factual knowledge it has stored up. Wisdom, on the other hand, is the sign of an open mind, and *Nirvāṇa*, which is freedom from hatred, greed and delusion and from all prejudices, means total receptivity to everything that life has to offer.

Part One

THE WORLD AND
ITS INTERPRETATION

The World and Reality

———

B ecause of the scientific progress in the present century, we may question the basis of our experience of the world, or the possibility of objectivity in our perception of things. In the external world, the only reality we can really speak of is the world of our experience. It is conditioned by our organs of perception and the nature of our consciousness. Accordingly, we can only speak of a subjectively-experienced world, the world of our imagination. Even the methodology of scientific investigation does not basically change this fact: in the last analysis this merely extends the range of our sense-organs. In saying this, we are not in any way questioning the existence of the world, but merely pointing out that the world as we experience it consists of action; it is not a question of some kind of "being." In other words, the world has a dynamic, not an objective character.

The objective reality of the world can be compared to the colors of the rainbow. The colors are perceived with the senses, but neither the colors nor the rainbow as a whole have any substance. Just as the sun is the cause of all colors, so too the consciousness that perceives the world is the cause of our perception of form and substance. We only see the various colors of the rainbow when we turn away from the source of light and look "without," much the same as we perceive a multiplicity of things when we look outward, away from the center, the inner part of consciousness.

If we turn to the source of light or of consciousness, then the variety of colors and the world of things disappear. The colors of the rainbow join together in an arc round an invisible center which is different for every observer. Seen against a different background, the idea of the world of things is grouped round an ideal center of reference that we experience as "I." Neither the center of reference, the arc, nor its colors have any permanent substratum, and the same concept applies to consciousness—light and consciousness appear as projections against a fleeting, universal background that consists of momentarily arising and vanishing droplets (quanta and atoms). Although we observers experience ourselves as being in the center of the arc of the rainbow, the form in which it appears is not subject to our whim, but obeys rules that can be established. This rule of law within subjective systems of reference gives the world (as we perceive it at any time) the character of something apparently existing independently of ourselves. Thus the objective is not opposed to the subjective: the objective is really based upon a subjective system of laws and upon the stable relationships within that system, from which derive the "material objects" perceived by the senses and felt to be "out there" and "not me." To speak of an objectively establishable reality that exists in and by itself is a contradiction, because its functioning is merely a relationship that embraces innumerable interconnections. For example, the table I see before me is, in the form in which I see it, just as real as, or no less real than the atomic structures of which, according to the physicists, the table consists. But what *is* this table when it is viewed neither by the human eye nor by the mind of the physicist, nor from the perspective of an ant or a woodworm?

The Buddhist answer would be: in itself it is nothing, it only becomes something through the shaping, selecting, presenting consciousness. And since the kinds and possibilities of consciousness are infinite, we can go a step further and say the table is the sum of all the possible ways of perceiving it. And so, we can say with equal justification that the table in itself is nothing—and everything—meaning that there is no such thing as a table "in itself," for this "in itself" is a pure thought-construction that has no basis in experience.

It was this recognition that led the Buddha to establish his doctrine of *anicca* and *anattā*, which abolished the "thingness" of things and the "I-ness" of the individual in favor of the living dynamic of unlimited relatedness or reality in an infinite universe. The only reality that is *immediately* accessible to us is that of consciousness, without which neither this world nor the other would exist.

> Indeed I tell you that within this your body, though it is mortal
> and only a fathom long, but endowed with consciousness and
> mind, there is contained the world, the arising of the world
> and the passing of the world, and also the path that leads to
> its cessation. [1]

With this the Buddha defines the world as that which presents itself to our *consciousness* as the world—without going into the question of its objective reality. Since he rejected the concept of substance, he cannot have meant, even when he spoke of that which is material or bodily, that this was essentially opposed to the psychic; this was used rather in the sense of the inner and outer manifestations of the same process, and was of interest to him only in so far as it came into the sphere of immediate experience and thus concerned the living individual, that is, the processes of consciousness.

Our world and the reality of which religions speak are two ways of experiencing, they are not two separate worlds. These ways of experiencing are distinguished by a difference of *direction*: as worldly beings we look outward to the multiplicity of sense-objects; as religious beings we look within, to the wholeness of the origin, to becoming conscious of the universal unity amid the multiplicity of appearances.

This has to do, not with two entirely different spheres of existence, but with two different ways of regarding the same reality. The former

---

[1] *Anguttara Nikāya* IV, *Saṁyutta Nikāya* II.

way is concerned with the differentiation of a reality projected in time and space—in other words, a secondary reality—while the latter seeks for its origin and goal. But these two ways of viewing are not mutually exclusive. They are complementary because universality can only be experienced in the individual consciousness, whereas individuality can only take on meaning in the consciousness of its universal basis.

The reality of which religions speak, then, is in the Buddhist view not a beyond—a different sphere from our world, or a future heavenly world—but that which underlies daily existence, but which we cannot see as long as our eyes are only turned outward. In order to recognize that other, primary reality, therefore, all that is needed is that we should look in a different direction, "a turn-about in the deepest seat of consciousness," as it says in the *Lankavatara Sutra*.[2] This is a reorientation, a change of attitude, a turning away from the external (the realm of objectified differentiation) to the internal—the totality—the all-embracing universality of spirit.

This inner turning-about is the only miracle that the Buddha recognized. But he was not satisfied to recognize this miracle. He showed us the way by which this primary reality can be experienced and made fully conscious: it is the way of meditation, of mind-training, of concentration and of the awakening of the mental powers slumbering in all people, whereby it is possible to expand the range of conscious experience beyond purely individual and temporally conditioned bounds.

The revelations, sacred scriptures and cultic traditions of all religions are the product of these experiences, which necessarily employ symbolic language and actions in order to give expression to experiences that are alien to an outwardly-directed consciousness. Many reported experiences give the impression that that "other reality" is exempt from the laws and conditions of the reality we know. This is true, in so far as these events occur within the sphere of inner experience, in which psychic and not physical laws prevail. But the question of how far the psychic affects the physical is one that has not been solved.

---

[2]*The Lankavatara Sutra,* translated by D.T. Suzuki (London: Routledge, 1932).

Although Buddhism does not deny the possibility of certain unexplained phenomena which, because we do not understand their causes, seem like miracles to us, it considers the attempt to acquire and practice such miraculous powers to be unwholesome and a straying from the path. A Buddhist aims not at gaining paranormal powers, but at reestablishing the balance of psychic functions that have been disturbed by one-sided attention to the world of the senses, by drawing upon depth-consciousness and activating it through the recognition of its potential universality. The only miracle the Buddha recognizes is the miracle of the turning-round within, for in that lies the first step toward enlightenment, the full awakening to reality.

The Development of Consciousness and the Goal of the Path

Human beings are the product of a development of consciousness going back to a beginningless past, which embraces the potentialities of all forms of life and includes the natural development of all living beings, or else makes use of them just as the germ of new life in the womb makes use of the nutritive and formative materials of the mother's body without thereby becoming their product. We are distinguished from animals and plants not because we possess a completely different nature or some kind of supernature, but by a higher level of consciousness which is not confined to external impressions (sense-functions) and inner emotions. This consciousness possesses the capacity for reflection, for abstract thought and for returning to the origins of its own consciousness. It is here that consciousness for the first time becomes aware of itself—of its potential universality. It is only when the consciousness comes to realization that we are liberated from the cycle of death and rebirth in the knowledge of our all-embracing completeness, in the state of enlightenment.

Since the Buddha rejected the concept of substance in favor of the momentary character of all the elements of existence and the dynamic character of reality, we must take care, when he speaks of matter and corporeality, not to understand this in the sense of an essential opposition to the psychic sphere, but in the sense of inner and outer forms of appearance of one and the same process. The connection of physical and psychical, the essential unity of mental and material laws, is here proclaimed, the material representing a secondary manifestation of the mental, or a special case of psychic experience. The organism consisting of mind-and-body (nāma-rūpa) is, according to Buddhism, the product of the constructive powers (saṁskāra) of consciousness, as it were the consciousness of past moments of existence crystallized, set firm, materialized and made visible. It is consciousness that—according to the principle of the effective, intentional deed (karma)—now appears on the scene as the completed result (vipāka). Thus, the mental aspect is not merely an expression and function of material and physiological processes, the body is also a product of the mental, i.e., part of the creative powers of consciousness.

An immortality that merely consists of the continued existence of the elements and processes that make up human beings would be entirely senseless, and would not be of the slightest interest to people. In fact we might ask ourselves, what is the purpose of all individuality, of all consciousness, if the experiential contents of every existence exhausted themselves in an empty continuity of unconscious processes and an eternal succession of elementary rebirths? The retention of energy and matter may satisfy the materialist intellectually, but spiritual people, aware of a deeper past and mental continuity with its potential for growth, are not impressed by such catch-phrases.

The question whether individual human beings existed in some form before birth, and how we should imagine the nature of postmortem existence, receives a clear answer in Buddhism, based on observation and inner experience (and capable of proof through meditative experience). This answer requires neither belief in another world nor any complicated metaphysical hypotheses, but speaks for itself by its simplicity and naturalness, and thus at least has the advantage for the unprejudiced mind of being an acceptable working hypothesis.

The Buddhist answer is that birth and death represent the same process, only seen from two different sides, just as the same door can be described as an entrance or an exit, according to whether we look at it from outside or inside. In other words, we have already passed innumerable times through the gate of death and birth, and our present life *is* the "beyond," or rather the continuation of our previous and all our former existences.

However, our continued existence is not to be understood as the continuation of an eternally identical soul-substance of unique, self-contained personalities, but rather as the continuity of an ever-growing power of consciousness which changes as it grows. Every new experience contributes to the expansion of its mental horizon, to the enrichment of its inner life and of its relation to the surrounding world, until the state of complete awakening to universality—the realization of completeness—is attained. The conservation of experience-contents of the consciousness is not the same as our capacity for voluntary recall of active, peripheral awareness, whose purpose is to serve the temporally and spatially conditioned needs and aims of our present life.

The depth consciousness memory is not merely a kind of storeroom where everything rejected by superficial consciousness is indiscriminately stored up. Rather, it has the capacity to assimilate and transform all the experience-contents in such a way that, divested of all chance temporal and personal features, they become crystallized into living archetypal symbolic forms that join in a network of endless relationships, whose center is individual deep-consciousness.

Since this center is not static, but is in constant motion because of the constant stream of fresh experience-contents pouring into it, it becomes a central axis of psychic growth that persists through innumerable existences, each conditioning the next in an unbroken chain. The transition from one existence to another, according to Buddhism, has nothing to do with metempsychosis, according to which one soul-essence or entity (in the sense of a closed, self-identical soul-unit) passes from one body to another. It should be understood as a kind of shifting of the center of a power of consciousness along the axis of a line of development that is not limited by space or time. Instead of a soul-transference (metempsychosis) we can speak of soul-transformation, the only constant factor of which is the direction or axis of its growth and development, depending on internal causality. The depth of our consciousness, both according to Buddhism and to modern depth-psychology, reaches back to a beginningless past, and has the entire universe as its basis, although the only contents that come into the perceptual field are directly related to the needs of our momentary situation, or to the interests and aims of our intellect.

Just as the depth-dimension of consciousness is not temporally limited, so too the breadth-dimension—the dimension of our present space—is not limited. This means that consciousness is individually centered (and needs to be individually centered in order to become aware of itself), but that it is not identical with the boundaries of the body or of the physical organs on which it is centered.

All the distant workings of mind and psychic perception (telepathy, extrasensory perception, telekinesis, etc.) which have been proved to exist by numerous experimental tests, point to the spatially unlimited nature of consciousness. Each individual consciousness is, so to speak, a center of radiation which (to a greater or lesser degree) penetrates all other simultaneously existing centers of consciousness, lives in or with them, and can influence them to the extent of their mental-spatial development or psychic disposition.

Just as we ourselves share in the consciousness of innumerable beings, to whose vibrations we react in accordance with the receptivity and affinity of our own nature, so too at the moment of our physical death there is no need for psychic transmigration or a search for a fresh womb. Rather, within the mental space already occupied, at the very moment when one particular center drops out or becomes inadequate as a basis of consciousness, another point of necessity becomes a center of consciousness—namely that one which corresponds most closely to our deepest nature, or, put negatively, offers the least resistance. Naturally, the least resistance can occur only when no independent organism as yet exists, but only the germ, or the appropriate conditions for one. And the greatest affinity or the closest approximation can only exist where the dispositional tendencies of such a germ (or the psychic conditions for its existence) are such as to provide the being or the nature of the consciousness that seeks incarnation with the greatest possibilities of development and expression.

Thus, the disappearing here and reappearing there (as death and rebirth are often described in the Buddhist texts) are not connected with any spatial movement or transmigration of a spiritual entity, and therefore present no temporal problems. The manner of the shifting of the center of consciousness can perhaps be made more intelligible by the following comparison. Our consciousness resembles a great banyan-tree which has innumerable aerial roots. The main trunk represents the present center of consciousness of each human being, in which that being is conscious of individuality. The innumerable aerial roots represent the relations of that consciousness, radiating in all directions toward other beings or potential life-centers. The main trunk grows old, and when one day it dies, the next largest aerial root automatically becomes the main trunk and center (or ego) of the tree. In this way a shifting of center can take place without any movement of the center.

It therefore depends on the maturity and direction of consciousness in what soil we take root: in that of a higher level of reality and being (a dimension of higher consciousness), which will bring us closer to awakening to completeness—and thus to our true immortality—or in that of a greater attachment to and identification with the petty goals and limits of mortal existence, or transient personality.

Mortality and immortality are contained within human consciousness. But immortality does not mean the preservation of personality; it consists rather in the rediscovery of the components of imperishable wholeness. It is in the rediscovery that our psychic growth finds its expression, and individuality is the necessary transitional point on the way toward the experience of universality and to the awakening to the highest reality.

> Our self to live must go through a continual change and growth of form, which may be termed a continual death and a continual life going on at the same time. It is really courting death when we refuse to accept death; when we wish to give

the form of self some fixed changelessness; when the self feels
no impulse which urges it to grow out of itself; when it treats
its limits as final and acts accordingly.[3]

Growth means not only continual change and transformation, but
also continuity; and it is this continuity that gives an aim and sense to
change and transformation. Continuity cannot be achieved by clinging
to the past or what is transitory, but only through the conscious direction
of our forward march, in which, out of the organic connection with the
past, there grows an understanding of the present and a meaningful
shaping of the future. The Buddhist doctrine of rebirth, whether or not
it becomes possible to prove it scientifically or experimentally (although
much experiential evidence speaks in its favor), is therefore of the
highest importance, because it draws the individual into those larger
life-contexts, which in their totality, give individual existence meaning
and breadth. The continuity that embraces all forms of life and weaves
all experience-contents into an organic whole is that universal oceanic
consciousness (*ālaya-vijñāna*) which, includes and supports all individual
currents.

Human salvation, according to Buddhism, consists in awakening
to reality—to completeness—by the conquest of greed, hatred and
delusion. Delusion consists of an erroneous belief in a separate "I-
ness" which, in the struggle for self-preservation, hates everything that
opposes it and craves for whatever gives it pleasure or serves its selfish
ends. Only insight into the potential universality of being (and into the
laws of all life) can deliver us from this false belief and its painful
consequences. This insight can be gained by the triple path of world-
experience, world-transformation and world-conquest. The path of
world-experience culminates in the recognition of suffering and its
causes; the path of world-conquest reaches its peak when the causes
of suffering are removed by overcoming of self; the path of world-

---

[3]Rabindranath Tagore, *Sadhana: The Realisation of Life* (India: The Macmillan Company
of India, 1972), pp. 81–82.

transformation ends in the realization of that totality in which the duality of world and ego are removed. These are not three different and separate paths, they are three phases or aspects of the same path, and can be regarded as occurring either successively or simultaneously.

From early Buddhist times these three phases or aspects were recognized as the basis of the Buddhist path to deliverance, and were formulated as *paññā* (Pali, Sanskrit, *prajñā*), *sīla* and *samādhi*; *prajñā* (wisdom) being the harmony between mind (or cognitive powers) and the laws of real life; *sīla* (morality) being the harmony between convictions and actions; and *samādhi* (concentration) being the harmony between feelings, knowledge and wishes, or the integration of all creative powers. In other words, *prajñā* is the principle of understanding, *sīla* the principle of morality, and *samādhi* the unifying principle of integrated experience.[4]

Thus, the path set out by the Buddha embraces the whole human being. By the perfect and exhaustive development of mental gifts we develop the power of understanding, by the fulfillment of individual and social duties we develop ethical qualities, and by concentration on that which is within we develop those powers and qualities that bring us into contact with the "other reality." Thus it is not a question of an either/or of the outer or inner path, of a choice between the active and the contemplative life, but a both/and situation. What we have gained within must be proved without, and what we have experienced in the outer world must be worked on and transformed within.

It is not sufficient for Buddhists to simply follow the ethical demands of their religion if they have not understood their justification, or if their own conviction is not involved. The recognition of the essential truths is the first step on the religious path, and ethics is the natural consequence. Good behavior that is based merely on conformism or fear of the disapproval of others may have some temporary advantage, but has no spiritual value. On the other hand, understanding that does not bear fruit in corresponding action is not the understanding of real

---

[4]See Lama Anagarika Govinda, *The Psychological Attitude of Early Buddhist Philosophy* (London: Rider & Co., 1961).

conviction—at best it is just "considering to be true," and mere belief in this sense in regard to religious dogmas is of no more value than good conduct based on conformism.

Suffering and happiness are the touchstones of character, the positive and negative signs of experience, and test what we have come to understand. Joy and sorrow are not related to each other in terms of what is valuable and valueless: there are joys that are valueless if not positively harmful, and sorrows that are highly profitable for development, and therefore of lasting value. In general joy is a sign of harmony and sorrow a sign of disharmony, so that both are measures of right or wrong attitudes.

We suffer primarily on account of our own imperfections. By suffering, we become conscious of it, and it arouses in us the desire for perfection. In the measure that we overcome our imperfections and limitations, so we become freer and happier. Thus a perfect human being ought to be completely free from suffering and completely happy. But is it possible to feel happiness without the contrast of suffering?

The Buddhist answer is this: the perfected one does not call any suffering his or her own, but retains the capacity for compassion, as well as the joy of helping and the shared joy that arises by taking part in the well being of others. Thus, compassion becomes the *raison d'être* of the perfected person, and is one of the most essential signs of inner maturity. The further one advances in mental development, the more free he or she is from limitations, the wider becomes the spiritual horizon—and the less is it possible to seek happiness for oneself, or to seek liberation or salvation without including all other beings in it.

This has nothing to do with social welfare; it is concerned with an inner attitude, out of which actions relating to other beings arise unsought and spontaneously, just as the circumstances of life demand. And further, in the Buddhist view, there is no unchanging ego, no self-existent soul-entity (but, instead, an omni-relational soul-continuum), so any striving for "one's own" happiness or "one's own" liberation is not even theoretically possible without including all beings.

This is the basis for the *Bodhisattva* ideal of the Great Vehicle or the Great Way (*mahāyāna*) in Buddhist teaching. It is not satisfied with attaining liberation as speedily as possible for oneself by fleeing the world—as taught by the proponents of the Lesser Vehicle (hīnayāna)—but right from the start makes its aim the liberation of all beings, having as its ideal perfect enlightenment (*samyak-sambodhi*). With this attitude, our evaluation of the suffering that inheres in all life becomes different. The moment we take it willingly upon ourselves instead of fleeing it, suffering not only loses its terror and power over us, it becomes a source of new strength.

However, to take upon ourselves the suffering of the world does not mean that we should look for suffering or inflict it upon ourselves in the belief that we are thereby purified, or to do penance. This would only strengthen our egocentric attitude and lead to diseased states of mind or psychic imbalance. If we feel at one with all that lives and feel the sufferings of others as our own, we merely find our own discomfort trifling, and from this inner solidarity with others there flows a power to strive for the liberation of all beings, and to find our own liberation in this striving. To strive for the liberation of all mankind does not mean we should set ourselves up as saviors of mankind. Rather, we should regard personal spiritual and ethical perfection *sub specie aeternitatis* and put these at the service of the development of mankind. And now the question arises—is there such a thing as human development in the sense of essential human qualities, and not merely in technical know-how and intellectual understanding?

In spite of the vast expansion of technical and intellectual knowledge, and in spite of all the progress of civilization, we have still not advanced a single step beyond the wisdom of a Buddha, a Lao-tse, a Plato, a Christ or a Mohammed. And yet we cannot say that these great teachers of mankind lived in vain. Millions of people were led by them on the path of self-realization, and mighty cultures that still exist and grow today were brought into being by them. And these cultures were not only the property of certain nations and races, they are in process of becoming the possession of all mankind.

In place of the battles between various religious and cultural communities, an exchange and mutual understanding between religions is gradually taking place. Different denominations are being forced to consider the essentials of their religious life and experience, and are breaking through the incrustations of dogmatic certainties and outmoded concepts. It is here that we can speak of a development of mankind in the sense of spiritual progress. Because the experiences of past and present are becoming the common property of everyone, a maturation process is taking place in human consciousness, the consequences of which cannot yet be foreseen.

Religion and Truth

————

Religion and exact science both seek after truth, and they can both exist side by side without contradicting or hindering each other. This does not mean that the two can be fused into one, or that their statements must always agree. Their differences are based, not so much on the objects of their consideration or their aims, as on their *method* of consideration. The research method of science goes outward from within, that of spiritual investigation goes inward from without. And each can only achieve the highest results by following its own laws.

The essence of science is deduction from that which is perceptible to the senses, while that of religious understanding is the immediate experience of psychic contents, that is, those that slumber in the depths of consciousness. This immediacy of religious experience is related at a profound level with art. Just as art does not need to prove its value through agreement with scientific observations—though this may occasionally happen— so, too, religious experience has no need of confirmation by science. Science, in consequence of its dependence on external facts, will always remain an incomplete, fragmentary structure, whereas the religious worldview, like every genuine work of art born of the depths, is, on account of the intuitive character resulting from its unity of experience, always one whole, resting in itself.

Just as the spontaneity or immediacy of artistic experience is not affected by its methodical representation or the process of creation; so, too, the immediacy of religious experience is not affected if certain methods are used to produce and develop it. The discoveries of a Buddha, or of other great beings in the world of the spirit, are based on strict method and mental training, which are in their own way capable of producing observations and results that are just as objective as the methods of science. And though these results—just like those of science—are beyond the understanding and capacity of the man in the street, they should not be called transcendental, because they can be checked by anybody who has taken the trouble to develop his or her latent faculties.

The scientist requires strict training in his or her particular sphere, and the investigator of the human spirit and religious experience needs a serious course of schooling as well. Such schooling teaches that the boundaries of human consciousness are not a constant quantity, and that they do not coincide with the boundaries of thought, logic or imaginative power.[5] The religious person and the scientific thinker are not mutually exclusive. Religious experience may give new meaning and greater depth to many results of scientific research while the scientific way of thinking, freed from all personal considerations, may help the religious thinker gain greater clarity and distance from self, thereby achieving greater power of judgment concerning inner experiences.

Truth is a condition of the mind. It is not merely the agreement of a statement or perception with an object existing independently of that perception, because the conception or perception of the object is itself already a mental act of selection, delimitation and forming, a "creative" act (although usually of an unconscious and impersonal char-

---

[5]Kant showed theoretically where, within a given consciousness, the boundaries of knowledge lie, but the Buddha teaches the practice, the way by means of which that given form of consciousness can be transcended. Not logical thought, but a *higher consciousness* (*bodhi*) resolves the contradictions in which the lower mind, bound to the senses, is hopelessly trapped. *Tr.*

acter). Truth is just the adequate (i.e., non-contradictory) expression of the perception of an object or the content of an experience. The latter refers above all to the metaphysical truths of religions. Robert Reiniger said that the mark of metaphysical truth is its capacity to form the intelligible expression of a living world-feeling.[6]

The truths of religion are significant not because they represent objectively provable facts, but because they go back to primeval experiences common to all mankind, and are thus the expression of a living world-feeling. The universality (or the effective range) of a religion depends on the degree to which this world-feeling is generally intelligible and not conditioned by a particular time or nation. The truth-content of a religion consists in its experience-content. Even the most profound statements of a particular religion are valueless if they evoke no experiential response. This is the reason why so many ancient religions died away. They died out, even if their statements, symbols, and ritual forms persisted for a long time, because they could no longer evoke an echo.

The general validity of a religion depends upon its capacity for evoking an experience corresponding to its contents, and not on some abstract truth-content. No religion can lay claim to sole possession of truth, nor can it claim a monopoly on the depth-experience of which all human beings are capable. This depth-experience, which can assume different forms according to the level of development of the individual, is that inner certainty that we call faith—faith not in the sense of believing a dogma or an untestable revelation to be true, but faith as a *direction of the heart*.

Faith differs from belief just as religion differs from dogma. Religion is the expression of a life-feeling that has become a worldview, whereas dogma is its intellectual, abstract-logical formulation. Faith stands to religion as does individual experience to a supra-individual worldview, in which the experiences of many people have combined to form a higher unity. There is no religion without faith, though there can be faith without religion.

---

[6]Robert Reiniger, *Metaphysik der Wirklichkeit*, Vienna 1947–8, p. 209. The translation is mine. *Tr.*

The difference between faith being interpreted as an intellectual "believing to be true" and as a "direction of the heart" is especially clear in Buddhism. The Buddha warned his followers not to believe mere hearsay, not to follow his words blindly or to accept them merely for the sake of personal loyalty or attachment to him. They should only accept his teaching when they had put it to the test of their own experience and insight, and found it to be true. But at the same time he pointed out that an inner openness, as expressed in *saddhā* (Pali; Sanskrit, *śraddhā*), trusting faith, was the first step on the way to understanding and coming to experience his teaching. Its motto is, "Come and see!" Convince yourself by your own experience! Just as we cannot see without opening our eyes, we cannot understand without opening up inwardly. Without confidence we cannot learn even from the best teacher. And, just as inner and outer seeing are not necessarily contradictory, inner experience does not have to contradict the laws of reason and clear thought. Buddhism respects both and does not fall into the error of believing that we can attain to an understanding of reality (or "prove" this) by reasoned thought alone.

Recognition of the truth of a religion depends on the moral maturity of an individual rather than on intellectual development because this understanding is based more on experience than on discursive thought. The religious understanding of the world, on the other hand, depends on an individual's attitude to the world, and this is largely dependent on intelligence, the power of observation, range of knowledge and social conditioning. Primitive people think in symbols, intellectuals think in concepts. Spiritually developed people who pass beyond the boundaries of conceptual thought (though not despising it and recognizing it in its legitimate sphere) return to the symbol, but this time with full recognition of its symbolic character. This leads, not to a diminution of its reality-content, but to an understanding of its multidimensional nature. Higher mathematics, too, is a purely symbolic language and for that very reason is well suited to push forward into dimensions that lie beyond the bounds of experience in the world of the senses. But whereas the symbolic language of mathematics and physics go beyond the bounds of what can be experienced, the symbolic language of religion leads us back to an awareness of that reality out of which all religious experience flows. The word "back" does not mean that we refer to the past, to past experience-contents or primitive states of consciousness to try artificially to return to this level. It means regaining an experienceable reality that has been always accessible to us, but has been temporarily neglected. Going back allows us to start out from our present level of consciousness and includes all the experiential values we have acquired in the meantime. Thus we see this same reality with fresh eyes, from a different viewpoint, enriched by many dimensions of experience. There can be no "going back" to archaic forms, but rather a re-experiencing, a making present, of the same forms in a living relationship to the here-and-now. That which for archaic humanity was still unconscious (or only a kind of intuition, a premonition derived from the symbol), becomes a conscious perception for people of a later age. As long as this perception is not reduced to a concept, the character of its reality remains intact.

When we try to take hold of religion through conceptual thought, we miss the essential content of religion. Concepts isolate a single aspect out of the multiplicity of what is experienced, and thus rob it of its life. Only when we understand the symbolic language of religion can we come to terms with its content. The life of a symbol depends on whether it has a universal character or one that is conditioned by cult, race, society or the individual, i.e., the stratum of consciousness to which it belongs.

The more universal the symbols of a religion are, the longer their life and greater their importance for mankind. But no religion can restrict itself exclusively to the deepest zone of depth-consciousness without losing contact with the peripheral consciousness of daily and individual life. Accordingly, every religion presents a hierarchically ordered system (or an orderly range of symbols) starting with universal archaic symbols of the deepest zone and reaching to those that are traditionally and historically conditioned and thus characterize a unique situation in time and place. In the deepest zone lies the common origin of all religious experience, and from it *radiate* (extend in different directions) the individual forms of faith that establish the connection with the periphery in accordance with the cultural milieu in which they arose. Therefore Buddhism regards *no form of religion, no doctrine capable of being expressed in words, as final or exclusively true.*

The Buddha called his teaching a raft for crossing the ocean of life. The raft is merely a device for reaching the other shore, that other, more complete reality, and is not something we should hang on to as a precious possession. As soon as it has served its purpose, we should let it go. For example, if a man escaped over a great body of water by means of a raft and, having reached the other shore, continued to carry that raft around on his head, we would think him ridiculous. And how much more ridiculous are we who—before we have even crossed the flood—start arguing about the material the raft is made of or the way it is put together, instead of making the best possible use of the available material! The majority of people cling to the wretched fragments of their "raft" while still wandering about on the hither shore, forgetful of the Buddha's words:

> I will teach you *dhamma*, monks, as a raft, for crossing over,
> not for holding on to. (*Majjhima Nikāya:*22).

Feeling (or sensitivity) is of primary importance in the religious life, because feelings are not hemmed in by the obstacles and prejudices created by the intellect. Feeling lies closer to deep-consciousness than the intellect which calculates and judges and which is primarily directed outward, being concerned with the world of concepts and objects. In feeling we open up spontaneously to the prime reality that slumbers in our deep-consciousness waiting to be awakened.

Neglect of this feeling side of human nature is the main reason for the failure or the meagerness of most of the psychological or parapsychological experiments concerned with ESP, prenatal memories, telekinesis, ectoplasmic materializations, telepathy and other paranormal phenomena. The majority of these scientifically performed experiments display an almost childish naivety, because they overlook the principal factor of the religious depth-experience and the psychic powers released by this: the supra-individual sphere of religious emotion, which is activated and awakened through deep-rooted symbols that act as catalysts of creative power. The intellectual curiosity and the cold objectivity which seek to investigate and register psychic phenomena by means of statistics and physical measuring apparatus actually destroy the very conditions under which such phenomena can appear. Scientific method and religious experience belong to two completely different spheres. Just imagine somebody trying to prove or measure the spiritual, aesthetic or emotional content of a Beethoven symphony with scientific instruments!

Although the *technique* of music (the vibratory range of every note and the rules of harmony based on this) is based on mathematical laws and can be explained with mathematical exactitude, science has no access to the *experience* of music, and cannot approach any closer to this than a group of blind men who should try to describe an elephant when each has touched only a part of his body. This parable of the Buddha's fittingly illustrates the total inadequacy of conducting psychic research on a materialistic basis by using intellectual methods which fail to perceive the essential.

Natural religion, art and literature are of much greater significance for a religious understanding than such scientifically primitive experiments and investigations. The fact that many of the greatest works of art and literature were inspired by religious experience, and that many of the greatest sages and saints drew their inspiration from their close bond with nature, shows the great value that nature and art, poetry and world-philosophical literature possess for religious life. Art and poetry are the flowers of religion. A religion without art is dead.

The language of religion is not the language of concepts but of symbols. When these symbols are conceptualized, they lose their vitality, their multidimensionality, and are reduced to mere clichés. The multidimensionality of a symbol makes it the representative of a higher reality, in which a religious person, like a true poet or artist, is at home. Symbols are the key to that "other reality," they open up for us new dimensions of experience. Wherever Buddhism established itself, art and literature flourished. Sculpture, painting and architecture, poetry and philosophy, music and the dance-drama became forms of expression for a religious world-feeling, and nature herself became a living textbook of inner vision, as the Zen and Taoist landscape painters and poets of the Far East show us.

The mystic experiencing of that "other reality" appears in thousands of works of religious literature, poetry and art. The evidence alone of this immense creative power ought to convince us of the reality and importance of the underlying experience. This is mystical, not because it is dim and vague, but because it is direct, immediate and spontaneous—and therefore not accessible to the judging intellect. The mystic of antiquity (as of old Tibet) was no fantasist but one who was initiated, with knowledge, who had passed through experiences and tests—one whose lips were sealed in order to preserve the sacred experience from profanation, from intellectual curiosity and from its destruction by uncomprehending chatter. This wisdom can only be gained through contemplation, meditation and self-dedication. To the extent that self-dedication is put into effect, the knowledge outgrows the boundaries of personal character, of all individual limitations—and of the psychological factors determining these. Since, in the Buddhist view (especially of the Vijñānavādins) depth-consciousness is the reservoir of universal experience—just as memory is the container of personal experience—the possibility arises, in states of absorption or contemplation (i.e., when the intellectual, outward-turned superficial consciousness is cut out), to bring to light knowledge-content that has not been gained in this individual life and that does not depend on personal experiences or qualities of character. The claims of modern depth psychology, which credits the unconscious (i.e., depth-consciousness) with the same qualities that Buddhists ascribe to the "store-consciousness" (*ālaya-vijñāna*) are further evidence for the correctness of this view.

This "other reality" cannot be described using the categories and concepts of our secondary everyday consciousness, it can only be discovered by means of certain symbols or archetypal forms of our consciousness and culture. The word "God" is one of these symbols—a cypher for something which defies all description. That is why it says in the Bible, "Thou shalt not make an image of God." Such an image is only a concrete sensible representation, a logically or qualitatively limited concept such as that of a person with such-and-such attributes. Therefore, Buddhism rejects all such statements of this sort, and confines itself to discovering the divine in the symbol of light, understanding and compassionate love of one's neighbor in one's own heart, instead of arguing about all the various possible interpretations of the god-concept. Buddhism is the only one among world religions that has not profaned "god-experience" by dogmatic conceptualization—a profanation which has avenged itself all over the world through bloodthirsty persecutions and bitter struggles.

Buddhism has been accused on the one side of being atheistic, while on the other hand there have been charges of idolatry and even polytheism. Both charges are totally wrong. The teaching of Buddhism is neither agnosticism nor atheism, because it denies neither the possibility of the highest understanding or supreme enlightenment (*gnosis*) nor the value of the god-experience, which assumes different forms according to the level of human understanding, and thus cannot be the subject of any intellectual definition. Therefore, the Buddha left all the god-ideas of his contemporaries to one side and showed mankind, beyond all theistic theories, the way to the experiencing of the divine within. This consists of the conquest of our egoistic restrictions, through the cultivation of such immeasurables as feelings of loving-kindness, compassion, sympathetic joy and the establishment of such complete mental balance or equanimity as is untouched by personal joys and sorrows. The Buddha called these the four "divine abidings" or "dwellings in God" (*brahma-vihāra*). He proclaimed a teaching that had nothing to do with the materialistic atheism of our time, but was a *nontheistic* teaching, one which aimed not at imagining God, but at the realization of the divine, the infinite, in every human being.

The image of the Buddha is the symbol of the perfect human being, one who has become aware of and has fully realized the divine within. This is the symbol of the highest perfection to which the Buddhist pays homage. Buddhists identify inwardly with this symbol and so fill it with the power of their own devotion, with their own life-blood. Thus the cult-image is not the locus of a god to be worshipped, but a means to the awakening of the inner vision which transforms the people perceiving it, and delivers them from the ossification of the conceptual. The essence of a symbol is that it is capable of growth and opens up a new meaning on every level of consciousness without exhausting itself on any.

For Buddhists there are no religious statements that are to be taken verbally, because words, too, are symbols of something that lies beyond them. Hence it is said in the Laṅkāvatāra sūtra that the disciple should avoid clinging to words:

> . . . let the son or daughter of a good family take good heed not to get attached to words as being in perfect conformity with meaning, because the truth is not of the letter. Be not like the one who looks at the finger-tip. For instance, Mahāmati, when a man with his finger-tip points at something to somebody, the finger-tip may be taken wrongly for the thing pointed at; in like manner, Mahāmati, the people belonging to the class of the ignorant and simpleminded, like those of a childish group, are unable even unto their death to abandon the idea that in the finger-tip of words there is the meaning itself, and will not grasp ultimate reality because of their intent clinging to words which are no more than the finger-tip to them.[7]

---

[7]*Lankavatara Sutra*, section 7. See also D.T. Suzuki, *The Lankavatara Sutra* (London: Rider & Co., 1932, rep. 1956), p. 168. Tr.

Faith and Tolerance in Buddhism

The ethical conduct of a religious person is determined by faith or inner conviction. Humaneness, on the other hand, is a capacity possessed by each individual independently of religious ideas. This capacity can be greatly strengthened and deepened under the influence of a religion that believes in the dignity and freedom of conscience of each individual. The humanizing influence of Buddhism appears most clearly in the history of Tibet, which, in the course of a few centuries, moved from being one of the most warlike and feared nations of Asia, to become one of the more peace-loving and religious of communities. In spite of the most profound religious conviction and the existence of a well-organized hierarchy (to which the simplest peasant could gain admission), there was complete mutual tolerance between the various schools and sects. The liberty of individual conviction was never questioned. Even Christian missionaries were hospitably entertained; they were not only tolerated but even encouraged to present their teachings. The fact that the missionaries, in spite of the interest with which they were received, had no lasting effect in Tibet was not because they were strange, but because their teachings were too similar to Tibetan teachings, and therefore did not contribute any enrichment to the Tibetan outlook. A further reason was the Christian claim to exclusivity, which imperiled the liberty of individual belief.

Religions that concede complete liberty of judgment to the individual automatically advance humanity, while those that claim to be in sole possession of the truth and are scornful of the judgment of the individual can be enemies of humanity. And this is all the more the case when religion becomes a question of political or social power.

The more a particular religion separates away from people of other faiths, the greater the danger of onesidedness and intolerance. Living together with people of other faiths is a touchstone of the value of a religion. It forces each individual to pay attention to the problems of his or her own (as well as other religions), and to become conscious of the motives and reasons of his or her own religion. Both the resemblances and the differences between religions can be an inspiration. Every group has found its own particular approach to the deep experience of religion itself, and has developed practical ways of development which can be of benefit to those who follow other forms, without damage to their special qualities.

The active charity and helpfulness of Christianity, the inclusion of the body in prayer, and of the prayer in daily life in Islam, the meditation training of early Buddhism, the variety of images of God within an all-embracing feeling of unity in Hinduism, the way to inner unity in Yoga and to spontaneity in Zen, the closeness to nature in Taoism and the deep humanity of Confucianism, the parallelism of worldly and supramundane events in Tantrism, the profound fear of God and the personal sense of responsibility in Judaism, the universalism of Mahāyāna Buddhism with its inclusion of all beings in the process of liberation—all these are features of a nondogmatic character which can be applied to any religious practice, and from which every religion can profit, just as every tree, in spite of the variety of its form and the nature of its fruits, can profit from water, light and air.

Therefore the existence of various tendencies within a religion does not conflict with its claim to possession of the truth, because this very truth (or reality) has as many different forms of expression as it has dimensions. And since there cannot be such a thing as "one true faith," a person can also find an individual answer to religious questions outside of the established conventions. It is more important for a person to find some approach to religion than to belong to a recognized sect. The deeper one's understanding of the religious question the greater the capacity for recognizing the real.

It is not necessary to be informed about all the possible religious ways of interpreting the world, although this knowledge is useful and saves us from intolerance and intellectual narrowness. Religious communities ought to encourage such knowledge, in order to be sure that those who joined them did not do this from ignorance of other religious paths, from mental laziness or because of social advantages or prejudices, but out of honest conviction. Religions should limit membership to those who really accept them. If there were an organized religious exchange, various religions would have greater understanding of each other. Perhaps they would draw closer together. This activity would not lead to a fusion, or to the victory of one religion over the rest, for one religion can no more conquer another than one temperament can gain victory over another. All religions are dependent on certain primal forms of the human psyche that are conditioned by climate, race, language, and the cultural or national community. The importance of these primal forms or supra-individual symbols of depth-consciousness cannot be underestimated. Western psychology has degraded these symbols to the unconscious, and thus in the eyes of contemporary people the symbols have been devalued, despite Jung's heroic efforts to free this concept from Freud's negative prejudices.[8]

The same symbol can have opposite meanings in different religious systems. The aura of flames, which in Christian symbolism is ascribed to a hellish emanation, is regarded in the Tibetan Buddhist system as

---

[8]For more on this, see p. 204 of Jean Gebser's *The Ever-Present Origin* (Athens, OH: The Ohio University Press, 1984) where he says that modern psychological terminology—which postulates an unconscious in opposition to consciousness—is guilty of the falsification of primary psychosomatic facts. This terminology and the falsely structured phenomena resulting from it are classic examples of the false conclusions that arise from a radically applied dualism. There is no so-called unconscious; there are only various kinds of consciousness.

a symbol of wisdom. The dragon—in the West the archetype of all that is evil—is in the Far East a symbol of the highest spirituality. The sun, which in the North is the friend of mankind, has in the hot regions of tropic and subtropical zones become an element that is hostile to life. Therefore Islam, which was born in the hot deserts of Arabia, elevates not the sun but the moon to the highest symbol; and in the mysticism of Indian yoga the solar power of the outward-turned, individual life bears within it the poison of death, whereas the lunar, inward-turned power contains the elixir of immortality. Many more such examples could be found.

The majority of misunderstandings or misinterpretations of religious symbols are caused by language, and here, too, it is often not the recognized differences of terminology that lead to misunderstandings, but precisely those concepts and ideas that look alike. The same word does not have the same meaning or the same feeling-tone in different religions or cultures. Can there be anything more susceptible of different interpretations than the word God? For one it denotes a person, for another a principle, a law, an impersonal or suprapersonal power. And even among those for whom God is a person, his character is a very different one according to the position he occupies in their emotional world or their world-view. In the Old Testament, God is a strict and often frightening ruler and judge, and according to the Christian faith a loving father; in certain Hindu sects God plays the part of a lover or beloved, while according to other Indian ideas God is the creator of the world, and the world is his dream in which he experiences himself in innumerable different beings created by himself—till he wakes from that dream. Still greater is the diversity of conceptions among those who see in God an impersonal or suprapersonal power. Here, God can be regarded as either immanent or transcendent, as permeating the world or towering over it, or God can be considered as an expression of interior human experience, a symbol of inner reality or a psychic projection.

There may be a common element, indefinable, that underlies all these concepts—for this is characteristic of every symbol—but the symbol only gains its meaning through its relation to the remaining parts of whatever world-view prevails in each instance. Thus, the essence of every religion or world-view consists of its particular relationship to concepts and experienced symbols, and not in mere statements which can be compared in solation with the statements of other systems, and possibly disproved by these.

> It is natural that anyone who claims to have found a truth is also convinced that it is not merely a truth for him, but is valid for all, to the extent that they have succeeded in grasping his reasons. But this presupposition of a general validity is not a primary mark of truth, but only the natural interpretation of the irresistible nature of one's own experience of acceptance.

> It cannot therefore be a case of penetrating into a somewhere existing realm of truths valid in themselves, but simply and solely of building up such a realm of truth irrespective of all accidents and errors that occur in our actual thinking, while that prior conception of its perfection can act, as a never fully attainable ideal, to be striven for in the service of the idea of truth.[9]

In other words, the truth of a religion or worldview can never be the object of proof any more than can be the existence or nonexistence of a God. A God who was proved would be a finite god and so divested of its Godhead. Similarly, a religion that could be proved would be robbed of its character of infinity, and thus of its religious value. "A proven God, worshipped as fact, would be a worse fetish than the golden calf," as Keyserling once said.

Truth consists in the meaningful coordination of given contents of experience in the human mind, and thus in a creative act, whose reality-value and effectiveness (like that of a work of art) depends on the perfect, i.e., noncontradictory agreement of all its components with

---

[9]Reiniger, *Metaphysik der Wirklichkeit*, Vienna 1947–8, pages 203 and 197. The translation is mine. *Tr.*

each other and with the resulting total picture; for the idea of the whole must never be overlooked in discussing the details. From this point of view we can understand Kung Fu-tse's dictum: "It is not truth that makes man great, but man who makes truth great." Similarly, we can say it is not religion that makes humanity great, but people who make religion great; for it is not belonging to this or that religion that makes us better human beings, but what we make out of religion by filling it and giving it reality with our own lives. The value of a religion, therefore, is shown only through the spiritual and ethical level of its followers.

As long as a religion (*re-ligio*, from *re-ligare*, to join again) is able to link its followers to that universal depth-zone of their consciousness, the nontransient, all-embracing "divine ground of all being" that is not limited by time and space, it has fulfilled its function. For a religion must be capable of giving some meaning to existence. It must also point the way beyond the data of the senses and individual limitation toward a higher reality which can be attained by personal effort. Such a religion has value.

In the future, the criterion of a religion may no longer be a dogma based on intellectual considerations or dogmatic revelation, but the religious experience whose reality-content gives direction and dignity to human life. It is to this goal that present day development of interreligious interaction points. Despite dogmatic differences, hitherto competing and warring groups have buried the axe in the realization that a mutual exchange of experiences promises each group more gain than loss. Such an exchange of experiences, as was organized by the Fondazione Cini in 1960 at their cultural center on the Isola San Giorgio Maggiore in Venice, and at which the present writer was able to take part as a representative of Buddhism (Mahāyāna), was clear evidence of the great change that has come over religious life in Europe in the course of the last few decades. Representatives of Christianity, including some of the most senior dignitaries of the Catholic Church, sat side by side with those of Islam, Hinduism, Buddhism (both northern and southern), Shintoism, Judaism and Jainism, in order to exchange religious experiences in which prayer and meditation played a leading role. It was a joy to see how, after centuries of religious struggles and misunderstandings, the supporters of different religious communities had come together in the spirit of mutual respect and good will, not to demonstrate the superiority of one faith over another, but to understand each other better and strengthen the common factor that links all people who believe in the life of the spirit.

During the exchange of ideas it soon emerged that the group had a great deal in common. We were concerned, not with dogma, but with the religious experience itself. Intellect, thinking, the interpretation of the world and our position in it (and in relation to it) are largely determined by cultural, historical, and sociological factors, but our deepest experiences belong to a realm that is common to all human beings. It is the common ground on which we all stand, and from which all religious movements have taken their origin. It is only on this basis that the spiritual exchange and collaboration between different religions can bear fruit. On common ground the clear and honest recognition of differences presents no threat, but represents an enrichment of cultural life.

As I have already pointed out, the truth of a religion—like the beauty of a work of art—is the unique and inimitable interrelation of living form-symbols that combine to express spontaneous experience, a harmonious whole, an organic world-picture. Just as there is no single art that is valid for all times and all people, or no single work of art, however perfect, that can exhaustively represent the meaning of art or beauty, so, too, no religious form, however perfect, can be valid for all times and all people.

That is why (even within one religion) new tendencies and schools must continually arise, if that religion is to preserve its liveliness and its closeness to reality (which we interpret as truth). For life means growth, and growth is continual change according to an inward law. A religion incapable of change is dead. But since transformation is not arbitrary change, the essential identity of a religion remains despite all transformation. In fact we could say that it is in its capacity for transformation that the strength of its individuality and its special spiritual stamp clearly emerge. For growth is both a process of un-foldment of inherent qualities, and one of assimilation and integration—a process of enrichment. It is the mystery of life which passes by those who resist change and deliver themselves to spiritual death.

It is not the differences between religions that creates problems; it is the frantic urge to fuse them into a unity, to equate one with another, to force some common denominator or subordinate them to the same dogma that is the problem. Just as the value of different fruits consists precisely in their varied characteristics, and just as this value is not increased but destroyed by indiscriminate mixing, so a mixture of religious forms of expression and symbolism will not lead to a higher religion, but to the destruction of religious values.

The common factor shared by all religions is not an abstract basic truth (i.e., an intellectual formulation or abstract principle), it is the experience of a supra-individual reality. This reality—even if it could be grasped as a whole—must also embrace the developmentally-conditioned spiritual standpoint and temperament of the experiencing individual. This experience can only be presented in the living symbols that are intelligible to a particular time and culture.

The uniqueness and singularity of every such experience does not mean a reduction in reality-content, but actually an increase or intensification. For example, the creative formation of a work of art does not exhaust the nature of a landscape, yet the painting is more than a mere reproduction of it. A thousand skilled artists would represent the same landscape in a thousand different ways, and the value of the paintings might relate to the differences of expressive form, even though each painting was a competent representation of the landscape. The same thing happens with religious experience.

The inner world experienced by a Buddha, Lao-tse, Christ, or Mohammed is not merely a reflection of reality, but a reality intensified in the focal point of a mighty experience, whose irresistible power of conviction carried contemporary people along, and continued to work for thousands of years in ever wider circles. The written or orally-preserved traditions of the contemporaries of these great men or their successors give only a pale reflection of the dazzling brilliance of the spirit that originally moved them. If we can succeed in raising ourselves to that level of experience we can come face to face with the great ones of the spirit and attain to that which unites all religions. All people can make use of that all-embracing depth-experience that every religion offers. Prayer, contemplation, meditation, visions, atonement, ethics, helpfulness, compassion, love of one's neighbor, sympathy with all that lives, self-denial, truthfulness, investigation of one's conscience, will to understanding, insight, equanimity, patience, and so on are all approaches that can be used. Thus beside the imponderables of visible and linguistic symbols which are peculiar to every religious system (and which cannot be arbitrarily transplanted or translated into conceptual and logical terms) there is a lot of practical collaboration and spiritual understanding that makes all religions into members of one great human family. On the basis of mutual respect and recognition of the personal character of each individual member, a family of various religions can endure. As for that which remains the incommensurable kernel of each religion, or which is not revealed to our understanding, we can only approach it with reverence.

Ethical values that are recognized by all religions are the basis on which the rights of humanity, as proclaimed in the UN Charter and in the constitutions of all civilized states, rest. It is the task of religion to keep these values alive, so that they are observed out of an inborn respect for the dignity and liberty of conscience of all people of whatever class, race or religion. No external compulsion, no national or political intervention can *produce* ethical values. They must flow from the depths within, unforced as from a natural spring which pours forth its wealth and its "superfluity" into the world, finding freedom and liberation in this flood of self-giving. This kind of liberty protects us all from the arbitrariness of selfish goals and leads to liberty for all.

Science and the Doctrine of Rebirth

Ascientist was once attracted by the ethics of Buddhism, but could make nothing of the doctrine of rebirth. He decided that if this doctrine had any real basis it must eventually be *scientifically* provable by means of fully confirmed and tested recollections of past lives, such as the Buddha himself claimed to have, and which are supposed to have occurred in our own time as well. This demand is fully justified. Actually incontrovertibly proven cases of such recollections have often been presented, and if scientists were to take the trouble to follow up these proofs and investigate the existing factual material, science would very soon be as well informed on this score as about the life of microbes or the starts of the Milky Way.[10] The fact that scientists have not taken the trouble to do this merely shows the prejudices and the gaps in the scientific world-picture—but not the impossibility of rebirth.

A scientist should logically adopt the following position: "I have so far not had any experiences of this nature and I have not learned if others who claim to remember previous births can give convincing proof

---

[10]See, for instance, M. Willson, *Rebirth and the Western Buddhist* (Boston & London: Wisdom Publications, 1987). *Tr.*

of this. I therefore leave the question open until I am in possession of sufficient proof." But here we see the lack of genuine scientific impartiality. The scientist usually goes straight on, without any logical basis, to the opposite assertion: "If science knows nothing of rebirth, then that means that no such thing exists, and that the Buddha therefore made an incorrect statement."

Is it true that microscopes and telescopes can give us evidence of a reality that is objectively more real than that experience of reality reported by the Buddha and countless others who have followed his path? Is the way of science, looking outwards, any less anthropocentric than that of the inward vision? Who makes use of the microscopes and telescopes but the person who interprets what is seen with the mind? If you let a Tibetan, untouched by modern science, look through the microscope, he would find confirmation there for his "demons of sickness"; if he looked through a telescope, he would recognize the radiant worlds of his visions.

The scientist who regards his views as objective, and as absolutely true, is a good deal more naive than the unscientific Tibetan who, despite the far stronger reality of his visions and meditative experiences, is clear in his mind that no visible, audible or imaginable form has absolute reality, but that all are presentations of a reality which finds expression at every level of understanding in a different form—*in accordance with the instrument of observation.* This relativity does not destroy the value of the observation or experience, but simply puts it in its right place. It makes it possible to understand—each in its own way—the observations of science and of religious experience, and to value them according to their character. This "both-and" attitude is acutely painful to Western dogmatists, whether of science or of theology, because they are, as C.G. Jung puts it so nicely in his preface to the *Tibetan Book of the Dead*, ". . . still in the mediaeval, pre-psychological stage where only the assertions are listened to, explained, defended, criticized and disputed, while the authority that makes them has, by general consent, been deposed as outside the scope of discussion."[11]

---

[11]W.Y. Evans-Wentz, tr., *The Tibetan Book of the Dead*, C.G. Jung's "Psychological Commentary," p. xxxvii (London & New York: Oxford University Press, 1927).

Opposed to this science that is limited to concepts, and that forgets the conceiver of the concept, is the reality of experience. Thus Paul Dahlke says:

> The artistic moment of experience is in its profoundest depth free of concepts—reality as it takes shape, reality *in statu nascendi*. We can only judge science from the conceptual standpoint. But the essence of the concept is that it presents reality only in a provisional, hypothetical form. A tree is a tree in the conceptual sense only in its momentary form. The definition "tree" exists only for a time. There was a time when that which I now define as a tree was a seed; there will be a time when that which I now define as a tree will no longer be a tree, but either again a seed, or dead wood, or something else. The essence of artistic (as of meditative) intuition is finally this, that one sees, *looking beyond the conceptual form*, the *connecting link* (*das verbindende Band*), as Goethe saw in his *Metamorphosis of Plants*.
>
> One should therefore be clear that the factor of the hypothetical, the conditioned, attaches to all science; that every definition, every conceptualization, is something non-definitive and provisional; and one should quickly accustom oneself to measuring the true worth of science accordingly. The strictness with which science works, or can work, changes nothing in this conditional evaluation. Logic can be applied not only to hypothetical but also to fictitious suppositions. In fact logic can be applied all the more strictly, the more purely hypothetical, the more purely fictitious these preconditions are, that is to say the less they are mixed in with reality, and the less reality spoils the game. . . . Pure logic is only to be had at the cost of reality-content. . . . And so it comes about over and over again, that man sacrifices the spiritual life of humanity for the mess of pottage of reason, and thus throws away the best part: reality itself.[12]

---

[12]Paul Dahlke, *Heilkunde und Weltanschauung*, p. 15. The translation is mine. *Tr.*

The admission that science, despite its future ultra-microscopes and super-telescopes, is only able to show and explore the world of appearances and not the world as it really is, is not "a borrowing from the transcendental," as the scientist mentioned at the beginning supposed. It is sound common sense, which in spite of all the triumphs of scientific understanding, has preserved sufficient objectivity and modesty to recognize that there is not "only one world, namely the world which presents itself to our senses," but as many worlds as there are dimensions of consciousness, i.e., innumerable.[13]

This understanding allows science to remain valid within its own sphere, without thereby excluding other methods and fields of research such as psychology and meditative experience. And even when the methods of the exact sciences such as physics and mathematics cannot be employed, and where purely logical thinking is insufficient to achieve results or proofs, chance still does not rule, as our scientist assumes when he declares that in such a case "every assertion, and its opposite, may be correct."

'The discoveries of a Buddha, and other great ones in the realm of spirit, are built on a strict methodology and mental training which—in their way—can lead just as much to "objective" observations and results as the methods of science. But the scientist, who is his own field demands a strict schooling, imagines that in the matter of psychic experience he is capable of passing judgment without the slightest effort or training. This is just as if a schoolboy who scarcely knows his multiplication table were to pass judgment on Einstein's theory of relativity—which, after all, obviously conflicts with Euclidean logical thinking.

It is a widespread mistake to regard immanence and transcendence as two mutually exclusive opposites, instead of welcoming the fact that we are here concerned with relative expressions, just as in the case of "objective" and "subjective." Those who regard immanence and transcendence as constant factors proceed from the wrong assumption

[13]The mathematically-inclined reader is recommended to read J.M. Dunn, *The Serial Universe*, 1927.

that the boundaries of human consciousness are unalterable and that therefore whatever goes beyond them is transcendental. The dogmatists of science do not see that consciousness can change and grow beyond the arbitrarily assumed frontiers, or beyond those typical of the average human being.

> Not logical thinking, but only a *higher consciousness* (*bodhi*) solves the contradictions in which the lower thought that is bound to the senses becomes hopelessly trapped.[14]

Anyone who denies the possibility of this higher consciousness in order to turn Buddhism into a handmaid of science, depresses it to the level of a simple moral teaching, decked out with arbitrary formulations like the Noble Eightfold Path, the Four Noble Truths and, perhaps a doctrine of causality misunderstood in a materialistic sense, in which the *connecting link*, namely the universal connection and multirelationality of consciousness, on which depend both the doctrine of rebirth and that of *anattā*, is lost from sight.

Anyone who believes that the Buddha only "took over" the idea of rebirth for missionary purposes, i.e., for outward advantage and against his better conviction—despite the fact that the Buddha expressly claimed to know this by his own experience (and indeed this understanding formed a major part of his enlightenment process)—is declaring the Buddha to be nothing better than a wretched charlatan. It is difficult to understand why anyone who takes this view should consider it worthwhile to water down the "unshakable facts of science" with the Buddhist doctrine.

Anyone who has only come to Buddhism in the belief that it agrees with the findings of modern science (which tomorrow will no longer be modern!) would do better to stay with science. The fact that Buddhism agrees with so many things discovered by science is beyond question. But it is not Buddhism that is confirmed thereby, but science, which at

---

[14]H. Beckh, *Buddhismus*, 1928, p. 120. The translation is mine. *Tr.*

last, after 2500 years, has begun to catch up with the discoveries of Buddhism.

Let us at last find the courage to stand by our most inward and profound convictions without the crutches of science—whether our contemporaries agree with us or not.

Potentiality and Reality
in Hinduism and Buddhism

When the Upanishads say "Thou art that" (*tat tvam asi*), the stress is not on the word "art" in the sense that "thou" and "that" (the individual and his surroundings) are identical, but rather that the two are inseparably linked—like the positive and negative pole of the same power or reality. To say the two are the same would be just as much a distortion of reality as to say the two were two entirely different things having nothing to do with each other. They have a common root, they are expressions of the same truth, of the same stream of life and consciousness (or of the conscious life that penetrates the entire universe).

Recognizing oneself in others (as the Buddha once convincingly put it) does not mean denying the importance of the individual: this is a necessary condition for actual consciousness as well as for organic life. It actually stresses the common origin and essential unity of all that lives. Unity does not mean identity. Unity presupposes variety, and this variety is just as important as the concept of unity or wholeness. If we raise unity to the status of the sole reality and thus debase variety to an illusory condition, we are indulging in arbitrary abstractions and falsifying the character of the universe and of all life.

It was this one-sided tendency that falsified the truly experienced and poetic ideas and formulations of the Upanishads. It created the purely intellectual doctrine of the abstract *Advaita* (non-dual) philosophy, according to which the individual is reduced to a mere wrong development of the universe that, in the form (or non-form) of the universal Brahman, is regarded as the sole and absolute reality. Can there really be such a thing as "reality in itself?" Is not precisely the notion of an "absolute reality" a purely conceptual abstraction based upon the naive assumption of an unchanging substance, a "thing in itself?" "Real" means that which exists as something, and derives from the Latin word *res*, which literally means "thing, matter." But ever since science discovered that behind the phenomena that go to make up our world no matter can be discovered—that behind the most massive matter nothing exists but immaterial fields of force moving with unimaginable speed, which come together to make up different forms of longer or shorter duration—the whole conception of reality has turned out to be a view which itself possesses only relative validity.

There is water in solid, liquid, or gaseous form—as ice, steam, clouds, or moisture in the air, and so on. Can we say that ice is more real than water, or that water is more real than steam or clouds? Or that atoms of hydrogen and oxygen are more real than the above-mentioned forms of H_2O? Reality is a relative concept, and ultimate reality is a purely abstract idea.

Where there is no form, there is no reality in the sense of something "really there." The reality of an atom manifests in the form of its motion, the speed of its electrons and their distance from the nucleus. Speed and distance lead to the experience of space-and-time. There cannot be any "space in itself" any more than there is "motion in itself," i.e., without any point of reference or any kind of relationship. Therefore to speak of "absolute reality" is merely playing with words. "Absolute reality" means nothing, has no relationships and can therefore not be experienced in any way. It cannot perform a function in either a religious or a meditative context. The Buddha, who had no interest in philosophical and metaphysical speculations, but only in the realities experienceable by the human mind, never mentions the idea of a *universal* Brahman.

It is something quite different when we speak of the principles of universality and individuality as two poles of the same reality, which condition each other in such a way that neither can be experienced without the other, both being of equal value. Universality, as such, is meaningless as long as it is not experienced in the individual, just as the individual is senseless unless it is brought into relation to something outside itself. There is no "I" without an "it." As long as we have not come to *experience* this with our whole being, we have not realized it, but have merely recognized it as an intellectual or logical conclusion. It is quite an achievement to transform a rational consideration into immediate experience; and since this does not strengthen our feeling of separateness, but rather makes us feel at one with our surroundings and our fellow-beings, it does not lead to intellectual arrogance but to humility.

When we are told that such an experience cannot be brought about by any effort on our part, but that it falls into our laps like a gift from the gods or, in other words, that it is an unintended, spontaneous event, then it must at once be pointed out that hard work and continual practice or effort are the conditions which prepare the ground for the capacity to accept and integrate this lightning-like occurrence. For what is meditation—and still more, contemplation—but that condition of readiness to accept, in which we open our minds and keep our sensitivity alert by getting rid of everything that hinders us and hems us in? We have to place ourselves in an intuitive state of mind, an inner attitude in which we are more ready to hear than to argue, more ready to be moved than to move.

Just as a seed dies when it falls on unfruitful ground, so, too, the inspiration or intuition that comes to an unprepared mind will die and leave not a trace behind, unless it becomes a creative capacity of the human soul. This is a transformation into a life-giving vision that finds its expression in creative thoughts and symbols, as for instance in poetry or painting, music or dancing, in sculpture or architecture: in short, in that which gives form to the formless, bounds to the unbounded, corporeality to the not yet embodied. It is through form that the formless becomes visible, it is with words that we hint at what lies hidden beyond words; we display the boundless through its limitations, for no spiritual power can become effective unless it achieves embodiment. Therefore it is more important to materialize the spirit than to spiritualize matter. The latter is all the more superfluous because what we call matter is already more spiritual than we suppose. Matter is, in the last analysis, a solidified form of cosmic energy which, in comparison with the endless emptiness of the cosmos, is one of the rarest and most grandiose phenomena of the universe. At the same time, however, matter is also a precondition (the *conditio sine qua non*) for the individualized and focused consciousness, through which the universe comes to be aware of its own existence.

Although intuition (and inspiration) cannot be called forth by an act of will, intuition gains in strength, and can appear more easily, through the constant exercise of all our faculties. This exercise can be pursued to such a stage of mental sensibility and adaptability that these faculties react to the slightest impulse. By attaining this state, we can translate and transform our intuitions into a creative form of expression so that the original impulse in them can fully develop its indwelling qualities in a continuous process of growth and transformation. This is comparable to the process of growth and transformation of a seed into a plant. Therefore form (or the production of form) must never be understood as a "solidifying;" or "setting" of intuition or inspiration—like some sort of crystallization. Form and its production are really just the start of another process of transformation that moves in a prescribed direction—a continually expanding, living, organic stream of conscious energy.

Inspiration is not merely a gift but something that can be developed. Music critic Ernest Newman once said that great composers do not work because they are inspired, but are inspired because they work. Beethoven, Wagner, Bach, Mozart sat over their work day after day with the same regularity with which bookkeepers sit over columns of figures. They did not waste any time waiting for inspiration. Even if inspiration is a gift of heaven (or "the grace of God"), we cannot receive such gifts or make any use of them if we are not open to receive them. We cannot accept gifts with closed fists, and presents are of no use if we don't know what to do with them. The wisdom and compassion of the Buddhas and Bodhisattvas are freely given to all receptive beings— just as is the grace of God, of which other religions speak. But only those can profit who are willing and ready to receive it; only when the flower opens up to the sun of its own accord can it receive the benefit of its rays. Neither merit nor unworthiness determine whether we receive grace or not, but only maturity and the readiness to receive in humility. That's why "the sinner is nearer to it than the self-righteous man."

Maturity is the fruit of experience. Those who (like Ramana Maharshi, the great Indian saint of our time) are born with this self-realization, or seem to be suddenly gifted with it, have probably acquired this maturity through the experience of many previous existences. These experiences need not necessarily be the result of conscious striving for enlightenment or self-realization—they may well be the outcome of profound suffering, which, just as much as the greatest joy and happiness, can be the grace of God in disguise.

Those who accept suffering in the spirit of humility can turn it into a liberating power, a blessing. This was one of the great recognitions of Mahāyāna Buddhism. Mahayana Buddhists do not seek to flee from suffering by turning their backs on the world in order to gain their own liberation in the shortest possible way, but change their attitudes and say: "I would rather take the sufferings of the whole world upon myself than leave my fellow beings in the lurch for the sake of my own happiness. My striving for liberation and enlightenment must include the liberation of all suffering beings."

Paradoxical as it may seem, the acceptance of suffering *is* precisely the shortest way to its conquest. When we accept it in its universal aspect and share it with our fellow beings, considering their sufferings and, in consequence also their joys, as our own, then we not only withdraw our interest from our own personal affairs, we also consider them from an expanded viewpoint that frees us from the prison of our limited egoism and awakens the positive qualities of love and compassion.

The grace of God and personal effort supplement and condition one another. They are not two different ways of liberation, but two equally important factors of spiritual life. Since there is no independent self—that is, no self that can be separated from its surroundings, from the world in which it lives and obtains its nourishment— "own-power" and "other-power" are complementary, like the left and right sides of the same thing. They can never be separated from each other. We have received and gift of Buddha-Dharma and the blessings of those who have passed it on. But until we practice and realize the Dharma in our own lives, this gift will be of no use to us.

If anyone says, "The Self, the Ātman, is the Godhead, is Brahman, and this has ever been so from the beginning. Your attempt to realize it is equal to rejecting it, to refusing the gift, because you ignore the existing reality," then I fear that he or she is just playing with words, or else taking the finger that points to the moon for the moon itself. Originally, Ātman stood for the breath of life (corresponding to the German atmen, to breathe, and to the Greek pneuma). It denotes the universal power that inspires the individual and fills it with life and floods it with the uninterrupted flow of in- and out-breathing. As such, the Ātman links the individual with the greater life, and makes this universal life conscious in the individual of whom it is the origin. This power, this living breath of the universe, can no more be captured and possessed than one can take hold of a river with a bucket and carry it away.

Therefore, to identify the Ātman with the Self (except as a poetic metaphor) is the cause of great misunderstanding, namely that the individual is the same as Brahman, the totality of the universe, the Godhead, and so forth. But the very fact that we cannot move the heavenly bodies in the same way we move our arms and legs ought to teach us that (however much we might feel ourselves as an expression of the universe from which we have sprung) this potential and essential universality of our inmost being is more like the focusing of sunlight through a lens which (though it combines all the features of sunlight) is not the sun itself.

From our potential universality to the real experience of this universality, the path may be long or short, although perhaps only a hair's breadth separates us from this experience. The whole thing can be compared to the situation of a poor man in whose house—perhaps directly under his feet—a treasure is hidden. As long as he is unaware of this, he remains a poor man even though the treasure is within his grasp.

If we do not know of the existence of hidden treasure, or don't have the will to remove the obstacles that block the way to it, then we will never be able to take possession of it. As long as we cling to the idea of a Self—whether we regard it as a physical or metaphysical reality, or as a mere point of reference in a psychological or philosophical system of relations, such as the relation between center and periphery—we are creating a completely unnecessary misunderstanding. It is for that reason that the Buddha rejected the concept of *Ātman*. For *Ātman* had lost its original dynamic meaning, and had degenerated to an ossified metaphysical abstraction. Accordingly, he replaced the *Ātman* concept with that of *Anattā*, based on the fact that there is no reality in the form of any kind of Self or I, and that nothing in the world can exist in or from itself alone. All forms of life, all things, and all phenomena depend upon each other, are related to each other, and are so interwoven that the individual becomes the point of intersection of all the crossing lines of force of the entire universe.

The potential for the transformation of our universal nature into effective reality, that is to say into living experience, is the way of the Buddha. As long as we are not aware of this universality, we remain prisoners of the ego-state, although we have the potentiality of gaining enlightenment. Potential is not the same as reality. And even if we say, "You are Buddhist," or "You are Brahman," that does not turn us into Buddhas, or into the embodiment of the universe. It is only poetic language for, "That is your real being, your potentiality." As long as this is not realized, we are like the poor man sitting on his treasure without knowing it.

Part Two

THE INWARD PATH

Buddhist Meditation

Recently, I was asked what meditation really is. I replied, "Meditation is the way to re-connect the individual with the whole, to make us aware of our continuing connection and communion, which has never really been broken off." The way of meditation is the only way open to us so we can see through the ego-complex and thus overcome the illusion of a soul or selfhood that is separate and independent of the whole—something that neither pious sermons nor solemn admonitions can accomplish. Meditation brings about a change that allows us to give up our fixations on the ego that sets itself apart from the universe, the ego that is so full of desires, so we can enter into the freedom of an ever-changing individuality which, rooted in the universal, is continually developing. To give up something small and petty for something greater is no real sacrifice. It is the gaining of freedom, just as when someone steps out of a cramped prison cell into the world again. The selflessness that arises from the conquest and rejection of the ego-illusion is not an attitude produced by an act of will, nor is it one that despises joy. Rather, it develops in us quite naturally without our doing anything about it, and is free from all feelings of moral superiority or arrogance. The compassion and sympathy that arises in us because of meditation is a spontaneous and natural expression of solidarity with all life, and not—as can so often be observed today—an ideologically stimulated emotion.

Meditation is not only a means of experiencing our connectedness with the whole. It is also a way of coming to realize that one is oneself, like every other individual, a focal point in which the universe becomes aware of itself in unique fashion. In order to have such an experience, a focusing of consciousness is necessary. In the West, this is generally termed concentration. But, as is well known in the East, there are different kinds of concentration. For instance, we can turn our undivided attention to a job we are doing. On the other hand, if we need to solve a problem, we have to concentrate on the various aspects of this problem, in which case the focus of consciousness must be constantly changing. A third kind of concentration occurs when we approach an object or thought in ever-smaller concentric circles. In this way we create an inner direction toward the object under consideration, without fixing on a particular point and without binding ourselves to a particular point of view, thus experiencing and getting to know the meditation-object "from all sides," and its totality. It is this type of concentration and contemplation that forms the basis of Oriental meditation.

Western thinking, on the other hand, sets it sights on its goals from a particular position, and then marches toward it in a straight line, leaving everything else aside to right and left, or neglecting it. Oriental thought moves round the object in ever-narrowing circles. The Western method has proved successful in the field of science; but because it wrests its objects out of their environment, it has also caused much pain and distress. If we circle round the object that interests us and see it in the web of all that surrounds it, we then see it as a whole, embedded in a whole, and therefore have a better understanding.

People speak about meditation and often equate concentration with meditation, but this is a misunderstanding. A simple example will make this clear: every bookkeeper concentrates on details—but he is certainly not meditating! Concentration and meditation are different things. Some people wish they could concentrate better during meditation and this can also become a hindrance to meditation—especially if this wish assumes a compulsive character.

It is, therefore, at least when we *begin* to meditate, a good thing to simply observe the flow of thoughts, to watch the flow, before turning to specific meditation objects and before we approach any nearer to those regions which form the basis of our existence. In this way we offer no resistance to the dynamism working within us, everything flows freely, all agitation ebbs away, and we attain a state of inner calm in which—as if automatically—we find our inner direction.

If, in the course of meditation, we come to experience ourselves as one of the "focal points" of the universe, then this experience of universality and of the uniqueness of the individual fills us with a growing feeling of responsibility toward the bearer and instrument of this experience. Therefore, true meditation cannot lead to self-destruction or dissolution into a nebulously conceived totality, nor can it lead us into a state of indifference toward the world we live in, or indifference toward the body and its sense-organs through which we experience this world. On the contrary, meditation enables us to see everything in a wider framework, in a wider context. It actually shows the trivialities of our worldly life in a new light, transformed as it were, as profoundly important aspects of a great cosmic game, in which we are at once active participants as well as spectators.

If we speak of a cosmic game, this term can also be easily misunderstood, since the idea of a game is frivolous for many people. A game for them means something in which they can simply let themselves go. But a little consideration would convince them that every game has its own rules. In the great universal game, the rules are what Buddhists call *dharma*. Without an understanding of *dharma* we cannot make full use of our freedom in this game that we all play. Again, we should bear in mind that everyone who plays a part on a stage must know the part perfectly, and this means that we can only play it properly when we understand how the part fits in to the overall context of the play.

Thus, one of the reasons for meditating is that through meditation we gain certainty about our roles in life, about the starting position, and the responsibility, because—to anticipate slightly—*there is no freedom without responsibility*. That's why so many people are afraid of freedom: they are afraid of responsibility. Freedom does not mean doing and not doing whatever we like. It means that we do the right thing according to the situation of the moment, which is to say, in accordance with the rules of the great game in which we are all involved.

In India they have a special expression for this great cosmic game— *līlā*—a term for which there is no adequate translation in Western languages. *Līlā* is the polar opposite of what we call *karma*. *Līlā* and *karma* relate to each other like freedom and necessity, or spontaneity and the rule of law. Neither pole can stand alone. Without the rule of law, life would be unthinkable. It is only through the limitation imposed on us by the rule of natural law that we are enabled to be free so that— within the limits of that law—we can make our own decisions.

For example, if a composer wants to write a piece of music, he must know the rules of harmony, as well as the capacity of the instruments, and so on. It is only when he has fully grasped the laws which underly music, that the very laws themselves enable him to give free expression to that which he feels as an individual. Thus individual self-expression is not in conflict with the universal rule of law of the world we live in. In this sense, the greatest art is always *līlā*. It pours out of the artist like a bird's song, not for the sake of profit or reward, and not for ego-boosting. It is the free and spontaneous expression of an overwhelming inner experience! The great artist is one who transforms his or her whole life into a work of art and thus matures into a perfect sage.

We cannot believe in freedom without at the same time believing in *līlā*. Without freedom there is neither the possibility of ethical behavior nor of virtue. When we speak of *līlā* and *karma*, or of freedom and necessity, the question arises of how *līlā* relates to the law of *karma*. If we understand *karma* as that which necessarily arises from an intentional, ego-related action (*karma* as *cetanā*, i.e., intentional), then, as long as our activity is egocentric (with reference to self or imagined ego), we are by that very fact tied to our act, be it unwholesome or wholesome. It remains, so to speak, centripetal all the time, so that it continually rebounds on us.

Līlā, on the other hand, is spontaneous, ego-free activity that is not determined by intentions. It is something that freely pours out of us. It overcomes *karma* in the sense of the *karma-vipāka* ethic. Literally, the word *karma* means action. If we use the word *karma* in accordance with general usage, then in Buddhism we think of an action based on will and intention, which produces a re-action. Thus we should really speak of *karma* and *vipāka*, that is, of the intentional deed and its consequences. This explains why every act that we have previously carefully considered, and which we repeat in the same way, finally becomes a spontaneous and therefore karma-free action. Also, the intentional act of concentration on a particular point, object, or idea can turn into a concentration that is simply centered in itself, which becomes spontaneous and so leads us to an inner wholeness that is the goal of all meditation.

Karma-free—that is to say, intention-free and selfless action—is only possible if we succeed in shaping our lives in the same way that a good actor plays the part, by forgetting ourselves. An actor who, during the performance, thinks and lives in the reality of his or her own individual existence, who thinks about what he or she is and what, as an actor, he or she ought to be, is a bad actor. In the same way, in this game of life (*līlā*) we can only play our parts properly when we completely forget selfhood, our separateness from the whole, and in self-forgetfulness just play the part in relation to whatever happens around us. That really makes for Buddhahood.

Buddhism teaches that we are interrelated with everything that is. The whole world can be compared to a mighty net of interrelations. There is nothing that is not akin to everything else in the universe and does not have a relation to it. Accordingly we can say that every individual is a crystallization point of everything the universe contains. All the powers of the universe are required to create a single human being, a single tree, or a single insect; without the basis of all the powers of the cosmos no being can come into existence. From this point of view we have to ask ourselves whether the coming-to-be of the innumerable forms of life is not the mightiest achievement of this entire universe. And when we then consider the universe as a whole and recognize the endless emptiness that exists in both the macrocosm and the microcosm, and see how extremely rarely those crystallizations of forms occur (that we call matter), and if we then consider how much rarer still are the conditions under which living, conscious beings can develop, then perhaps we shall understand that individuality is just as essential as universality. Indeed, universality can only be experienced through individuality, and so we can perhaps say that the universal had to produce individuals in order to become conscious of itself!

To mature into an individual does not mean to become egocentric. This is also one of the many misinterpretations people invent for themselves. They think that in order to overcome egocentricity, we merely need to deny individuality. This idea rose from a misconception of what we call the soul, and, indeed, from current psychological thinking. In order to correct these misapprehensions with the aid of the Buddhist understanding in regard to consciousness, here is a simple comparison.

Imagine a circle and its center. We see a periphery (the circle) and the center (the point). Concentration is the relationship between the periphery and the central point. In the center is the point in which all concentration becomes one. The periphery, on the other hand, is that part in which concentration is individualized. If we live entirely in the periphery, we are cut off from the center and are cabined, cribbed, confined—we are cut off from the source of all life. But if we were to live only in the center, we would deny all individuality, and the whole universe would not be conscious. Therefore, in meditation we must re-establish the connection between the periphery and the center. In so doing, our aim should be to find the middle (between periphery and center) where we have an equal share in both, or, to put it another way, where our individuality becomes a reflection of our universal center. In this way we achieve wholeness and also realize the full extent of our abilities.

At this point, in order to avoid misunderstandings, it should be made clear that the ego-function is by no means essential for the individual. Nor is it necessary for the totality of the human organism— for instance—in order to maintain and express its individuality. Every individual is, as we have seen, a unique manifestation of the whole, just as every branch is a particular, specific part of a tree. But in order to unfold its individuality, every twig and every branch must be intimately connected with the tree, just as our fingers, which act independently of one another and are separate from each other, must always stay in constant, close contact with the whole body, without which their individuality would cease to exist. And here we have reached a point that cannot be repeated often enough: *differentiation is not separate, independent existence.* Head and feet are quite different from each other, but as parts of the whole body they are not separated. And even if we were not quite so obviously bound up with the universe by physical links as the branches are with the tree, or head and feet with the body, nevertheless we are inseparably connected with the whole through innumerable physical relationships of a fascinating complexity.

In this connection, too, the death of the individual does not appear as the dissolution of existing connections and connectedness, but rather as a taking-back or "being drawn-in." The body is like a footprint or an echo; that is to say, it is like the dissolving trace of something that passed by. For we are not born into the world but out of the world. We are part of it, and the impenetrable mystery of its continuity (that we call eternity) lies at the root of our existence. Thus the universe is finally our self-created body. And this conception of the universe as our greater body found its expression in Buddhist terminology as *dharma-kāya*. It is said that every enlightened being exists in the form of three bodies, and that in a certain sense, we, too, live in three bodies. These are the *dharmakāya*, the *sambhogakāya* and the *nirmāṇakāya*: the universal body in which we all share, the body of spiritual rapture, and the body of transformation. This "body of transformation" is identical with the physical material body, in which consciousness is crystallized. But according to Buddhist philosophy we are not something different from the body, and we therefore do not regard it as a "garment" into which and out of which the eternal soul slips, as it taught by the doctrine of transmigration, according to which a "self" (*puruṣa, ātman,* etc.), monadically conceived, goes from one body into another and at death, so to speak, lays aside its "sheath."

If such ideas have spread to some extent in popular Buddhist belief, this is one of the greatest misunderstandings about the Buddhist doctrine of rebirth. The Buddha never taught anything of the sort. The Buddhist doctrine of rebirth says that consciousness becomes crystallized from the moment of conception in corporeality, and forms a whole with the body. The body is, so to speak, the crystallized product of a consciousness that belongs to the past. We therefore sometimes feel the discrepancy between the present body and the present state of our mental development. We feel that our body is lagging behind and perhaps hindering us, because it is the materialization of a process of consciousness that lies behind us, which we have transcended. But the discrepancy we feel between body and mind does not really exist. We ourselves are simultaneously representatives of two distinct time-elements or time-sections, which manifest on one hand in the form of material crystallization, and on the other in that of our ever onward-flowing consciousness.

Whereas the change in consciousness is fairly obvious, it is much harder to recognize that the body, too, is in a state of continuous change; after about seven years not a single particle is the same. And yet, although not a particle is the same, the continuity of physical form remains. This points to a central formative principle within us, which, despite all change, continually restores physical form and maintains a definite direction. In this way the change of form is never an abrupt alteration, but a gradual transformation. And so we can say that a transformation takes place from the body of a child into that of a grown-up, even though the body of the child is not the same as that of the adult that develops out of it.

The continuity that we noted in the body finds a complete parallel in the continuity that occurs in the mental psychic realm. Consciousness does not remain the same for a single instant. However, the change that takes place here, although it is the same flowing transformation, occurs more rapidly than in the body.

If we include our bodies in meditation, we see, in so far as we are willing to become conscious of the totality of the body, how the universe is mirrored in us, and how the stream of constant transformation is active in us. In this way we can "tune" the body so it corresponds to the current level of our consciousness. However, this can only be done if we succeed in gaining that profound meditative absorption in which corporeality is fully included in the process. That is why we adopt special *āsanas*, special ways of sitting and holding ourselves, in meditation.

In order that the body can react correctly to our meditative experience, we need to establish a deep link, and the best such link between the body and the mental-spiritual is our breath. Breath is the connecting function between conscious and unconscious, because it can occur both voluntarily and automatically. We cannot, by an act of will, force our hearts to change rhythm, nor can we voluntarily influence the process of digestion, the circulation, and so on. All these vegetative functions operate automatically, and even our breathing is a function mainly directed automatically by the vegetative nervous system. But breathing is more subtle than all the other vegetative functions. It is closest to the mind and can, when its relationship to consciousness is recognized, be made into a voluntarily regulated or experienced function.

Because the breath forms a living link between mind and body, we can, if we treat breathing as something experienced and not just an automatic habit, become aware of our breathing function, and follow the breath in the whole body. Then we feel how it penetrates the entirety of our body, and in experiencing this we finally feel how consciousness pervades the whole body and how the body takes part in our meditative experience.

Buddhist meditation, especially in the form in which it is practiced in the *Vajrayāna*, brings us into contact with the deeper layers of consciousness. These deep layers embrace not only our individual consciousness, but also that sphere of consciousness that is connected to the entire universe. In this way we come to know regions that are not confined to the human realm, but embrace the whole world, the whole universe, thus giving us the possibility of finding ourselves.

Spontaneous experiences, embracing our whole being in the sense of this meditation method are brought about through the great Tibetan rituals, which, as dramatized meditation, beyond all rational calculation, immediately bring the deepest layers of consciousness into play. Thus in the deep notes of the temple music—reminiscent of the mantra OM, the universal sound—we experience the elemental—rocks and mountains, the breadth of the high plateaus of Tibet, the roar of the sea. We recognize the human voice in the oboes and intuit in the high notes that rise above them how life is reflected in all its manifold forms and appearances which condition and swallow up one another, while all the time everything proceeds uninterruptedly toward that background which embraces and bears the whole.

Tantric meditation is not a static fixing, but a dynamic happening. Frightening and peaceful forms penetrate one another and turn into each other, for the divine and demonic forces are not fundamentally different. They are merely different aspects of the same energy appearing to us in various forms. When we feel goodness and beauty, we feel akin to the gods, whereas the other aspect of the divine seems to us terrifying, just as the forces of nature sometimes appear to us as benign and at other times frightening. But why do we experience certain forces as terrifying? Because we do not understand them, because they seem strange to us. Then we imagine an evil intent behind them, although they, like other powers, can at times produce good effects, because a power operates without intent, and therefore beyond all value judgments of good and bad. Thus meditation as a dynamic process—as a process of our own consciousness—sets free powers that manifest in the form of gods and demons, of peaceful and terrifying shapes.

Once we have come to this realization, we are aware that nothing remains at a standstill; everything is in constant motion. And so, in Tantric meditation, too, all the shapes we have created turn into one another. Consciousness cannot be fixed at one point. It is continually in a state of flux, continually changing, and we cannot control the change as such. We can only influence the *direction* of this constant change, and thus achieve a "directed motion" through all the changes. The purpose of meditation is to achieve this directed motion. As long as a definite direction is maintained, every change, every transformation, serves the purpose that is prescribed by that direction. Then we recognize that we are not isolated, that consciousness in fact reaches further than we thought. We discover ourselves in the consciousness of all beings, and equally, all beings in our own. Otherwise no mutual understanding would be possible, because, although we use words as symbols in conversation, there is something in every one of us through which we can understand each other even without words. In fact, our speech is often so quick that without this other consciousness within ourselves, we might not be able to understand each other.

When I first entered a Tibetan monastery, I did not yet understand the Tibetan language. But to my astonishment I discovered that entirely by itself, without language, another form of understanding developed. And this was a far deeper communication than I had ever had in any language. How was this? Because language operates in concepts, and so causes the living flow to petrify into abstraction. Therefore, in meditation we must not allow ourselves to cling to concepts. Buddhist meditation (especially in the forms developed by the *Vajrayāna*) accordingly works very much with pictures. Conceptual thought is replaced by thinking and experiencing in pictures, because it is only the picture that enables us to have direct experience. The concept as an abstraction, on the other hand, provides us with second-hand experience, that is to say, experience that is derived from other experiences. The main task of meditation is to make first-hand experiences possible. And that, too, is the reason why—particularly in Zen—the demand is constantly made not to remain stuck with rational deductions, but to pass beyond them.

How *can* we get beyond our thoughts, our words and concepts? This can be done, for instance, through the experience of inner pictures, through visualization. If we are going to follow this path, we should always heed the warnings of the Tibetan texts: that in all visualization we should never fall into the error of imagining that what we see is a reality outside of ourselves. All the things we see are projections of our own minds. We must be constantly aware that visions are not a gift from the gods, and that they do not exist anywhere outside ourselves and do not "come over us." What we see in a vision in the play of our own consciousness, our own creation, the product of our own minds, born this instant. It is not some ultimate reality, and yet in another sense it is real, because whatever our power of imagination produces is based on something previously given. Consider, for instance, the picture of the rope that was mistaken for a snake. At the very moment we recognize that it is not a snake but a rope, our fear vanishes. But the rope is still there. And that, too, is an illusion. In other words, the rope is an illusion, and the snake is an illusion of an illusion. The moment we recognize the illusion as an illusion, we are freed from it. But if we cling to our illusion and believe it is real, we are trapped and bound. It is important to recognize that what we call an illusion is based on certain laws of consciousness, and that our consciousness in turn rests on the laws of existence, that is to say, universal laws. That means, however, that the laws underlying all illusions in fact lead us closer to reality. If we can manage to see through the illusion, it turns into a helper that aids us in our search for reality.

We must learn that the gods and demons of all the worlds dwell within ourselves. They are not some sort of powers working from without that can arbitrarily determine our fate. We follow the laws of our own karma, and it is our own karma that shapes our future.

Many people think meditation consists of investigating what they once were in some previous life or lives. Many imagine they were famous—kings, great writers, and so on. They hardly ever consider that they might have been washerwomen or street sweepers, or very ordinary people. But is not the simplest job, which is often disregarded, just as important as those that are held in high esteem? We should not care whether we were kings or queens or simple workers in the past. What we should be concerned about in meditation is the realization that here and now, at every moment, we are sowing the seeds of our future. This is something that Buddhist meditation has always stressed.

If we use mantras in meditation, we should not do so because we believe in their effectiveness. To have belief is in certain cases valuable. We know that belief can mislead as well as help people. For the sake of belief, we have burned, waged war, and murdered others because they believed something different. Thus belief, although it is a valuable faculty, can also turn into a terrible danger. Buddhism is the only religion in which belief has been assigned to its proper place. The Buddha said that we must have a reason for beliefs (Sanskrit *śraddhā*, which also means confidence, or inner conviction). Whoever believes blindly in something—whether good or bad—is not master of it. If belief or confidence has arisen after due consideration, then we know why we believe why we hold this conviction or pursue particular ideas.

Accordingly, the Buddha stressed that we should not follow him out of love or respect, but only if our own experiences coincided with what he taught. Thus Buddhism is one of the few religions that follow the guidance of our inmost being, that is to say not the guidance of the intellect but that of our deeper nature which contains and embraces everything.

Tantric Buddhist meditation makes use of mantras as a means to an end within the framework of a specific technique. The background is a mantric science, which demands more than faith, and above all an understanding in depth. Thus for instance we must know, when we chant a particular mantra, which visual form it is related to. This does not mean that the mantra depends on the vision. It simply means that we conjure up a particular vision with the aid of the mantra, and that the vision thus obtained is more profound than the form associated with it. For through the mantra our deepest feelings are released, which may emerge through trusting faith, but which are rooted in understanding.

If, for instance, we recite the sound OM, we feel that is something all-embracing, universal. On the other hand, ĀH expresses a horizontally extended motion, and with HŪM there is a feeling of going into the depths. That is, with these three mantric sounds we touch on three levels—the universal, the human, and that of the subconscious, or that of nature in its deepest sense. When I speak of nature, I mean those forms of life that reach far beyond our purely intellectual existence, which fulfill us inwardly, and at the same time link us with others. These three levels are expressed in OM—ĀH—HŪM. If, when we recite a mantra, we are not aware of the network of relationship of which it forms a part, then the sound or the word that we repeat, however fine it may sound, has no inner value, and conveys nothing.

If we want to penetrate deeper into this mantric science, we will soon find that every mantra is connected with a particular cakra (wheel) or physical center within us. And if we want to stimulate one or other of the cakras deliberately, we have to use the corresponding mantra. Without the knowledge of their interconnections, the mantras are just sounds that appeal to us because of their rhythm, but which cannot initiate any more profound process.

It is also important to know that each one of these psychic centers has to be stimulated and activated afresh every time. We wish to be perfect and complete because we feel that we are not yet complete and whole human beings. And we can see this goal that we strive after realized in the Buddha, who is for us the figure of a perfect human being—the image not only of someone good, but of one who has become whole. That is much more than being a god, for a god stands far below the range of possibilities that slumber within us. The status of a god is that of one form of existence in the cycle of becoming, which is probably very happy, peaceful and beautiful. But such a condition is not the one really worth striving for, because in such an ivory castle of happiness we cannot experience the other side of life with its suffering, and without this, compassion cannot develop in us.

Only when we have developed the capacity to suffer with others shall we succeed in understanding others and feeling with them, forgetting our own suffering—or at least disregarding it—in the face of theirs. Compassion constitutes the essence of the Buddhist way of life, and is always inextricably linked with wisdom. For compassion without wisdom leads nowhere, and wisdom without compassion leads to spiritual ossification. Therefore we must develop wisdom and compassion harmoniously and together, because they are the pillars of Dharma. If we have developed them, then we are on the path of the Enlightened One.

The Importance of Ritual

Attachment to moral rules and rituals (*sīlabbata parāmāsa*) was regarded by the Buddha as one of the greatest hindrances on the path to liberation. The stress lay not so much on moral rules and rituals as on the *clinging and attachment* to them. Even in the earliest Buddhist communities there were many ritual cult-practices that were an expression of either faith or tradition. These were forms, such as the triple refuge in the Buddha, the Dharma and the Sangha in the ordination ceremonies, for which a special consecrated place was chosen. These rituals were performed in the absence of anybody who did not belong to the monastic order. Likewise there were special *pūjās* and *parittas* (held for the protection of health and mind). Whenever we cling to something, even if it is something entirely good, it becomes a fetter which inhibits our forward march to freedom. This includes the five *sīlas* or rules of conduct that the Buddha gave his followers.

This, too, is the reason why it is said that Zen masters follow no moral rules and no tradition, and even reject Buddhist scriptures for the sake of mental spontaneity and honesty. In spite of this, Zen followers have to submit to strict rules and a code of ceremonial behavior demanding the greatest concentration and mindfulness. Western admirers of the unorthodox ways of Zen, which appear to open the gates to all possible individual opinions and weaknesses, would only need to spend a short time in a Japanese Zen monastery to be cured of this misconception!

If we accept the five *sīlas* as rules for our lives, we should not turn them into commandments that must be observed at all costs, irrespective of whether or not we are convinced of their worth. Otherwise we would be like the monk who, by obeying the rule not to touch a woman, allowed his mother, who had fallen into a well, to drown. Only when we understand the reasons why the rules were made and are in full agreement with them, should we accept them as our own and act accordingly. The Buddha did not want blind devotees. He was the only founder of a religion who allowed criticism and even encouraged it. He wanted followers and successors who came to his way by their own experience and conviction. And so he said to Ānanda, his favorite disciple: "If you only follow the Dharma out of love for me or because you respect me, I would not accept you as a disciple. But if you follow the Dharma because you have found out its truth for yourself, and if you understand it and act accordingly, then you have the right to call yourself a disciple of the Exalted One."

Moral rules and rituals are acceptable when they are practiced in the right spirit, that is to say, after complete understanding and with clear awareness. If we celebrate a ritual simply as a matter of routine, or because it is prescribed by tradition or convention, then it is not only useless but a hindrance. If a ritual is carried out consciously, conscientiously, and with a complete understanding of its meaning, then it becomes an act of meditation—a meditation that is transferred without and turned into action.

If we offer candles to the Buddha, we should not imagine that we are doing the Buddha a service, but rather that we are doing something good for ourselves and our fellow beings. It is an expression of striving for enlightenment for ourselves and for the whole world. This also applies to incense and other offerings that express our gratitude, devotion, and a readiness to follow in the footsteps of the Enlightened One in order to awaken the still sleeping qualities of enlightenment within ourselves. In other words, *we should look on a Buddha image as on something that reminds us of the Buddha within ourselves, as an expression of that great ideal that the historical Buddha realized in his life, and that we, too, can realize in ours; for this goal lies within the range of possibilities for all conscious beings.* We are not doing the Buddha a favor by honoring his image, but we are strengthening our own determination to follow his path, to bring the Dharma to realization, which is not only his teaching, but is also the universal law on the human plane.

Accordingly, the Buddha image is not just a representation of a personality who walked the earth 2500 years ago, but the image of a perfect and, in this sense, complete human being, the embodiment of that humanity we are striving to realize. When we bow to the Buddha image, we do not honor the Enlightened One, we overcome ego and pride. Devotion rids us of the main hindrance to meditation—our overestimation of ego—and opens us up to a greater life.

When we look at a statue of Buddha, even if we know nothing about Buddhism, we will see a representation of a perfectly spiritual human being, a human being who never lost the firm ground of reality, because he accepted and ennobled his bodily existence without clinging to it, without depending on it, and thus lived at peace with himself and the world. What inner bliss and happiness are mirrored in his face, what equanimity and calm appears in every limb of his body, what profound silence and harmony! This harmony is infectious and suffuses the on-looker. Here there are no more wishes, there is no desire, no restlessness, no insecurity, no chasing after material things, no dependence on anything at all. Here is the highest bliss: in a word—completeness, perfection.

There are, and always have been, enlightened beings who achieved this universality. We can give expression to our veneration by raising our joined hands to our foreheads or above our heads, to honor their highest realization, to call to mind that we, too, can realize it by stimulating and activating these higher centers of consciousness to a similar awakening.

This form of veneration is a common feature of all ritual devotions as practiced all over the East, often accompanied by prostrations in which the forehead touches the ground. This is an exercise in humility that often comes only with difficulty to Westerners. It hurts our pride, our vanity, our ego and our false sense of dignity. In reality, this touching of the ground with the highest center of consciousness is not only an act of humility but also a symbol of the fact that *the highest consciousness has to descend into the depth of material existence; that the lowest and the highest are interchangeable (being one in their essence, and only distinguished in appearance and function); and that the earth is the basis, the womb, and the matrix of all development and spiritual realization.*

As long as we consider matter and spirit as irreconcilable opposites, we split the world into two halves and lose the ground under our feet. It has been the tragedy of most religions that they have tried to alienate us from the world in which we were born. Instead of—as was their duty and their proper task—encouraging us to develop the world, they taught us to condemn and neglect it. What we call matter is one of the rarest phenomena in the universe. It only appears where energy is concentrated and condensed in visible form, which can take billions of years. And this matter serves as a basis for all forms of life to develop, which again requires billions of years. Since no organism can exist without matter, and no consciousness can develop without an organism, mind, in the sense of a consciousness that is conscious of itself, cannot develop without the tension between matter, thinking, and feeling. Matter is just as important as that which we call mind, in fact it is the basis of all that exists. It is the mother (*materia*, from the same root as mother) of the world we live in.

It is more important and more sensible to materialize our minds than to try to spiritualize matter. If mind cannot find expression in material form, or in some action or achievement in life, it remains a mere thought or a vague emotion that remains within our heads or hearts and never finds any expression in words, deeds or works of art. If Michelangelo had never given expression to his ideas and feelings in sculptures, paintings and poems, the world would never have received the gift of his creations, and he would not have become what he was. And the same thing is true, according to circumstances, for all human beings. Those who do not give form to their feelings and thoughts by expressing them in some shape or other have lived in vain, whereas those who expressed their feelings and thoughts in works or deeds both enriched their own existences and contributed something to the well-being and development of their fellows.

Ritual is one form in which we can express our deepest thoughts and feelings. But it must be the expression of clear thought, or of genuine feeling. Otherwise the ritual is just the empty repetition of conventional forms, and becomes a hindrance on the way to enlightenment.

The Act of Will and
the Practice of Meditation[1]

W e are told that the world is going through an energy and power crisis. Only a few people realize that this is true in a far deeper sense than might be assumed from a purely economic point of view. Energy has become a kind of obsession, and has turned into a self-destructive principle. That in turn his led to a psychological revolt against the deepest roots of all energy, power, and force—against the intellect and the will that led to such control— and to such misuse of the powers of nature that leads step-by-step to the destruction of the ecology of our planet, and thus of the whole of humanity.

This psychologically understandable revolt has taken on two forms. One is the attempt to escape from the intellect and from all forms of responsible action by taking drugs. The other seeks to overcome the intellect and its volitions, dictated by desire and craving, by turning away from the external world and trying to take refuge in meditative practices through which the sub- and unconscious powers are awak-

---

[1]*In memoriam* to Dr. Roberto Assagioli, the founder of psychosynthesis, who passed away in September 1974, age 86.

ened—but without gaining a clear understanding of the nature of these powers, and without possessing the ability to integrate them.

It is not surprising that the human will has been discredited and is identified with a concept of energy and power (and especially with the power and force of the ego), which either separates the individual from the universal or else represses a particular aspect of human nature. As a result of this misestimation, the importance of the human will has been relegated into the background by modern popular psychology, with the resultant impression that human beings are nothing but a product of biological urges, drives and compulsions, determined and conditioned by forces and circumstances beyond the control of the individual.

Because of this misunderstanding, it is good to be reminded, by works such as *The Act of Will* by Dr. Assagioli,[2] that despite all unconscious drives and conditioned reflexes, the role of the conscious will is of decisive importance not only for the intellectual life of the individual, but still more for the completion of our spiritual strivings and the development of creative faculties. Our conscious will is the basis of our sense of personal responsibility, and therefore the basis of all ethical values, without which human existence would be unthinkable and senseless. The will is also the foundation of all religious thinking and experience. The assumption that the will was "something stern and forbidding, which condemns and represses most of the other aspects of human nature"[3] created the present-day misunderstanding of the nature and function of the will, since will cannot be separated from the distinguishing and goal-oriented functions of consciousness.

Through the artificial separation of these functions in our conceptual terminology we create a non-existent problem. No impulse of will can take place without a distinguishing consciousness. Therefore a differentiating and directed consciousness is the precondition for the production of a goal-oriented power of will, which is not a biological

---

[2]Roberto Assagioli, *The Act of Will* (New York and London: Penguin, 1974).
[3]Assagioli, *The Act of Will*, p. 10.

force (like those drives of the sub- and unconscious), but a psychic one. Assagioli says:

> The will has a *directive* and *regulatory* function; it balances and constructively utilizes all the other activities and energies of the human being without repressing any of them.
>
> The function of the will is similar to that performed by the helmsman of a ship. He knows what the ship's course should be, and keeps her steadily on it, despite the drifts caused by the wind and current. But the power he needs to turn the wheel is altogether different from that required to propel the ship through the water, whether it be generated by engines, the pressure of winds on the sail, or the effort of rowers.[4]

In this image, the wind, current and other forces correspond to biological drives, the influence of surroundings, and all those general forces by which the individual is *conditioned*, but *not* totally and without exception *determined*. This is where the principle of free will comes in, which makes possible an alternative between a right and a wrong decision, between a more and a less favorable choice, or between two equally acceptable possibilities. The action of the helmsman (the conscious individual) is based on *knowledge* of what course the ship has to take in order to reach the chosen harbor of destination. In other words, the nature of the will depends on the state of knowledge and understanding. As long as we see ourselves as independent or separate egos, the will is going to be egocentrically determined and limited. The moment we realize and perceive ourselves as beings, the will is transformed into a transpersonal faculty. And if we recognize that it is an exponent of the wholeness of the universe, then the will becomes an expression of that universal law that Indian philosophy calls *Dharma*, and that reveals itself in the human heart (or its inner core) as the realization of the

---

[4]Assagioli, *The Act of Will*, p. 10.

highest spirit or the universal consciousness. Here, the aspect of energy and power—the will to dominate, control, suppress or resist—disappears, giving place to a condition of profound harmony. Assagioli continues:

> Thus, a proper understanding of the will includes a clear and balanced view of its dual nature: two different but not contradictory poles. On one hand the "power element" needs to be recognized, appreciated, if necessary strengthened, and then wisely applies. At the same time it must be recognized that there are volitional acts which do not necessarily require effort. [5]

That is the case, for instance, in the more advanced stages of meditation and absorption, in which inspirational or intuitive forces take the place previously (and in the beginning stages of meditative practice with justification and rightly) occupied by conceptual and goal-oriented motivations. But in the higher stages of absorption, the personal will is effortless because

> . . . the willer is so identified with the Transpersonal Will, or at still a higher and more inclusive level, with the Universal Will, that his activities are accomplished with free spontaneity, a state in which he feels himself to be a willing channel into and through which powerful energies flow and operate. [6]

The concept of will takes on different meanings at different levels of consciousness, and accordingly Assagioli distinguishes various aspects of the human will, such as strong will (in which we experience the will as a dynamic power), skillful will (which we can define as "the ability to obtain the desired results with the least possible expenditure of energy"), good will (in which appropriate means are used for altruistic

---

[5] Assagioli, *The Act of Will*, p. 21.
[6] Assagioli, *The Act of Will*, p.21.

results), transpersonal will (equated with the urge to find a meaning in life—the urge for the highest realization: Sanskrit *dharma-chanda*), and finally universal will (in which the will is in perfect harmony with the universal law or *dharma*).[7]

This concept of different aspects of the will at different levels of consciousness solves one of the problems that are always arising in the definition and practice of meditation. We are told on the one hand that meditation requires willpower in that it must be practiced deliberately, with orientation on a goal, and with concentration. On the other hand, it is a condition of complete freedom from thought, concept, idea, impulse of will, aim and striving—a condition without distinction, calculation, or any other intellectual attitude—simply a state of pure awareness, of absorption, of pure being. To illustrate the spiritual attitude, here are a few sentences from a recent essay on "Contemplation" by Alan Watts:

> You—understood as that "ego"—cannot attain to the polar vision or cosmic awareness. It may suddenly break through in you, as if by the grace of God—but there is nothing, nothing at all that you can do or not do in order to produce it.
>
> When that has been understood, then the effort to transform the mind will collapse, and with it the entire illusion that one is a separate center of consciousness to which experiences occur and for which these events are problematic. And this collapse will then lead to the state of absorption—to the recognition that everything is one.[8]

If we follow the advice of the Buddha (which has proved its value for thousands of years and is equally valid now) to avoid extremes, both in thought and in life, then we must recognize that one extreme is to consider ourselves as something different from the universe we live in.

---

[7]Assagioli, *The Act of Will*, pp. 14–18.
[8]The essay the author is referring to may be from Alan Watts, *The Art of Contemplation* (New York: Pantheon, a division of Random House, 1973). The translation is mine. Tr.

To suppose that we are identical with that universe is the other extreme. In truth we are neither the same nor different from the universe (rather in the same way that we are neither the same as, nor different from, the personality we had yesterday or when we were children), because we are not simply self-contained and unchanging units or monads, but are the outcome of endless interconnected causes and effects which in their sum equal the wholeness of the universe.

The individual can be compared to a whirlpool in a turbulent river, inseparable from it but not identical with it. Although of the same origin, yet different in form and appearance, the whirlpool, like the individual, creates its own center through its own unique form of motion, and still remains a part of the greater (universal) stream. This is beautifully put in the opening sentence of the previously quoted essay by Alan Watts:

> The individual is an aperture through which the whole energy of the universe becomes conscious of itself—a vibrating point in which the universe knows itself as man or beast, flower or stone—yet not separated, but as the center of all that surrounds it.[9]

How much closer this symbolic and poetic language comes to reality than all the purely logically constructed theories! Is not "the hole" (emptiness) in the center of the whirlpool the very opening through which the individual becomes capable of developing into the most perfect vessel for the universe to become aware of itself in? Such an image justifies and legitimates individual existence and at the same time shows the importance of the individual as the opposite pole of the universe, and thus also the inseparability of the two poles. The Vedānta position, which speaks of absolute unity, attempts to ascribe reality only to the universal pole and, by relegating the individual pole to the status of mere illusion, condemns all individual life as meaningless and thus rejects all individual striving after self-realization. But the mere assertion

---

[9]Watts, *loc cit.* The translation is mine. *Tr.*

that all is one cannot abolish the fact that uniqueness without differences, like unity without multiplicity, is senseless, and that multiplicity itself is born from an endlessly progressing polarity.

Reality is not to be found in the abstract concept of undifferentiated unity or equality, but in the recognition of creative polarity, in which the tension between the positive and negative poles enables that uniting spark of life and consciousness to appear, in which alone unity can be *experienced*. Therefore what we call reality can best be described as actuality (*Wirklichkeit* from *wirken* to act), because only that which acts on us can be experienced. Whatever cannot be experienced exists merely as a concept.

The slogan "all is one" is just as one-sided as "all is different." Both are equally conceptual extremes; one denies (or at least minimizes) the value of the individual and all individual effort, while the other denies the universality dwelling in the individual and thus overestimates the role of individual willpower. The first-named standpoint regards all techniques of meditative training as superfluous, if not absurd, and deprives the individual of divine grace or the spontaneity of intuition. The second relies too much on strength—both routine training and personal achievement—and by its arbitrariness, suppresses the spontaneous powers of intuitive insight.

Here, too, it seems to me, the middle way (as propounded by the Buddha, and as recommended in Assagioli's presentation) is the best method on the path of realization, a path in which human striving and effort on the one hand, and intelligence in the form of clear thinking and lofty aspiration on the other, are used as the starting point for meditation. The Buddha's enlightenment, too, was as Assagioli stresses, the result and the reward of his efforts of will. D.T. Suzuki said that enlightenment includes *both will and intellect*, because it is an intuitive act of completion, born of the will.

Of course, this "will" is no longer the ego-motivated will of the ordinary self-seeking individual, but that which Assagioli would call the transpersonal will. It is a will that has been sublimated and transformed into a power that, far beyond all petty aims and goals, transcends individual limitations, and finally turns the individual into a ready channel through which the powerful energies of the universe flow and work.

As long as people block this channel with the ego-centered will or the illusion of separateness, or because they simply are unaware of this potential source of energy, they cannot make any use of it. Therefore, meditative practices have no other purpose than to awaken awareness, to develop and strengthen it, and, further, to eliminate the obstacles that stand in the way of the free flow of creative and life-giving energy. In addition, they should open up the mind for unlimited possibilities of experience, at the same time making it a tool capable of integrating these experiences into everyday life.

Even the greatest genius (whether artist or thinker) must have command over the organs of perception, the means of giving them creative expression, and the laws governing these. Such training leads to a condition in which the employment of the conscious will, of effort, directed striving and concentration do not obstruct spontaneity, but work toward preparing the ground for the reception and integration of intuitive experiences and spontaneous insight into the nature of reality. Thus meditative training has no other purpose than to put us into a state of increased receptivity to strengthen our sensitivity and turn us into "ready channels" for the powers of inspiration. But inspiration *alone* would waste itself in momentary feelings of elevation and liberation (or in mere emotionalism), if it were not integrated into our being through the creative act of giving it form and expression, for no power can work unless it has form and direction. It is here that we see the importance of art, of clear thought, of profound vision like the realization of a new dimension of consciousness, which can change our attitude to life, giving it a new direction by giving life a new and more profound meaning. Without the creative activity of transpersonal will, neither drug-induced visions (which are not expansions of consciousness but merely the result of a confused transmission of messages from the nervous system) nor self-hypnotic trances (the result of misdirected meditation practices) have any spiritual value. They are only attempts to escape from the realities of life. Another attempt to escape the realities of life is:

. . . the attempt to escape it by returning to a primitive state of consciousness to be reabsorbed into the "mother," into a prenatal state to lose oneself in the collective life. This is the way of *regression*. The other is the above-mentioned way of *transcendence*, of "rising above" ordinary consciousness . . . so we need to face courageously and willingly the requirements for transcending *the limitations* of personal consciousness, without losing the center of individual awareness. This is possible because individuality and universality are not mutually exclusive.[10]

The union of these two in the realization of the human mind—in a state of enlightenment—is not only the goal of Assagioli's *psychosynthesis*, but also of all creative meditation that finds its expression in an attitude of mind that seeks not to avoid life's problems but to solve them. Psychoanalysis is a valuable tool for exploring the human mind, but if it is not followed up by a synthesis, its therapeutic effect is of limited value. That is why Assagioli's psychosynthesis seems to be especially valuable at the present day, because the analytical tendency of an all-inquiring and distinguishing intellect can lead to the destruction and devaluation of all creative effort, unless we again come to recognize the role of the human will as a conscious power that depends on the level of our knowledge and power of imagination, and which alone is capable of delivering us from the tyranny of blind drives and compulsions.

Knowledge and imagination are two poles of consciousness. Knowledge is based on experiences that are stored in memory. Imagination, on the other hand, is the creative application of this knowledge, or the intuitive enablement of consciousness—here in a quasi-playful attitude—to bring about, step-by-step through its internal impulsion, an inner direction of mind through which all the works of art and all the great discoveries made by the human mind were born. This function and the power of will are not mutually exclusive any more than are the

---

[10]Assagioli, *The Act of Will*, p. 113.

spontaneity and training required for mental or technical skills, both being necessary for the shaping, formulating and realization of intuitive insights. This is demonstrated by the life and work of great artists and thinkers, whose creations are based on uninterrupted effort, persistence and intense concentration.

The greatest creative principle and source of strength is the power, force and energy of the *imagination*, which inspires and leads human genius. According to Jacob Bronowski,

> These images play out for us events which are not present to our senses, and thereby guard the past and create the future— a future that does not yet exist, and may never come to exist in that form. By contrast, the lack of symbolic ideas, or their rudimentary poverty, cuts off an animal from the past and the future alike, and imprisons it in the present. Of all the distinctions between man and animal, the characteristic gift which makes us human is the power to work with symbolic images: the gift of imagination.[11]

This is the real basis of Tantric meditation, which was practiced in India and Tibet, and whose sphere of influence extended over the greater part of Asia including the Far East, where it everywhere gave the impulse to works of art and to a literature that is only now beginning to be investigated.

According the William James "every picture of the imagination contains a motor-like element within it." And Assagioli formulates this as a basic law as follows:

> Images or mental pictures and ideas tend to produce the physical conditions and external acts that correspond to them. . . . Attitudes, movements, and actions tend to evoke corresponding images and ideas; these, in turn . . . evoke or inten-

---

[11]Jacob Bronowski, *A Sense of the Future: Essays in Natural Philosophy* (Cambridge, MA: The MIT Press, 1977), p. 25.

sify corresponding emotions and feelings. . . . Attention, interest, affirmations, and repetitions reinforce the ideas,
images, and psychological formations on which they are centered.[12]

Here we have in a few words a competent account of the main
elements of meditation and mental training, in which both will and
intuition have their place, and that demonstrates that training and
spontaneity do not conflict with one another, for:

Great is the power of images, and they can be said to constitute
a necessary intermediary between the will and other psychological functions . . . the will possesses no *direct* power over
the intuitive function . . . the will can perform a most helpful
indirect action; it can create and keep clear the channel of
communication along which intuitive impressions descend.[13]

But, just as the power of imagination stimulates the will in relation to
the realization of the imagination, so, too, the will is able to call forth
powerful and significant images, and to give them direction. Assagioli
uses for his therapeutic method what he calls *directed imagination*. As
already mentioned, this technique was practiced and developed earlier—especially in Tibet—with this difference: that here the guidance
of imagination was not left to the choice and judgment of the individual
practitioner or the spiritual teacher, but was based on the collective
experience of countless generations of sādhakas (practicers), a living
tradition more than a thousand years old.

The West still has much to learn from this store of experience. But
a psychological approach on the basis of the depth and wisdom of
Assagioli's psychosynthesis will finally enable understanding to be
reached, and hopefully prove the importance of the act of will for daily
living as well as for the art of meditation.

---

[12]Assagioli, *The Act of Will*, pages 51, 52, and 56.
[13]Assagioli, *The Act of Will*, pp. 194–195.

Love and Attachment

————

The word *attachment* is frequently used by Buddhists in English. It is intended to express the idea that we bind ourselves through our passionate, demanding possessiveness, and that we therefore necessarily suffer by being so bound when, sooner or later, the object of desire eludes our grasp. It is therefore in non-attachment, in giving up and letting go (the sign of the true love that wishes to make not itself but the loved person happy) that the way to the overcoming of suffering is to be sought.

This basic Buddhist attitude that teaches people to show first real love, real compassion, and unrestricted joy in the joy of others (while at the same time, we attain to an inner equanimity in regard to whatever happens to ourselves), was at a relatively early date reinterpreted and taken to mean that *every* kind of human attachment and love was devalued. This concept arose because of the wide range of meanings in the English word *detachment,* but the German-speaking Buddhists followed suit, using the words *Verhaftetsein* or *Anhaften* for all forms of love and affection, irrespective of whether it was a matter of passionate desire and possessiveness or of loving devotion. In this way, Western Buddhism was turned into a gloomily ascetic anti-world doctrine. But being attached in the sense of inner devotion and love is a very different thing from possessive attachment (*taṇhā*). If a person close to me has an accident or dies, that causes suffering. And to accept this suffering is far better than to remain unmoved in cold equanimity.

It is true that at some fairly early date certain Oriental Buddhists also aided this development by equating quite different emotions. In so doing, they appealed to the words of the Buddha, who is said to have declared to one of the great female supporters of the Sangha, when she was in despair over the death of her grandson, to whom she was greatly attached: "Whoever has great love has great suffering. . . . Whoever has no love has no suffering." These words, torn from their context—which was to help a person who in a particular situation could not free herself from what had been irretrievably lost to her—has since then served ideological critics and opponents of Buddhism who wished to represent the Buddha's doctrine as one of coolness, of inhuman coldness and lack of feeling. And it must be admitted that there have been, and are, Buddhists in East and West who profess non-attachment in this sense. But it becomes clear how far from the real spirit of Buddhism their conception is when we consider the definition of love (Pali *mettā*, Sanskrit *maitrī*) which the Buddha himself gave in the central verses of the *Karaṇīya-Mettā-Sutta*:

> Thus as a mother with her life
> Might guard her son, her only child,
> Would he maintain unboundedly
> His thought for every living being.
> His thought of love for all the world
> He would maintain unboundedly,
> Above, below, and all around,
> Unchecked, no malice with or foe.[14]

Buddhist authors in the past have always hesitated to translate the word *mettā* or *maitrī* as love, choosing instead, probably with some

---

[14]Verses translated by Nanamoli.

embarrassment, such as terms as kindness (*Güte*), friendliness, and so on (in English most usually loving-kindness). It is true that a mother is also kind to her child, but in the first instance she *loves* the child. Therefore, the rejection of the word love for *mettā* or *maitrī* is quite unjustified, especially since this word perhaps expresses the highest capacity of mankind which—when perfected—reaches its culmination in *cetovimutti* (liberation of heart and mind), and finally in *mahākaruṇa* (supreme compassion) and *muditā* (sympathetic joy).

Returning once more to the passage quoted (so often out of context) from the Pali Canon: "Whoever has no love has no suffering," it will be clear to anyone who has absorbed the spirit of Buddhism that, in isolation, it totally contradicts the essence of the Buddha's teaching. This becomes even clearer when we turn it round: "Whoever has no suffering has no love." Is it not a matter of course that we are lovingly attached to our friends? And naturally, we do not feel in any way guilty about being attached to them. But as always when we have to make use of words, we have again fallen into the trap of words and concepts. There is scarcely a single word in any language that has only one meaning. If we want to be clear about the question of attachment, we must first ask what kind of attachment we experience in this particular instance. We must test our attachment in regard to its specific nature and characteristics, for only by doing so can we determine whether it is wholesome or unwholesome. If we cling to things or beings with passionate possessiveness, we will experience suffering and learn the unwholesome nature of our actions. But if we are inclined toward things and beings with an inner freedom and with loving sentiments, that is wholesome.

However, it's not quite as simple as that. If we assume that a person is attached or devoted to the Dharma (the great universal rule of law) and to the highest goals of perfection, we must admit that that kind of attachment is not any kind of wrong attachment. If the attachment to the Dharma takes the form of clinging to some particular formulation of that Dharma, if scholasticism overwhelms and suffocates every new manifestation of Dharma, then everything is easily turned into its opposite, and leads to intolerance and narrowness and orthodox claims to knowledge instead of the openness of spirit, like that of a beginner, which is the essence of spiritual discipleship.

In Buddhism we make a distinction between *kāmacchanda* and *dharmacchanda*. *Kāmacchanda* is the passionate possessive attachment to sense-objects or involvement in sensual love. *Dharmacchanda*, on the other hand, denotes loving inclination and a devotion to the highest goal. *Kāmacchanda* and *dharmacchanda* are both *chanda*, a word which can be translated as attachment (in the sense of possessiveness), but also as loving inclination or devotion.

The Buddha as well aware of the danger that people might misunderstand even such a high ideal as *dharmacchanda*. And so he used the parable already mentioned, according to which the Dharma as a concept or formulated doctrine—including his own—was to be regarded as a raft to cross a stream.

> This *dhamma* has been taught to you, monks, to be used as a raft for crossing over the river, not for holding on to. You monks who have understood the parable of the raft should give up even the true teaching—how much more then the false. [15]

On the basis of these words of consolation spoken by the Buddha, many Buddhists declare that one must suffer all the more, the more loving attachment one feels for other beings. Here the question must be asked: is not suffering a small price to pay for the privilege of loving? I personally would rather take upon myself the suffering arising from loving others, than to be incapable of love. For it is only from this basic attitude that we can develop the capacity for compassion and sympathy with other beings. And if there were really such a thing as the state of so-called perfection in which those who have attained it remained untouched by all the suffering round about them, then I frankly admit

---

[15] *Majjhima Nikaya: 22.*

that this kind of so-called holiness leaves me cold, and that I have no desire for it.

In my long life I have again and again met people who were in despair because they did not know how they could ever attain inner freedom because they had so many attachments. It seems important that they should first ask what was the nature of their attachment. If they are greedily attached to money, goods, objects, particular places and all sorts of possessions, then of course this fondness becomes an attachment that will keep them bound as prisoners. But if a man is devoted to his wife, a mother to her child, children to their parents, a chela (pupil) to his or her guru, and a guru to a chela, then such devotion is an expression of love, and as long as this does not degenerate into a desire to possess, it is a positive quality. People with no attachments of this kind, who have developed no personal relations to anyone based on love, even if they should be perfect saints, doing harm to none and committing no evil deeds, would, to me, be cold and monstrous beings with no human features. Therefore I prefer the weeping Ānanda to all the cold-blooded Arahants who—according to the *Mahāparinibbāna Sutta*—sat round the dying Buddha with stony, unmoved countenances, wrapped up in their own holiness and perfection.[16] I would give all these frosty Arahants for a single tear of Ānanda's, for he was the only one who had remained human, who, despite his profound understanding of the Buddha's doctrine, had preserved his human qualities. He was the only one who loved the Buddha and realized the enormous loss of all that the personal and physical presence of the Buddha had meant to him, something dearer to him than all the doctrinal explanations. The others considered that they had absorbed these so perfectly that there was nothing further that was unclear or problematic for them, and so they had no further questions to ask the

---

[16]The account in the *Mahāparinibbāna Sutta* (*Digha Nikaya*: 16), like many other passages, was probably revised at this point at one of the councils, so that the image of the Arahant was idealized to conform to that of an imperturbable stoic. I have far too great a respect for the Buddha's chief disciples, who, as other passages show, were indeed capable of profound emotions. How could they not have felt moved and sad at the passing of the man who had been the light of their path?

Buddha before his passing. But are people who feel no attachment to anyone still living human beings? It seems to me that such people are perfect egoists—spiritually dead, and therefore incapable of any further spiritual growth. They may be "perfect," but they have entered a cul-de-sac and turned into perfect fossils.

We must distinguish between possessive attachment and attachment that forms an inner bond between beings who love each other, are concerned for each other and feel for each other. That loving attachments and brotherly love was highly regarded in the Sangha in the Buddha's lifetime is shown by the following extract from the Pali Cannon:

Once the Blessed One went to the East Eastern Bamboo Park, where the Venerable Anuruddha, the Venerable Nandiya and the Venerable Kimbila were living. The Venerable Anuruddha went to the Venerable Nandiya and the Venerable Kimbila and said: "Come out, venerable sirs, come out! Our Master has come." . . .

The Blessed One said to them: "I hope that you are all keeping well, Anuruddha, that you are comfortable, and that you have no trouble on account of alms-food."

"We are all keeping well, Blessed One. We are comfortable and have no trouble on account of alms food."

"I hope that you all live in concord and agreement, Anuruddha, as undisputing as milk with water, viewing each other with kindly eyes?"

"Surely we do so, venerable sir."

"But Anuruddha, how do you live thus?"

"Venerable sir, as to that, I think thus: It is gain for me, it is great gain for me that I am living with such companions in the life divine. I maintain bodily, verbal and mental acts of loving-kindness towards these venerable ones both in public and in private. I think: Why should I not set aside what I am minded to do and do only what they are minded to do? And

I act accordingly. We are different in body, venerable sir, but only one mind, I think."[17]

The Buddha received the same answer from the venerables Nandiya and Kimbila. At the same time, we should always remember that the Buddha's path is a middle way. And so, however wonderful the love between husband and wife, between mother and child, or between two friends may be, we must always be on our guard lest it turn into possessiveness. Even mother-love can be possessive, and the moment affection turns to possessiveness, it becomes a hindrance.

Let us state the position once more, quite clearly. Chanda as inclination, attachment, or affection cannot be judged solely on the nature of its object. It is far more important to know whether it is based on a tendency to possessiveness. But even possessive love can, in certain circumstances, be a factor that evokes and develops the capacity for genuine, freely-given love. Therefore we should not dismiss even possessive love as something totally negative and reject it altogether—it can be the seed from which true love and true sympathy burgeons and bears fruit.

Chanda—of whatever kind—is an essential factor on the spiritual path, which we should not condemn or set aside because it contains impulses aiming at possessing and grasping in the beginning. It is only with the destruction of the illusion of an eternal, unchanging ego that chanda can develop its full potential. As long as this breakthrough has not yet occurred, chanda—even if it is affection born of purified love—can and will cause suffering again and again. Not to allow love in order to avoid suffering is nothing but an extreme form of selfishness that is no better than the selfishness of possessiveness. To avoid suffering by not loving is a flight into indifference, which may be a stoic ideal but not a Buddhist one. It is better to accept suffering than to live a loveless life. The qualitative leap from Hīnayāna to Mahāyāna is marked by the fact that the Hīnayānist seeks at all costs to avoid suffering, while the Bodhisattva ideal teaches us to be ready to accept all suffering for

---

[17]*Majjhima Nikāya:* 128, translated by Ñānamoli.

the sake of love. Without *karuṇā*—feeling and suffering with others—Buddhism is unthinkable. Any Buddhist who does not make *maitrī* and *karuṇā* the central force of his or her life is betraying the essence of Dharma. Fellow-feeling with every creature, whether a dog, a bird or a cat, is a thousand times better than unfeelingness. The pain that we take upon ourselves for the sake of others ennobles us, makes us deeper and lifts us out of our isolation. That is the suffering out of which great characters grow.

Therefore, we should allow all our love, as well as our affection, both personal and arising from inborn affinity, to flow toward those who respond to our inner call—those who have awakened our deepest feelings and our noblest strivings, and also those who cross our karmic path in a karmically determining and decisive situation. Our good intent may be universal and all-embracing, but our *love* can only find expression in a *personal* relationship. And whoever loves, whoever does not hold back from such love, must be ready to take on in full knowledge the sorrow that this love might bring. Does not the power to love thus outweigh all our suffering? Is this suffering not a small price to pay for the spiritual fullness and breadth that love pours out over us?

The problem of *chanda* as attraction, affection, and finally devotion is also one of the central problems of meditation. We should not think of meditation as something separate from life that we can practice in detachment from our feelings and inner inclinations. If, in our meditation, we try to develop love and compassion for all sentient beings, then it seems to me that this can only happen out of the feeling, and knowledge, of our immediate relationship to all the beings that surround us. When people speak so much about universal love, then I fear they have made a wonderful *concept* for themselves that enables them not to love. Love always presupposes a personal relationship. Under certain conditions we can perhaps feel friendship, empathy and sympathy (literally, suffering with) without having a direct relationship with others. This type of sympathy is a kind of openness. Love, however, is always a direct relationship to another being.

If we want to develop feelings of love for other beings in meditation, then we must first test ourselves to see how far, without self-deception, we are capable of this. We shall soon discover how hard it is to love certain people, while with others it is easy. In the course of our self-examination, we shall also come to realize that we only love certain people because they agree with us, let us have our way, or provide us with advantages, while we cannot love, and may even hate, those whose thinking and feeling is different from our own, who oppose us or put obstacles in our way. Therefore, if our meditation on loving-kindness (*maitrī* or *mettā*), is really to bear fruit, we must first start by visualizing that direct relationship to particular people we know, instead of going off into purely abstract ideas of universality.

Such self-examination, based on thought and consideration, is the necessary precondition for all following steps in the meditation on the "four immeasurables": love, compassion, sympathetic joy, and equanimity (Sanskrit, *maitrī, karuṇā, muditā, upekṣā*). Because, in the beginning stages, meditation is always supported by thought. Why is this? Because our thoughts are a constantly occurring process as long as we are aware of ourselves. We cannot stop this activity even if we try. If we attempt to put it to an end by force, we have finally to admit that the process is still going on. All we can do is to watch over this activity, either by observing its movements in the constant interchange of coming and going or by following up the flow of thoughts to see where they lead. A third possibility is to channel the stream of thoughts in a particular direction by creating in our minds a clear picture of the object of our contemplation or meditation, the essential thing being that we become one with the meditation-object.

All these processes can, once set in motion, be continued indefinitely. But then there comes a point when we are suddenly aware of our consciousness as being here-and-now. In this experience of fully conscious present time and presence, we discover that there is something more profound than our thoughts. And from this experience comes the decisive change: we suddenly open up, and the miracle of the ever-renewed beginning occurs in us—the opening-up that is the beginning of real meditation.

Back Doors to Enlightenment? Thoughts on the Expansion of Consciousness Through Drugs

N otoriously there are no limits to human folly. But it remained for our age to regard the limitlessness of folly—
the unlimited expansion of a consciousness that is already
confused and incapable of forming judgments—as a valuable expansion
of consciousness, or even as the attainment or realization of a higher
dimension. The principal means of this so-called expansion of consciousness is LSD, which is put forward by certain gurus as a means of
meditation. Characteristically, however, it is only propagated by those
who lack any real meditative experience, or the basis of serious spiritual
discipline or traditional training (*sādhana*).

In the process of meditation, that is, in the process of integration,
there is never a question of an expansion of consciousness but only of
an intensification of consciousness. In his book *The Ever-Present Origin*,
which is so important for us at the present time, Jean Gebser writes:

> The error made today, which results from the quantitative em-
> phasis of the rational attitude, is the notion that this material
> increase must be countered by an increase of consciousness.

> Such an increase must always be understood as one of reflective
> cognition with its quantitative character, and never one of

consciousness itself which is qualitative. For this very reason we emphasized earlier (pp. 99–100) that we must not lapse into the error of aspiring to an expansion of consciousness. Mere expansion of consciousness leads to decline and destruction in exactly the same way as material quantification; it corresponds on the non-material plane to the atomization on the physical or material.[18]

The images of psychedelic art, which are put together as if from a thousand splinters and fragments, or the works of modern artists influenced by this, provide a clear idea of fragmentation. However, the principal difference between states of consciousness produced by LSD and those resulting from meditation—as I can confirm from personal experience—is that LSD deprives us of all control, so that we are willlessly and helplessly cast hither and thither by emotions and fantasies, and our attention is broken up and confused by a thousand fragmentary imaginings. Meditation is a creative activity, which lets a meaningful cosmos arise out of the untamed conflict of inner powers, and which, by centering, and by unifying and integrating all our spiritual powers, leads us purposefully to the inner core of consciousness.

It is only by the creation of this inner center that we become conscious spiritual beings lifted above blind nature (the chaos of Saṁsāra). LSD, on the other hand, leads away from the center into an ever more fragmented multiplicity of unrelated and constantly changing projections of unconscious contents, which may momentarily engage our attention, but which merely turn us into totally passive viewers of a psychic film-show that proceeds without our volition, and which— the more surely, the longer we yield to it—suffocates all creative impulses that require our own effort for their accomplishment.

Goethe's saying: "What you have inherited from your fathers, you must *gain*, in order to possess it," applies here, too. The "inheritance from our fathers" is here the inheritance of our own past, and the last resort of

---

[18]Jean Gebser, *The Ever-Present Origin*, Noel Barstad & Algis Mickunas, trs. (Athens, OH: The Ohio University Press, 1986), pp. 139–140.

the entire universe that has brought us forth, or, as it is said in Zen Buddhism, "our original face before our parents were born." But this face is far from being the face of our already perfected or immanent Buddhahood, although it contains all possibilities within itself. It is the reflection of the universal depth-consciousness (ālaya-vijñāna), which contains within itself the experiences of all forms of existence, all manner of life, from the lowest to the highest levels of consciousness (or, from the most primitive to the most all-embracing dimensions of consciousness)—from the blind outpourings of bestial and demonic drives and brutal passions to the emanations of divine or enlightened beings, in which the unconscious powers and blind passions are sublimated into understanding knowledge and sympathetic compassion and love.

To equate this ālaya-vijñāna with the Buddha-nature and to suppose that by simply cutting out thinking and willing, all of our individuality and our intellectual capabilities, we can attain to the illumination of Buddhahood, is naive. It is an unproven hypothesis which is not supported by any facts of experience and runs counter to the entire Buddhist tradition, which aims to sublimate, harmonize and integrate *all* human qualities and capacities. This tradition finds it necessary to employ our own efforts (vīrya), clearly conscious practice (sādhana), creative unfoldment (bhāvanā), discriminative thought (dharmavicaya), understanding and clear knowledge (prajñā), capacity for decision and purposeful striving (samkalpa), practical application in daily life (samyagājīva), consciously directed concentrative meditation (ekagratā), loving devotion (maitrī and karuṇā) toward all beings, and trusting faith (śraddhā) in the enlightened ones who lead the way.

We cannot gain enlightenment by "sitting it out," nor can we "force it" through a convulsive struggle to repress all feeling and thought, nor through the desperate effort to find the solution to a paradoxical kōan, or through maintaining a rigid, motionless, correct bodily posture. The key to enlightenment lies neither in compulsive contraction nor in any artificially induced expansion of consciousness.

A simple narrowing of the mental horizon to a single point, a single object, concept or thought, a single logical chain of conclusions or series of associations, to the exclusion of all other connections or possible points of view, confines observation to a fixed perspective that views its object exclusively from one position and therefore fails to reveal its wholeness, its true nature, and in its organic context. Such a form of concentration (which corresponds to the scientific-logical thinking of the Western mentality) is no more fitted to lead to enlightenment than the indiscriminating expansion of consciousness of an inexperienced person who inevitably lacks judgment, who has no more idea what to do with the phenomena of this expanded consciousness than a scientifically unprepared and untrained person knows how to cope with the phenomena of space travel. The trained space traveller can interpret these phenomena. They give him important intelligible information about the nature of space and of the bodies in it, of the forces that operate in them and, not least, about his own relation to them. To untrained people, on the other hand, they convey nothing, but merely plunge them into confusion and alarm.

Even if the experiences that drugs produce were *similar* to those of meditation or mystical vision (of which there is not the slightest proof, because those who use drugs have not the slightest idea of real meditation), even then they would not convey to untrained people anything of the more profound meaning of what was seen and experienced. Such people do not know how to interpret the psychic language of symbolism, and are unable to establish any significant relationship between themselves and the phenomena that occur, between the universal depth-consciousness and the individual, superficial consciousness. This is because they have bypassed the path from the periphery of normal waking consciousness to the inner center of depth-consciousness, a way that makes use of all the functions of thinking, feeling and intuition in the gradual penetration of the meditative process.

Mere expansion of consciousness, therefore, has no point unless we have found our inner center and made it the point of reference for our experience. Dürkheim, in his book, *Hara*, says that this inner center lies between the poles of individual peripheral intellectual consciousness and the depth-consciousness that lies beyond all individuality. Our true center is nothing other than a condition in which the *whole* maintains itself in the tension between the poles.[19] The centripetal tendency is not only a biological and psychological necessity, it is a law of motion that prevails throughout the cosmos, equally valid for spiral nebulae or solar systems, planets or electrons. Every movement creates its own center or its own axis, as the only possible form of stability within the endless motion of all that lives.

When that which lives becomes conscious of itself, this again happens on the basis of a new, more subtle centering, in a focused consciousness that creates its own point of concentration that moves as if along an endless axis from a distant past toward a (for us) equally distant future; or rather, toward a present that for us is ever-changing.

The universal depth-consciousness is common to us all, but it depends on each of us what use we make of it, what we distill from it and bring to the surface. Just as the water of the ocean contains all substances in a state of dissolution, so the universal depth-consciousness contains all psychic qualities as potentialities. From the water of the ocean we can obtain both gold and ordinary cooking salt, according to the degree of concentration and the method employed. It is the same with universal depth-consciousness. We can draw from it demonic or god-like powers, destructive or life-giving, powers of darkness or of light.

Those who descend into the depths of this universal consciousness without having found their inner center are swallowed up by it or else drift like a rudderless ship, lost in the limitless wastes of the ocean and bound for destruction. It is only to those with understanding that the deep reveals its treasures. It is the mirror of the stilled consciousness that reveals the inner relationships of all things and leads to the opening up of our intuitive capacity for perception. As long as intuition does not find clear expression in our thinking, it can have no influence on our life, and is lost in the mists of vague feelings and dream-like impressions and visions.

---

[19]Karlfried Graf Dürkheim, *Hara: The Vital Centre of Man* (York Beach, ME: Samuel Weiser, 1965; and London: Unwin Hyman, 1965), p. 83.

Masters of the Mystical Path

A thousand years after the Buddha's *Parinirvāṇa*, when the Buddhist religion had grown old and lost its spontaneity, being trapped in a maze of monastic rules and regulations that separated the monks from the laity (or, in other words, the clergy from the rest of the world, or the scholar from the common man), a protest was launched from among those who had been shut out from the original message of the Buddha. They had never been monks and had never shaved their heads, but they represented the centuries-old tradition of the *śramaṇas*. These were religious wanderers and ascetics (*askēsis* = practice) who walked the roads of the Indian subcontinent. They obeyed no fixed rules, and followed their own convictions based on their own inner experiences. They stood for the highest ideals of spiritual and physical freedom against a background of organized society and institutionalized religion. They stood outside the narrow confines of caste and creed, in opposition to the Vedic religion. Under their influence there developed a secret doctrine—a revolutionary movement based on the *Upanishads*. But why were these doctrines secret? Because, in contrast to the *Vedas*, they taught that we are not dependent on the gods, but that we create our own fate in the form of *karma*.

How could such a teaching, which destroyed at a stroke the superior strength and power of the gods, and with this the original power and monopoly of the Brahmins and indeed of the entire caste system, come about? It had developed as the culmination of an underground movement that existed in India for ages, and it had been suppressed by the Aryan invaders who entered India from the north. They, too, had introduced the caste system in order to preserve themselves from becoming mixed up with and finally absorbed by the fruitful masses of the Indian subcontinent.

It is only now that we are beginning to realize that there was a highly developed culture long before the arrival of the Aryans in India, and therefore before the growth of the Vedic culture. The proof came only recently with the excavation of the Indus Valley culture, and especially through the discovery of Mohenjo Daro and Harappa. The great scholars of the last century (Deussen, Oldenberg, Jacobi, Sylvain Lévi, Max Müller, Grünwedel, and many others) being convinced that Vedic culture was the beginning of Indian thought and religion, took it for granted that everything began with the Vedas. They therefore regarded Buddhism as a mere reform movement within Brahmanism or the Vedic religion, rather as Protestantism developed out of Catholicism, or as Christianity could be seen as a reform movement within Judaism.

That seemed all the more clear because Buddhism did not simply do away with all the Vedic gods, such as Indra, Sakka, Brahma and so on. But it was observed that they were retained—having lost all power over the fate of mankind—as purely decorative elements, in exactly the same way as the old Tibetan local deities were incorporated in the Buddhist system as protectors and preservers of the Dharma, or as servants of the Buddha and his successors. In a similar way, early Christianity replaced local deities by saints, and converted all cult centers into places of Christian worship—a clever and psychologically astute move. If the Christians had attacked the old gods or the *spiritus loci*, the latter would simply have gained in prestige and power. By assigning them a secondary role, it was possible to push them slowly into the background. It was only the intolerance of later Christianity which, by trying to extirpate all traces of other cultures and religions, dug its own grave (as we can see in the present-day religious revolution, which will lead to either the destruction or the transformation of all the dogmatic formulations of Christianity).

The Buddha already declared that the doctrine he proclaimed was not his own invention, but a teaching that had been proclaimed from time immemorial by previous Buddhas. Scholars, obviously, did not take this declaration seriously, or else they thought he was referring to the rishis of the Vedas. But a close examination of the Vedas and *Brāhmaṇas* does not reveal the least trace of what the Buddha taught. On the contrary, these scriptures were based precisely on those principles the Buddha rejected, the institutions of caste and of animal sacrifice, which formed the principal pillars of the Brahminical system. The basic ideas that we regard as typically Indian—karma, rebirth, *ahiṁsā* (non-harming), *nirvāṇa, karuṇā* (compassion), the sanctity of all sensitive life, in whatever form, free access to scriptures and shrines, the dignity of the individual and our responsibility for our deeds—none of these are found in the Vedas. On the other hand, sacrifices were performed in order to bribe the gods, to assure worldly prosperity (such as children and possessions), and also to preserve against the dissolution of the individual into the elements of the cosmos.

That is why Yajñavalkya—who had declared that the eyes go to the sun, the hair into vegetation, the bones into the rocks, blood, semen and so on into water, breath into the air and the ears into space— was asked by Arthabhaga: "But what is left of man?" Then Yajñavalkya led him outside and explained what was then regarded as the great secret—the law of karma. This dialogue took place either at the time of the Buddha or soon afterward.

How did this anti-Vedic doctrine, which made gods, sacrifice, and the caste system superfluous, find its way into the Upanishads? Only through the influence of the old tradition of the anti-Vedic religions of the Buddhists and Jains, or through the influence of the *śramaṇas*. But who were these *śramaṇas*? It does not seem to be by chance that the Buddha called himself "the great *śramaṇa,*" or that he was recognized as such by his contemporaries.

His order was not originally established along monastic lines, but consisted of homeless wanderers—a kind of religious community "without fixed address." It was only when rich supporters provided accommodation, and when the number of followers became so great that they were difficult to control, that it became necessary to establish definite rules. But these rules, it seems were not imposed on the community by the Buddha; they arise from the necessities of the situation. Therefore, shortly before his death, the Buddha gave his disciples permission to either abolish or retain the rules that had been thus established. Since, however, by this time the majority of the disciples of his inner circle had settled down into monastic communities, having given up the wandering life for the greater comfort of established monasteries and acquired privileges, they voted to keep the rules, which ensured their predominance over the laity. Even Ānanda, one of the first disciples and companions of the Buddha, who was emotionally strongly attached to the Buddha, was at first excluded from the council that was held after the Buddha's *Parinirvāṇa*, because he displayed feelings for his lifelong friend. However, he was eventually admitted because he could repeat the Buddha's discourses from memory better than anyone else.

The entire Buddhist tradition was fixed according to the unanimous decision of the monks, and was only written down after 400 years of monkish rule. The Vinaya—the rules for monastic communities and the monks' discipline—is the oldest part of the *Tripiṭaka*. And so the revolt of the *Siddhas* was an attempt to restore the old *śramaṇa* ideal, to establish the freedom of the individual against a privileged class of professional monks and a consolidated, fossilized and established society.

The Buddha's teaching was based on individual experience, and therefore not on faith in theological principles nor on dogmas and current opinions. As Saraha sang: *"Na manta, na tanta, na deo, no dhāraṇā,"* "No mantras, no tantras, no gods, no *dhāraṇā*,"—only pure mind (*asamālā citta*) or spontaneous consciousness, can lead to liberation.

In the highly symbolic language of the *Siddhas*, meditative experiences are denoted by external events and external events are transformed into meditative experiences. Thus, if it is said of certain Siddhas that they held up the sun and moon in their courses, or had crossed the

Ganges by stopping its flow, this had nothing to do with the heavenly bodies or with India's sacred river, but was concerned with the solar and lunar currents of psychic energy and their union and sublimation in the body of the yogi. We must similarly understand the alchemistic terminology of the Siddhas and the search for the Philosopher's Stone or the elixir of life.

◇ ◇ ◇

In the center of the stories that deal with the mystic alchemy of the 84 Siddhas stands the guru Nāgārjuna (Tibetan, ḥPhags-pa Klu-sgrub), who lived around the middle of the seventh century, and should not be confused with the founder of the *Mādhyamika* philosophy, who bore the same name but lived some 500 years earlier. It is true that the Tibetans are convinced that he was the same man, just as some declare that Padmasambhava lived in the time of the Buddha and Aśoka, while others believe he was a rebirth of Gautama Buddha and an emanation of Amitābha. From this point of view one can find even today the Siddhas of a thousand years ago still living, because the spiritual succession is regarded as more important than a single lifetime or an historical fact. Thus it was said of Nāgārjuna that he had changed an iron mountain into copper, and would have transformed it into gold if the Bodhisattva Mañjuśrī had not warned him that gold would only arouse quarrelling and greed instead of helping people.

The justification for this warning, which from the Buddhist point of view had, as it were, deprived the material side of alchemy of its *raison d'être*, very soon became apparent.

◇ ◇ ◇

In the course of the guru's experiments it happened that even his iron begging-bowl turned into gold. One day, while he was taking his meal, a thief passed by the open door of his hut and, seeing the golden bowl, immediately decided to steal it. But Nāgārjuna, reading the mind of the thief, took the bowl and threw it out the window. The thief was so perplexed and ashamed that he entered the guru's hut, bowed at his feet and said:

"Venerable sir, why did you do this? I came here as a thief. Now that you have thrown away what I desired and made a gift of what I

Nāgārjuna (in Tibetan,
hPhags-pa Ḳlu-sgrub).

intended to steal, my desire has vanished and stealing has become senseless and superfluous."

The guru replied: "Whatever I possess should be shared with others. Eat and drink and take whatever you like, so that you need never steal again."

The thief was so deeply impressed by the magnanimity and kindness of the guru that he asked for instruction. Nāgārjuna knew that, though the other's mind was not yet ripe to understand his teachings, his inner conversion was genuine. So he said to him: "Imagine all things you desire as horns growing on your head (i.e., as unreal and useless). If you meditate in this way, you will see a light shining like an emerald."

With these words he poured a heap of jewels into a corner of the hut, told the pupil to sit down before it, and left him to his meditation. The former thief threw himself body and soul into the meditation practice, and as his faith was as great as his simplicity, he followed the words of the guru literally—and lo!—horns began to grow on his head! This visible success of his efforts filled him with pride and satisfaction. As the years passed, however, he discovered that the horns continued to grow and finally became so big that the could not move without knocking against the walls of the hut. The more he thought and worried about it, the worse it became. Thus his former pride turned into profound dejection, and when the guru returned after twelve years and asked the pupil how he was doing, he told the master how unhappy he was.

The guru laughed and said: "Just as you have become unhappy through the mere imagining of horns on your head, in the same way all living beings destroy their happiness by clinging to false imaginings while thinking they are real. All forms of life and all objects of desire are like clouds. But even birth, life, and death can have no power over one whose heart is pure and empty of all illusions. If you can look upon all the possessions of the world as no less unreal, undesirable, and cumbersome than the imaginary horns on your head, then you will be free of the cycle of death and rebirth."

Then the scales fell from the pupil's eyes, and as he realized the emptiness of all things, his desires, selfish wishes and false imaginings vanished—and with them the horns on his head! He attained *siddhi*, the perfection of a saint, and has gone down in the history of the Siddhas as guru Nāgabodhi, Nāgārjuna's successor.

Another Siddha whose name is associated with Nāgārjuna is the Brahmin Vyāli. Like Nāgārjuna he was an ardent alchemist who tried to find the *prima materia* in the form of the Elixir of Life (*amṛta*). He spent his entire fortune in costly experiments, till finally in disgust he threw his formula book into the Ganges and left the scene of his fruitless labors as a beggar.

But it happened that, while he was in another city lower down the river, a prostitute bathing in the river retrieved his book and brought it to him. This revived his old passion, and he started experimenting again, supported by the prostitute, who provided him with food. It chanced that one day, as she was preparing his food, she dropped the juice of some spice into the alchemist's mixture—and lo!—what the learned Brahmin had not been able to achieve in fourteen years of hard work was accomplished by an ignorant woman of the lowest caste!

◇　　◇　　◇

The symbolic character of this story hardly calls for comment. The inner essence of nature and life, the secret of immortality, cannot be found by dry intellectual labor and selfish desire, but only by contact with undiluted life, in the immediacy of intuition.

The story goes on to tell, not without humor, how the Brahmin, who was clearly not spiritually equal to this unexpected stroke of luck, fled with his elixir into solitude, unwilling to share it with anyone or let others in on his secret. He settled down on top of an inaccessible rock in the midst of a vast swamp, and there he sat with his Elixir of Life, a prisoner of his own selfishness—like Fafner, the giant of Norse mythology, who became a dragon in order to guard the treasure for which he had slain his brother, after they had won it from the gods!

But Nāgāruna, who was filled with the ideal of a Bodhisattva, wanted to acquire the knowledge of this precious elixir for the benefit of all suffering beings. By his magic power he succeeded in finding the hermit and persuaded him to part with the secret. The details of this story, in which the elements of popular fantasy and humor combine with mystic symbolism and reminiscences of historical personalities, do not matter. It is significant that the Tibetan manuscript from which the story has been extracted mentions mercury (*dnul-chu*) as one of the most important ingredients in these experiments. This points to a connection with the ancient alchemical tradition of Egypt and Greece, according to which mercury was closely related to the *prima materia*. Whoever has understood the *prima materia* of the human mind has found the Philosopher's Stone, the metaphysical emptiness of "plenum-void" which is the basis of the universe. It is this creative emptiness (*śūnyatā*) in which all forms are contained. It is not a substance, but rather a principle, the precondition for all that exists, just as space is the precondition for all material things. This idea is illustrated in the story of guru Kankanapa, one of the 84 Siddhas.

There once lived in the east of India a king who was very proud of his wealth. One day a yogi asked him "What is the value of your kingship, when misery is the real ruler of the world? Birth, old age, and death revolve like a potter's wheel, and nobody knows what the next turn will bring. It may raise him to the heights of happiness or plunge him into the depths of misery. Therefore, do not allow yourself to be blinded by your present riches."

The king said: "In my present position I cannot serve the Dharma in the garb of an ascetic. But if you can give me advice that I can follow according to my own nature and capabilities, without changing my outward life, I am willing to accept it."

The yogi knew the king's fondness for jewels, so he chose this natural inclination as a starting-point and subject of meditation. In this way he turned a weakness into a source of inner strength—a device often employed by Tantric teachers.

"Consider the diamonds in your bracelet, fix your mind on them and meditate like this: 'They sparkle with all the colors of the rainbow, and yet these colors that delight my heart have no nature of their own, in the same way imagination is inspired by multifarious forms of appearance, which have no nature of their own. *The mind alone is the radiant jewel*, from which all things borrow their transient reality.' "

The king did as he was told and as he devoted himself with his whole heart to this meditation, his mind attained the purity and radiance of a flawless jewel. The courtiers noticed that some strange change had

Kankana (in Tibetan,
Ḳankana-pa).

come over the king and, one day peeping through a chink in the door of the royal apartment, they saw the king surrounded by innumerable celestial beings. Now they knew that he had become a Siddha, and they asked for his blessing and guidance. The king said: "It is not wealth that makes me a king, but what I have acquired spiritually through my own exertions. My inner happiness is my kingdom." Since then the king was known as guru Kankanapa.

Thus the Siddhas were no mere magicians or wizards, as some European scholars have assumed, obviously not knowing that *siddhi* means "gaining the goal," or "perfection." Otherwise the Buddha himself, whose name was Siddhārtha, would have had to be described as a magician. With the same justification we could call Christ, to whom many miracles are ascribed, a magician.[20]

From this point of view we begin to understand the questions of the monk[21] in the Kevaddha Sutta of the Dīgha Nikāya, who traveled up into the realms of the gods in order to inquire about the dissolution[22] of the four elements—earth, water, fire and air. But none of the gods could give him an explanation, each one referring him to a higher heavenly authority. Finally he reached the heaven of Brahmā and asked him the same question. But Brahmā was reluctant to admit that he did not know the answer. Instead of replying, he sang his own praises, repeating over and over again: "I am Great Brahmā, Ruler of all the Gods, the Highest, Almighty, Chief of Gods and Men . . ."

But the monk persisted: "Dear sir, I did not ask who you are, but where the four elements come to an end." Finally Brahmā had to admit

[20]It is time to treat perfection outside of the Christian field with greater respect. Thus we should not speak of Medicine Buddhas (like Voodoo or the medicine-men of primitive cults). Rather, the Buddha is the greatest healer of human weakness, the savior (*Heiland*) who makes whole (*heil*) and complete. Likewise, we should not speak of ritual dances as devil-dances but as mystery plays. So, too, *Śūnyatā* is not nothingness but no-thing-ness— the source of all things, the pregnant emptiness from which all creation springs.
[21]There is a slight error here on the author's part. Kevaddha was the name not of the monk referred to (who is not named), but of the questioner to whom the Buddha told the story. Tr.
[22]The author here has *Ursprung*, "source"; also an error. Tr.

that he did not know the answer. The only one who could answer his question was the Buddha, the Enlightened One. So the monk returned to earth and asked the Buddha: "Where are earth, water, fire and air completely annihilated?" The Buddha replied: "That is not the right way, monk, that this question should be put, but rather: 'Where is it that these elements find no footing?'—And the answer is: 'In the invisible, infinite, all-radiant consciousness (*viññaṇam anidassanam anantaṁ sabbato pabhaṁ*); there neither earth nor water, fire nor air can find a footing (*ettha āpo ca paṭhavī tejo vāyo na gādhati*)'."

In this verse we can, in all probability, find the origin of the *Vijñānavāda,* one of the most important schools of Buddhist philosophy, whose exponents, without denying the highest principle of *sūnyatā,* maintained that for all practical purposes consciousness was the final instance of human experience, and therefore the most important factor for all living beings. The Yogācārins were the legitimate successors of the Vijñānavādins; they put this philosophy into practice and constructed the mighty edifice which came to be known as Tantrism. But this was only fully formed by the Siddhas.

However, the Siddhas played another important part; they were the first to use paradoxes in order to illuminate in a flash the unthinkable nature of life. They turned things topsy-turvy by using logic to refute logic, by putting reason into situations which could not be resolved by reason or epistemology, and they continually pointed out how reality lies outside the laws of linear logic and causal thinking. Their use of paradoxes was not willful or a matter of chance. It was used to create surprising situations which revealed the true nature of things in a flash. When understanding is confused and thrown off the track of normal thought, it can recognize the truth in an unexpected happening or situation. This was the real beginning of Ch'an or Zen, and I can show by textual references that there was a historical connection between the Siddha tradition and what we today know as Zen Buddhism. To prove this, I will provide a typical Siddha legend and its counterpart in the writings of Zen as reported by D. T. Suzuki. Here, first, is the Tibetan version:

◇   ◇   ◇

Once there was a hunter called Śavari. He was very proud of his strength and marksmanship. Hunting and killing animals was his sole occupation, so that his life consisted of one long evil deed. One day when he was out hunting he saw a stranger, obviously a hunter, approaching him from a distance. "Whoever dares to hunt in my area?" he thought angrily, and as the stranger approached, he saw that the latter was not only just as big and strong as he was, but—and this astonished him—he looked exactly like him. "Who are you?" Śavari asked in a fierce voice.

"I am a hunter," replied the stranger without losing his calm.

"What is your name?"

"Śavari."

"How can that be?" exclaimed the hunter, astonished. "My name is Śavari. Where do you come from?"

"From a distant land," the stranger replied, evasively. Śavari felt his self-confidence returning.

"Can you kill more than one gazelle with a single arrow?"

"I can kill three hundred at a single shot!" replied the stranger.

This seemed to Śavari like a vain boast, and he longed for a chance to show up the stranger's ridiculous assertion for what it was.

But the stranger, who was none other than the Bodhisattva Avalokiteśvara and had assumed this form out of compassion for Śavari, at once by his magic power created a herd of 500 gazelles.

Śavari was delighted when he saw the gazelles approaching out of the nearby forest, and with a triumphant smile he asked: "Will your arrow pierce all these gazelles?"

"It will pierce all five hundred," replied the stranger, as if it were the simplest thing in the world; so Śavari suggested: "Let your arrow miss four hundred, and only hit a hundred."

The stranger performed this miracle with the greatest of ease, and Śavari began to feel uncomfortable and to have doubts about the reality of what was happening.

"Go and get one of the fallen gazelles if you have any doubts," said the stranger, and Śavari did as he was told.

But alas, when he tried to pick up one of the gazelles, he found it was so heavy that he could not move it from the spot.

"What, you are supposed to be a great hunter, and you can't even pick up a dead gazelle!" laughed the stranger, and Śavari did not know

Śavari (in Tibetan,
Śavari-pa).

what to do. His pride was broken, and he fell at the stranger's feet, begging him to be his teacher.

Avalokiteśvara agreed and said, "If you want to learn this magic art of shooting, you must first purify yourself inwardly by abstaining from all flesh-meat for a month, and instead meditating on love and compassion for all living beings. When you have done this, I will return and initiate you into the secret of this skill."

Śavari conscientiously carried out his teacher's instruction. When after a month the guru returned, a great change had taken place in Śavari, although he himself did not realize it. He begged the guru for the promised instruction in the secret way of shooting.

The guru drew a magical diagram (maṇḍala) on the ground, adorned it with flowers, and ordered Śavari and his wife to examine it carefully. When they had both meditated earnestly for a month, they were able to devote their undivided attention to the maṇḍala, and behold!—the ground on which the maṇḍala was drawn seemed to have become transparent, so that they could see deep into the earth. And from the bowels of the earth there rose flames and smoke, and cries of pain were heard.

"What do you see?" the guru asked.

The hunter and his wife were so scared that they could not answer. But when the smoke had blown away a little, they could see the eight great hells and the torments of innumerable beings.

"What do you see?" the guru asked again, and when they looked closer, they recognized two faces contorted with pain among the tormented beings.

"What do you see?" the guru asked a third time.

And then, suddenly, the true meaning of the whole thing came home to them, and they cried out with a single voice: "That's us!"

They fell at the guru's feet and begged him to show them the way to liberation. And they forgot all about asking to be taught the magic way of shooting. Śavari continued to meditate, and became filled with love and compassion for all beings. Thus he became one of the 84 Siddhas.

It is interesting and instructive to find the main features of this story in the garb of Zen Buddhism, as told in Suzuki's translation of the *Chuanteng Lu.*

Shi-kung was a hunter before he was ordained as a Zen monk under Ma-tsu. As a hunter he detested all Buddhist monks, because they were opposed to his occupation. One day, while he was hunting a gazelle, he came to the hut where Ma-tsu dwelt. Ma-tsu came out and greeted him.

Shi-kung asked: "Did you see a gazelle pass your door?"

"Who are you?" the master asked.

"I am a hunter."

"How many animals can you kill with a shot?"

"One with each arrow."

"Then you are no hunter," said Ma-tsu.

"Well, how many can *you* kill with one arrow?" the hunter asked.

"A whole herd."

"Why should *you* (as a monk) kill a whole herd with a single shot? They are living beings too."

"If you know so much, why don't you shoot yourself?"

"I don't know how to do that."

"This lad," Ma-tsu suddenly cried out, "has today put an end to all his ignorance and his evil passions!"

Thereupon Shih-kung broke his bow and arrows and became Ma-tsu's pupil. When he himself became Zen master, he always kept a bow with an arrow in it, ready to shoot, and threatened his monks with it when they approached him with questions. San-ping was once threatened in this way. Shih-kung cried out: "Mind the arrow!"

Ping bared his breast, saying, "This is the arrow that kills, but where is the arrow that restores to life?"

Kung struck the bowstring three times, and Ping bowed.

Kung said: "For thirty years I have used a bow and two arrows, and now I have only succeeded in shooting down half of a wise man."

Shih-kung broke his bow and arrows for a second time, and never used them again.

From this story we can see that paradoxes are used at an entirely new level. They consist in the sudden and unexpected leap over a whole series of logical proofs and thus demonstrate the immediacy of spiritual understanding, or sudden enlightenment. Thus paradoxes confront the understanding not only with confused or weird situations, but also with something that at first seems to cut out logic, because it reaches a conclusion that leaps over several steps of consecutive logic, and thus seems paradoxical to us. This method is in complete agreement with the oldest Buddhist teachings. The law of Dependent Origination (*pratītya-samutpāda*), for instance, was not always taught in the usual twelve steps. We find that Pali texts often leave out several links, to show that any link in the chain can be followed by any other, and that our step-by-step logic is only a support for our thinking, and now a law of nature.

Another curious parallel, but this time from a much older source— from Jewish, Christian or Islamic tradition—is the story of Mīna-pa, which is obviously borrowed from the Biblical tale of Jonah and the whale. Both are swallowed by a big fish, which is later caught by fishermen who, on cutting up the fish, find the man inside still alive. According to the Buddhist version, the fish had swum down to the bottom of the sea, where he hid under the palace of the ruler of the seas. And so Mīna-pa was able to overhear the secret teachings which a god or Bodhisattva conveyed to the ruler of the seas. When, later, Mīna-pa leaped out of the belly of the fish, he remembered what he had heard, and so became a saint.

What surprises me about the pictorial representation of this scene (see page 120) is the use of a style that is not only entirely different from the classical Tibetan style as we know it from *thangkas* and frescoes, but which makes use of bold perspective foreshortening, in order to indicate rapid motion. In addition, we find typically Indian features, such as are characteristic of most of the old Tibetan stone-engravings of this series. This all goes to show that we do have a very old tradition here, and that these stone-plates were brought together long before being built into the courtyard of a monastery and painted over by later generations. It would have been logical to omit the name of this Siddha, Mīna-pa as a later invention, in order to obtain the number 84, which is a conventional number like our dozen, hundred or thousand. But the fact that this Siddha is well-known by his Indian name of Matsyendra-

Matsyendranāth (in Tibetan,
Mīna-pa).

nāth, and is closely connected with Goraraksa, another equally popular Indian saint, proves his historicity. To this day the caves in which these saints lived are visited by many pilgrims.

The miracles performed by many of the Siddhas are either symbols of spiritual realization or summary accounts of their teachings, although these are often given in the form of longer or shorter treatises. Much of what the Siddhas set down in writing has been lost. Only what was preserved in Apabhraṁśa or in Tibetan translations has been preserved. The Siddhas were the first to write in the language of the people of their time instead of Sanskrit, which could only be understood by scholars and clerics. They became the fathers of a local literary language, out of which developed, among other things, Hindi and Bengali. Thus their work was of far-reaching effect, and it is possible that some day further Siddhas may be rediscovered in Old Bengali literature. People like Sri Anirvan, a deeply religious scholar of our own day about whom the world-famous Swiss writer Lizelle Reymond has written at length, show that the teaching of the Siddhas has not yet died out.[23]

Swami Muktānanda, too, claims to be a successor to the Siddhas. Buddhists and Hindus unite in their praise. Although they possessed all kinds of magic arts and miraculous skills and powers, which they had gained by the practice of prolonged and intensive meditation, every one of these tales makes it clear that all these so-called *siddhis* or paranormal powers lose all value for those who have gained enlightenment. One who is fully enlightened has no need to demonstrate power over the laws of nature, because he or she has recognized the necessity for these laws, and knows that liberation does not consist of overcoming them, but in understanding them. Nirvāṇa is not eternal bliss or flight from this world, but—as Lobzang Lalungpa says—the complete understanding of *saṁsāra*. This is shown in many tales of the Siddhas, whose perfection was not based on their being able to perform miracles. On the contrary, it was based on their inner freedom from wonders and magic and on displaying a higher perfection, namely that of the highest liberation and

---

[23]Sri Anirvan and Lizelle Reymond, *To Live Within* (Masham, North Yorkshire, England: Coombe Springs Press, 1984).

Khaḍga (in Tibetan,
Karga-pa).

enlightenment. This is typified by the following story, the tale of the Siddha Karga-pa (Sanskrit, Khaḍga), the "sword-Siddha."

◇　　◇　　◇

Once a robber met a yogi and asked him how he could become invincible. The yogi replied: "There is a stupa at a place not far from Benares. Go there and circumambulate the shrine, which contains a statue of Avalokiteśvara, for three weeks, while reciting the mantra and doing the meditation practice that I will give you. If you do this with complete commitment and unbroken concentration, without ever wandering in your thoughts, then at the end of three weeks a deadly black snake will emerge from the opening in the stupa. You must at once seize this snake by the head, or it will kill you. But if you have performed your meditation conscientiously, the snake will not hurt you, and you will gain the magic power of invincibility."

The robber thanked the yogi and did as he was told. He performed the prescribed exercises with heart and soul, and when the dreaded snake finally emerged from the opening of the stupa, he seized it immediately at the back of the head, and lo! he held the invincible sword of wisdom in his hand!

But now he had no further use for magic powers, because he had attained sainthood. From that time on he has been known as the Siddha Karga-pa, the "saint with the sword."

◇　　◇　　◇

Something similar happened to Mahi-pa. He was a wrestler by profession, and it was his ambition to become the strongest man in the world. So he asked a yogi how to do this. The yogi said, "You must meditate on the infinity of space. As soon as you have realized that and become one with it, you will be invincible."

The wrestler followed this advice to the letter, and soon his mind was as wide as space. But at that moment there was no one with whom he could wrestle any more. He had become the universe, and so there was nothing that could oppose him. He became a saint and was known as the Siddha Mahi-pa.

◇　　◇　　◇

Not everyone was led to liberation through miracles or magic powers. The story of Nagpochöpa (nag-po chos-pa) shows that the gaining of

Mahi-pa

magic powers can also be dangerous because these can lead us away from our true goal. Magic powers are like blackberries that we pick at the edge of the wood, without leaving the path. Nagpochöpa is generally depicted with a parasol of honor, descending from heaven, but at the same time he rides on a witch. The parasol denotes his powers, but the witch indicates that he can still fall into temptation. For instance, it said that he once was walking over the water. Then the thought occurred to him: "See, I can walk on the water—what a great achievement!" At once he sank into the water and would have drowned if his guru had not rescued him at the last moment.

When his guru was dying, he gave his pupil, in spite of everything, the chance to save his life. He allowed him to fly to the Himalayas to fetch a life-saving herb which only grew at great heights. At once Nagpochöpa flew to the Himalayas, found the plant, and was about to return when he heard the sound of weeping and wailing, as if someone were in great distress. Overcome by compassion, he climbed down to the place from which the cries came, forgetting the purpose of his flight, and gave away the precious medicine that he had gathered for his guru. Scarcely had he done this when he realized he had been deceived by a witch. She had assumed human form in order to prevent him from saving his guru's life. When he finally returned from the Himalayas it was too late—his guru was already dead.

This legend shows that compassion without wisdom can have just as catastrophic results as wisdom without compassion. For this reason Dölma or Tārā is always shown with the eye of compassion in her giving hands, because giving without wisdom can lead to great misfortune and not to the noble purpose intended. We must give not only with open hearts, but with open eyes.

The stories of the Siddhas contain valuable truths, and if we understand them rightly, we can no longer regard them simply as fairy-tales about magicians, but as a valuable contribution to Buddhist literature and iconography. These few examples may suffice to convince future historians, and all who see more in Buddhist literature than a mere exercise in academic study.

The Mystery of Life
and Rebirth According to
The Tibetan Book of the Dead

———

Most people in the West take the view that no one who has not already died can speak with authority about death, and that, since nobody has yet returned from the dead, it is impossible to say anything about death or the state after death. We shall now discuss *The Book of Spontaneous Liberation from the Intermediate State*, known in the West as the *Bardo Thödol*, and the spiritual background of this literature.

The wise men of the East reply that there is nobody who has *not* returned from the dead. In fact we have all died many deaths before entering this life. What we call birth is only the other side of death, another name for the same process, seen from the opposite point of view.

It is really strange that not everyone remembers his or her last death. That is probably the reason why most people do not believe in this concept. But in just the same way they do not remember their birth, but still they do not doubt for a moment that they have been born!

Many people cannot even remember exactly what they did the previous day, what they said an hour ago or what they thought a minute ago—in fact most people cannot do these things. And yet the same

Kṛṣṇācārya (in Tibetan,
Nag-po Chos-pa).

people believe they can rely on their memory, and take their non-recollection of certain events of their more distant past as proof that these things never happened. It is quite true that, although we often cannot remember things in the immediate past, we are still able to recall events of many years ago, and that we carry with us a more or less connected picture of our life from early childhood to the present. This means that our memory is not a mechanical, static, or uniform instrument, but a capacity that depends on many factors and varies with the individual.

What then are the factors upon which memory depends? They are the depth of the impression or stimulus, and the degree of attention or concentration. These depend again on the attitude and disposition of the individual and his or her capacity for being impressed. An unusual occurrence is easily remembered, whereas habitual or routine impressions leave only faint traces behind, or none at all. An intelligent person will consider more things strange than a stupid one, and so his or her interests will be more extensive. The intelligent person will direct more attention to the things and events of his or her surroundings than the average person.

But in this purely intellectual attitude there is a danger that with an increased range of interests the memory becomes more burdened and is finally so overloaded that one loses control of it—with the result that one can no longer voluntarily call up memories, or can no longer keep them separate in their temporal or causal sequence and interrelationships.

The power of concentration is the really decisive factor in active remembering, because it makes receptivity greater and prevents distraction (or the indiscriminate scattering of attention over various objects), and increases the capacity to reproduce at will impressions and other contents of consciousness. It is this active remembering that distinguishes our waking consciousness from the subconscious. The latter possesses an automatic power of registering which, in contradistinction to our active memory, can be called our passive memory. This exists not only in human beings, but also in animals and plants as a race- or species-memory, and it regulates both habitual and spontaneous behavior. We term the latter "instinct" in the case of animals, and "genius" in human beings.

The fact that there are so few geniuses among us can be ascribed to the fact that we either overburden consciousness and active memory with indiscriminately piled-up sense-impressions and internal reactions, or that we have become dulled and unreceptive through routine. But if we were to direct concentration properly, and employ it with more discrimination and less egocentricity, we would not only profit from our present experiences. We would also be able to draw on the unlimited treasure-house of subconscious memory, in which are stored not only past existences, but the past of our race, the past of mankind and of all pre-human forms of life—perhaps even the first consciousness that made possible all life in this universe.

In other words, the power of concentration is the key to this hidden treasure. It is the power that enables us to raise the subconscious into the realm of waking consciousness, thus converting latent memories into active remembering, and so into knowledge that we can draw upon, command, and use appropriately. This is the capacity that distinguishes the wise from the merely intelligent. The wise person remembers the right thing at the right time. The wise person has the intuition of the genius and not the overburdened brain of the specialist or the nightmare mentality of the person who cannot forget anything, and who ends up either in suicide or in the madhouse.

If by any chance the doors of the unconscious were suddenly opened for any individual, the conscious mind would be destroyed. That is why the doors of the unconscious are guarded by all initiates and concealed behind the veil of mysteries and symbols. Those who have the strength and inner maturity to raise the veil and open the door are able to see the identity of birth and death, and to recognize the continuity and interrelation of all life. For them, rebirth is no mere theory, but a fact of experience which can be proved by all who take the trouble to investigate seriously and experiment.

Those who have not yet attained the strength and maturity to see the unveiled reality are led by way of symbol and initiation ritual with the appropriate exercises to gradual understanding and personal experience. That is why the *Bardo Thödol*, the Tibetan book of spontaneous liberation (*thos-grol*, pronounced *thö dol*) from the intermediate state (*bar-do*)—that intermediate state between life and rebirth that we call death—is written in symbolic language. It is a book that is sealed with the seven seals of silence, not because the knowledge it contains is to be kept from the uninitiated, but to protect them against their own ignorance, which could lead them astray through misunderstandings and destroy them through haste.

This is why European commentators have called the *Bardo Thödol* a secret book, a mistake that could only arise from ignorance of the religious life of Tibet, and which is disproved by the fact that the book is widely known and respected in Tibet. Like old family bibles in Christian countries, it can be found there in almost every home, especially among the followers of the old schools. But just as, for example, the Book of Revelation, although it is contained in every family bible, is a sealed book to the uninitiated, so too the *Bardo Thödol* is a book that cannot be understood without knowledge of its spiritual background and symbolic language. It reveals its meaning fully only to one who follows its instructions step by step. In Tibet, where this spiritual background is common, it only requires some personal effort under the guidance of a competent guru to penetrate to the inner meaning of the text and put its teachings into practice.

The reason for the great popularity of the *Bardo Thödol* (despite its profundity) is explained by the book itself in which it is expressly stated that one should not only read and reread it, master it and take it to heart, but that one should also "spread it abroad and proclaim it to all living beings, and even read it out in the midst of great assemblies."

It is therefore not a secret book or a secret doctrine, but a revelation of reality in profoundly symbolic language. This is the only language in which reality can be expressed, and it has no more to do with deliberate secrecy than has the language of mathematics, the purest form of symbolic language we know. And just as this purest and most abstract of all sciences addresses itself to all who can understand its language, so does the *Bardo Thödol* address itself to all who have ears to hear.

Who are those who have ears to hear? Here we come to the decisive point in our judgment of the *Bardo Thödol*: the "hearing" that is meant is not mere reception through the outer ear, but spontaneous grasping through inner hearing, described in the *Surangama Sutra* as an intuitive hearing that transcends the ordinary senses. In this text, Mañjuśrī says to the Buddha:

> We receive this doctrine of yours first through our hearing; but as soon as we are capable of fully grasping it, it becomes our own through a suprasensorial, intuitive hearing. This fact makes the awakening and perfection of such a supersensorial hearing of the greatest importance for every novice. The deeper the wish to gain *samādhi* is established in the mind of a pupil, the more surely can he gain it by means of this supersensorial organ of hearing.[24]

This is the spiritual background which makes intelligible the expression *Thödol* (*thos-grol*), which I have rendered as "spontaneous liberation," and which literally means "hearing-liberation." It is liberation through inner, intuitive hearing, through a spontaneous grasp of reality.

The understanding of the *Bardo Thödol* depends on one's inner maturity and readiness. While it is, for those who are unprepared, a book sealed with the seven seals of silence, it begins to reveal itself to those who have learned silence in the school of meditation, in the practice of self-absorption. For the ordinary person there is no hearing when there is no sound. But for the spiritually awakened, the inner hearing is most lively in stillness, in the silence of all the other senses, and above all, of one's own thoughts.

It is to such spiritually awake people who, in East and West alike, are to be found not only among the educated and scholarly, but also among the simplest people, that this book is addressed. It seizes hold of people where it moves and troubles them most—in the experience of death, in which lies hidden the mystery of life.

◇   ◇   ◇

The teachings of the *Bardo Thödol* are attributed to the great Buddhist apostle Padmasambhava, who brought Buddhism to Tibet in the middle

---

[24]*The Surangama Sutra*, Charles Luk (Lu K'uan Yü), tr., (London: Rider & Co., 1966).

of the eighth century at the invitation of King Ti-Song De-tsen, and founded the first Buddhist monastery (Samye) there. His remarkable personality made such a deep impression on his contemporaries that even today, after 1200 years, memories of his life and deeds are kept alive among the Tibetans.

That the essential ideas, if not the original version of the *Bardo Thödol* as they are preserved in the metrical parts of the work, go back to Padmasambhava is confirmed by the verses at the beginning of the book, which cast a light not only on the authorship, but also on the basic attitude of the work itself:

> To the Divine Body of Truth, The Incomprehensible,
>   Boundless light;
> To the Divine Body of Perfect Endowment, Who
>   are the Lotus and the Peaceful and the Wrathful Deities
> To the Lotus-born Incarnation, Padma Sambhava, Who is
>   the Protector of all sentient beings;
> To the *Gurus*, the Three Bodies, obeisance[25]

These verses presuppose knowledge of the maṇḍala and visionary symbolism as well as the doctrine of the "Three Bodies" (*trikāya*), which refers not only to the nature of manifestations of a Buddha (as we find it, for instance, in the profound presentation of the *Mahayana-Sraddhotpada Sutra* (Awakening of Faith in the Mahāyāna), but also to the three levels of experience and realization that occur in every human mind. It is only on this basis that the *Bardo Thödol* can be understood. It is therefore necessary, however briefly, to indicate the meaning of these words.

The nature of our inner being is not different from the nature of the Buddha. The difference between a Buddha and a worldling is that the former is aware of this nature, whereas the latter, because of the

---

[25]*The Tibetan Book of the Dead,* W.Y. Evans-Wentz, tr. (London & New York: Oxford University Press, 1927), p. 85.

veils of ego-illusion, is not. This inner nature is essentially *śūnyatā*—pure potentiality, the pure emptiness of the yet-unformed that is the precondition of all forms—and this *śūnyatā* is made conscious as *dharma*, as the highest reality, as suchness (*tathatā*), which is the immanent rule of law. This forms the spiritual essence of a Buddha, the *Dharmakāya* or Body of the Law, the highest, universal principle of Buddhahood.

The *Sambhogakāya*, the Body of Spiritual Ecstasy or bliss, is the experience of the *Dharmakāya* on the plane of intuitive vision. Here, the ineffable becomes a creative vision, a spiritual symbolic form, a blissful experience. It is the heritage that the enlightened ones have left us through their work in the world. They themselves constituted the visible physical manifestation of this experience, just as everyone who is filled with such a spirit gradually converts his or her bodily form into the expression of the inner experience; for the body is, according to Buddhism, nothing but the materialized form of consciousness made manifest. Therefore the visible body of an enlightened being is called the *Nirmāṇakāya* or Transformation Body—a designation applicable to the body of every human being who is treading the path of spiritual transformation.

Our verse therefore means that Padmasambhava is adored as the guru and protector of all who entrust themselves to him in the three "bodies" or principles of the Lotus Order: on the plane of universal law (*Dharmakāya*) as the infinite light of Amitābha, on the plane of heightened spiritual experience or vision (*Sambhogakāya*), as the manifestation-forms of kindly or fearsome Dhyāni Buddhas, etc., and on the plane of the physical body (Nirmāṇakāya) in his human form) which is nothing but the incorporation of all the previously mentioned forms.

In the human form then, it is not the human being—the historical personality—that is honored, but the inner principle—the imperishable—that finds its expression in that body. The same applies to the adoration of the Buddha: the Buddha was never an object of a religious cult, not a man for the Buddhists, as H. Kern rightly remarked. The historical figure of the teacher Sakyamuni is in fact called Buddha or

Tathāgata, but the object is not the deification of the man Sakyamuni.[26] It is what raises him above his singular manifestation and links him with all previous and following Buddhas, that is to say, that suprapersonal, all-embracing consciousness of enlightenment (*bodhicitta*), which is potentially present in all beings, that is honored in the Buddha.

As long as this consciousness cannot be experienced or realized as a totality (which is only possible for a Buddha), we must content ourselves with the reflexes perceived in our inner vision, in which the principles and qualities of enlightenment are broken down into their constituent parts like the rays of the sun through a prism. The symbolic forms of these visions are not arbitrary creations, but the shining traces which thousands of years of spiritual experience and perfection have left in the human psyche. They are the radiance of all the enlightened beings who have ever trod the earth, the body "created out of our merits," as the *Sambhogakāya* is also called, in the state of absorption (*dhyāna*), in which we create it afresh from within ourselves.

It is in this way that the Dhyāni Buddhas that one experiences in vision arise, each one of whom represents a particular aspect of enlightenment, and thus of one's own latent enlightenment-consciousness. In order to guard the mind against arbitrary aberrations, the teachers of the different schools have created the so-called *maṇḍalas*, concentrically arranged geometrical systems in which the positions and mutual relationships of the individual symbols and images are established. It is to this kind of an arrangement that the expression "Lotus Order" refers.

Without going into the whole maṇḍala, it may suffice to say here that the Dhyāni Buddhas and their corresponding Bodhisattvas and other companion-figures (who are collectively called by the Tibetan term *Lha*) are arranged in either four or five orders: the *Vajra, Ratna, Padma,* and *Karma* Order. The center of the maṇḍala, which summarizes

[26]H. Kern, *Manual of Indian Buddhism* (New Delhi, India: Motilal Barnasidass, 1974), pp. 66, 67.

all these principles, is called the Buddha Order, symbolized by the Wheel of the Law (*dharma-cakra*).

The *Vajra* (diamond scepter) denotes the indestructability and imperturbability of the enlightenment-consciousness, which knows itself to be identical with the Great Emptiness (*śūnyatā*) and is personified by the Dhyāni Buddha Akṣobhya. The Jewel (*ratna*) stands for the gift of the Three Precious Ones (*triratna*), in which the Buddha gives himself, his teaching and his community to mankind. It is personified in Ratnasambhava, who is represented in the gesture of giving. The Lotus (*padma*) stands for the unfolding of meditation, which is represented by Amitābha, who is shown in the meditation posture (*dhyāna-mudrā*). The double-*vajra* stands for *karma*, which here denotes the employment of knowledge in active love and compassion, and is represented by Amoghasiddhi in the gesture of fearlessness (*abhaya-mudrā*). The Wheel of the Law (*dharma-cakra*) stands for the potential presence of the four preceding qualities in the central Buddha Order represented by Vairocana.

Each one of the qualities mentioned can work on different planes: on the plane of universal law as potentiality, on the plane of spiritual experience as the creative idea, or on the plane of physical manifestation as the materialization or incorporation of the idea.

So, when Padmasambhava is understood as the incorporation of the Lotus Order, and indeed is, as his name implies, lotus-born, that means that by practicing the meditations based on the maṇḍala of Amitābha he has gained inner perfection and thus identity with the idea and the qualities of Amitābha. The teachings of such a man are not based on the repetition of philosophical theories but on the facts of meditative experience. What he wanted to leave to posterity was not a new system but the way to personal experience and realization of the goal, which is possible not only in the distant future, but in every human lifetime.

Only those who are ready to tread the path indicated and to put its instructions into practice can make anything of the signs and marks, symbols, and visions described in the *Bardo Thödol*. Those who seek to penetrate the secrets of this book out of sheer curiosity will only increase their own doubts and perplexities, or at best add another item to their collection of exotic curiosities.

The *Bardo Thödol* has become well known as *The Tibetan Book of the Dead,* a title that sounds very attractive and impressive, especially because it recalls the Egyptian *Book of the Dead,* but which, as we have seen, neither corresponds to the original title nor has any justification in the contents as we shall see. No comparison could be more misleading, for the *Bardo Thödol* is nothing like the Egyptian *Book of the Dead,* and in his commentary C. G. Jung hits the nail on the head when he writes:

> Unlike the *Egyptian Book of the Dead,* which always prompts one to say too much or too little, the *Bardo Thödol* offers one an intelligible philosophy addressed to human beings rather than to gods or primitive savages. Its philosophy contains the quintessence of Buddhist psychological criticism; and, as such, one can truly say that it is of an unexampled superiority.[27]

The word death does not occur at all in the title of the *Bardo Thödol,* and quite alters the stress of the work, which is on the idea of liberation—liberation from the illusions of our egocentric consciousness, which continually move back and forth between being and non-being, birth and death, desire and despair, without ever emerging from these intermediate-state samsaric illusions to reach a state of "objectivity" and the peace of Nirvanic awakening. To equate *bardo* with death would be a lapse into the most primitive world of ideas. The word *bardo* has a much wider meaning, and includes the concept of death only as a particular case. For anyone familiar with Buddhist philosophy it is clear that birth and death are not once-for-all events in human life but are taking place in us continuously. Every moment, something dies in us and something is reborn.

---

[27]*The Tibetan Book of the Dead,* W.Y. Evans-Wenta, tr., pages xxxi, xxxvii from C.G. Jung's "Psychological Commentary."

The various *bardos* are simply the various states of consciousness in life: the state of waking-consciousness, the state of dream-consciousness, the state of meditative-consciousness, the state of death-consciousness, the state of experiencing reality, the state of rebirth-consciousness. All this is made clear in the "Root-verses of the Six *Bardos*," which, together with the "Paths of Good Wishes," form the core of the original work, and this proves that the book deals with the reality of life and is not merely a guide to dying, or even a mass for the dead, to which it was degraded by later generations. It is not a guide for the dead, but for those who wish to conquer death and transform the process of dying into an act of liberation. For in dying we pass through the same stages as we experience in the advanced stages of meditation. As Plutarch said long ago: "In the moment of death the soul undergoes the same experiences as those initiated into the Great Mysteries."

Through the automatic cutting-out of corporeality and of all the hindrances of the superficial consciousness, death clearly gives us an extraordinary opportunity to liberate ourselves from the domination of our drives and mental blockages and, if only for a split second, to see the light of liberation. Whoever can hold on to this moment and keep to the height of such understanding can gain freedom. Sinking below this level means a greater or lesser degree of involvement in the cycle of rebirths.

Only those who have prepared themselves in this life can make use of the impetus of this moment. That is why the initiations into the great mysteries of antiquity and of earlier cultures took the form of the symbolic death of the initiand, and Padmasambhava also made use of this method, as we can see from the warning in the last of the "root-verses," where it says that we should not brush aside the thought of approaching death for the sake of the fleeting affairs of life, but should devote ourselves to the Dharma as long as life gives us a chance to do so.

For this purpose it is necessary to introduce death into daily life, not in order to arouse a distaste for life, but in order to come to know death as something inseparable from life and necessary to it. In order to penetrate into this sphere of experience, no concentration on corpses is required (its purpose is quite different), but a descent into the deepest core of our being, where life and death are in constant contact with one another.

◇   ◇   ◇

Vision is a Creative Reality. In the spiritual school of the *Bardo Thödol*, as in the mysteries of antiquity, the initiates must pass through the experience of death in order to achieve inner liberation. They must die to their past and to ego before they can enter into the spiritual community and the higher life and become "Sons of the Buddhas." The fact that the prose part of the *Bardo Thödol* is addressed to such initiates is confirmed by the constantly repeated address *Rigs-kyi byu*, (Son of a noble family, i.e., of the Buddha's family). The expression *rigs-lia* (family of five) is the regular designation of the five Dhyāni Buddhas, whose maṇḍala is at the basis of the *Bardo Thödol* as of most Tibetan meditation systems.

The initiate, who, through sincere devotion, has gained the vision of the Dhyāni Buddhas is thus a member of the community of the Enlightened One, having become a spiritual son of the Buddha, a *jinaputra* or "son of the victor," a son of the noble family. Similar expressions go back to the earliest times in Buddhism, as we see already in *Dīgha Nikāya* 27.9:

> Vaseṭṭha, he whose faith in the Tathāgata is settled, rooted, established, solid, unshakable by any ascetic or Brahmin, any deva or Māra or Brahmā or anyone in the world, can truly say: "I am a true son of the Blessed Lord, born of his mouth, born of Dhamma, created by Dhamma, an heir of Dhamma." Why is that? Because, Vāseṭṭha, this designates the Tathāgata: The Body of Dhamma (*dhammakāyo*, Sanskrit *dharmakāya*), that is The Body of Brahmā, or Become Dhamma, that is, Become Brahmā.

If, subsequently in the prose part of the *Bardo Thödol*, the dead or dying person is clearly being addressed (which led to later misunderstandings, and significantly does not occur in the metrical core-pas-sages), this can be ascribed to three reasons:

1) Because whoever seriously endeavors to put the teachings of the *Bardo Thödol* into practice should regard every moment of his or her life as the last. He or she should consider every moment of life with the same seriousness and ascribe the same value to it as if it were the last. "Live as if you had to die today—die as if you were immortal!"

2) Because when the last hour of an initiate is approaching, he or she should be reminded of the words of the guru and the experiences of initiation and visions should be recalled, in case in the decisive moment the mind should be clouded.

3) Because the attempt should be made to accompany someone who has just left this life with loving and helpful thoughts, as long as the mind is still uncertain and linked to the past, without allowing one's own emotion to become a hindrance for him or her or a cause of depression in oneself. This third point is probably a greater help to those left behind, as it clears and purifies their own attitude to the departed and to the fact of death.

In any case, it is a matter of remembering the right thing at the right time. In order to make this possible, it is necessary to prepare ourselves during life. Every quality that we want to make into a decisive directing influence in death (and beyond) must be produced, built up and culti-vated in life, so that when the decisive moment comes we are not confused and dismayed, but *spontaneously* enter on the right path, even if the conscious will be inhibited.

This spontaneity is not a characteristic of the surface of conscious-ness, but is deeply anchored in the subconscious. Accordingly, it cannot be produced through intellectual convictions and intentions, but only through the penetration and transformation of those levels of conscious-ness that cannot be reached through logical conclusions and discursive thinking. Such a penetration and transformation is only possible through the power of the "images" of inner vision, i.e., through the formative powers of inner vision, which, like seeds, sink down into the dark realm of the subconscious, there to germinate, grow and develop.

Some people may say that these kinds of visions are purely subjective and therefore are nothing ultimate. But words and ideas, too, are not ultimates, and the danger of clinging to them is all the greater because words have a constricting and limiting tendency, while the experiences and symbols of genuine vision are something living, growing, and inwardly maturing. They point us, and grow into something beyond themselves. They are too immaterial, too "transparent" to become reified and so to tempt us to cling to them. They can neither be "grasped" nor unambiguously described, and have a tendency to develop from form to formlessness, whereas that which is merely thought has the opposite tendency, namely to solidify into a dogma.

The subjectivity of the visions does not detract from their reality-content. They are not hallucinations, because their reality is the reality of the human psyche. They are the symbols in which the highest recognition and striving of the human spirit are incorporated. Their visualization is the creative process of mental projection through which inner experience is translated into visible form, just like the creative act of an artist, who transforms a subjective idea, emotion, or vision into an objective work of art which then assumes a reality independent of the artist.

But just as the artist must attain to a complete mastery of his or her means of expression, and makes use of various technical aids in order to gain the perfect expression of this idea, so the spiritually creative individual must have complete command of his or her spiritual functions and make use of certain aids in order to give the visions reality-value. These technical aids are *yantra, mantra,* and *mudrā,* the parallelism of the visible, audible, and tangible as exponents of the mind (*citta*), speech (*vāk*) and body (*kāya*). *Yantra* here stands for *maṇḍala,* the system of symbols underlying the spiritual vision, and which forms the visible starting point of the meditation. *Mantra,* the symbolic word, is the sacred sound which, passed on to the pupil by the teacher, creates an inner vibration in him or her, thus opening the pupil up to higher experience. *Mudrā* is both the physical gesture and the cultic act that accompanies the *mantra,* and the inner attitude which is stressed and expressed by this gesture.

Only through the cooperation of all these factors can the adept build up his or her mental creation, bit by bit, and so create a vision. For it is here neither a question of romantic wallowing in emotions nor of ecstatic fantasy, but it is a conscious, direct formation and creation in which there is nothing vague. According to von Glasenapp:

> The old Buddhist idea that actions which are performed *kāyena, vācāya uda cetasa* [by body, speed, or mind] can produce transcendental effects inasmuch as they are karma-producing expressions of the human will, gains a new meaning in the Vajrayāna; this corresponds to the new view of the enormous importance of sacral acts—the cooperation of the activity of body, speech, and thought makes it possible for the *sadhaka* to plug into the motive power of the cosmos and make it serve his purpose.[28]

But in the tantric view, the dynamic forces of the cosmos are not different from those of the human mind. Therefore, to control these forces and make them useful—not for our private purposes, but for the good of all living beings—is of the highest importance. As long as these forces slumber within us unrecognized, we have no access to them. Therefore they have to be projected into the realm of the visible as visions, and the symbols that are used for this purpose have the same effect as a crystallizing agent, through which a liquid is suddenly transformed into solid crystals, thereby revealing its true nature and structure. This mental crystallization process, which constitutes the creative phase of meditation, is call in Tibetan *skyed-rim,* and in Sanskrit *sṛṣṭikrama* or the process of unfolding.

If there were not some method of bringing these crystallized forms into the normal flow of life and consciousness, the fixed and visible

[28]H. von Glasenapp, "Die Enstehung des Vajrayana," *Zeitschrift der Deutschen Morgenlandischen Gesellschaft* 90 (1936), p. 553. The translation is mine. *Tr.*

forms would make the mind rigid, which would eventually deaden the mind instead of liberating it. This process is called the method of dissolution, or perfect integration (Tibetan *rdzogs-rim*, Sanskrit *laya-krama*). It shows the non-absoluteness (*anātman*), relatively and dissolubility of every form (*śūnyatā*). This is taught in every branch of Tibetan meditation training, so that there is absolutely no room for misunderstanding, or for clinging to one's own experiences and attachments, which is the bane of most non-Buddhist mystics.

Whoever discovers that reality is the product of our own activity (*manopubbangamā dhammā*, "Mind precedes all *dhammas*": Dhammapada 1) is liberated in the most clear and obvious fashion from the materialistic idea of the world as a self-existing or given reality. This is far more convincing than any theoretical or philosophical discussions. It is a matter of practical experience that has an infinitely more profound effect than the strongest intellectual conviction. Ludwig Klages said that vision *transforms* the visionary, which is clearly a complete contrast to the act of perception, for it merely distinguishes the perceiver from the perceived object and actually assures him of its limited self-existence.

A thing exists only insofar as it acts. Actuality (*wirklichkeit*) is acting (*wirken*, i.e., having an effect). An action symbol or vision is reality. In this sense, the Dhyāni Buddhas seen in meditation are real (just as real as the mind that produces them), whereas the historical Buddha when *thought of* simply as a historical personality in the past is, in this sense, unreal. An ineffective (non-*acting*) symbol or image is an empty form which is at best decorative. It also might be a remembered form of a concept, thought, or event belonging to the past. Therefore all the great Tibetan meditations already presuppose the universal goal, the great mystic synthesis, ideal Buddhahood, and only when they have identified the meditator with the goal do they leave him or her to the multiplicity of meditative experiences and methods.

Just as the archer first gets his or her eye on the target and becomes one with it—in order to be sure of hitting it—so the meditator must first of all envisage the goal and become completely one with it. This gives his inner striving the direction and impetus, so that, no matter the way and method chosen, whether constructive or separative, based on feeling or reason, creative or analytic, he continually proceeds toward the goal without either losing himself in the desert of fragmentation or by clinging to the creations of his own imagination. The latter danger is, as we saw, avoided through the dissolving and integrating action of the assimilation process. This capacity to create and then destroy a whole world proves the true nature of all appearances and the uselessness of all clinging and grasping—more than any mechanical analysis of the intellect.

◇   ◇   ◇

In the previous discussions we have seen that the *Bardo Thödol* is first of all a book for the living, because it is only through the application of its teachings during the lifetime, and in regard to life, that it can be of any use at the time of death and beyond. In case there should be any doubt, the first of the "root-verses" which outline the nature of the work makes its attitude unambiguously clear. It is directed not only at those who see the end of their lives approaching or imminent, but equally to those who still have their lives before them and who are just becoming conscious of the full significance of their existence—their human existence. To be born in human form is a privilege which the Buddha already recognized as such, because it provides the rare chance of deciding our fate, of conversion, and thus of liberation:

> Now when the bardo of birth is dawning upon me,
> I will abandon laziness for which life has no time,
> enter the undistracted path of study, reflection and medita-
>   tion, making projections and mind the path,
>   and realize the three kāyas;
> now that I have once attained a human body,
> there is no time on the path for the mind to wander.[29]

Study (hearing), reflection and meditation are the three stages of discipleship. That the Tibetan word for hearing, *thos* (*tho*), in this

---

[29]*The Tibetan Book of the Dead,* Francesca Fremantle & Chogyam Trungpa, trs. (Boston: Shambhala, 1975), p. 98.

context, as well as in the expression *Thödol* (*thos-grol*), should not be confused with mere physical hearing, can also be seen from the expression *nyan-thos*, corresponding to the Sanskrit *śrāvaka*, which denotes a disciple—that is to say, a direct disciple of the Buddha, not just one who has "heard" the doctrine but one who has wholly given himself up to this doctrine in trusting faith (*śraddhā*), one who has "heard it with his heart" and grasped it inwardly. This is the first step of discipleship. At the second stage, that which has been intuitively felt is worked through intellectually and confirmed by the test of reason; whereas at the third stage, that which has intuitively felt and intellectually accepted becomes reality through direct experience. Intellectual knowledge then becomes inner certainty. It is this that lifts the disciple above the realm of death and enables him or her to see through the illusion of dying and to become free from fear.

The illusion of death has its roots in people's identification with their temporal and transient form—whether physical, psychic, spiritual or emotional—from which arises the false conception of a personal, independent ego, and with that, the fear of losing it. But if we, as disciples, learn to identify with the eternal, the Dharma, the abiding light of Buddhahood that slumbers within, then the terrors of death vanish like mists before the rising sun. For then we will know whatever we may see, hear, or feel at the time of leaving this life are reflections of our own minds, projections of our conscious and unconscious powers, which have no power over us when once we know their origin and see through them.

The disciples are then in the position of detached observers who recognize the play of those forces and forms for what they are—that which we ourselves have built up in this and previous lives by thoughts and deeds, which seeks now either to drag us down into lower forms of existence or to raise us to higher spheres.

Just as the embryo of the physical body repeats all the stages of an age-long past development from the beginnings of organic life through plant and animal forms to *homo sapiens,* so too at the dissolution of the body the conscious mind sinks down, in reverse order, as if according to a spiritual law of gravity, through the various levels of consciousness to that level from which a new embryonic, or equivalent, form can develop. When consciousness gives up its hold on the dying body and is thus freed from the fetters of corporeality, it gains for a moment (which for the dying person can represent an "eternity," or any other period of time) a surprising and unusual state of freedom and clarity, accompanied by a feeling of transcendent peace and intense bliss (which is generally reflected in the facial expression of the dying person in the moment of death or immediately afterwards).

It is of the utmost importance to prevent the mind from slipping away from this illuminated state, and to turn it into a springboard for leaping even higher, if not to highest liberation. But only those who have learned to control the mind and who have developed its highest capabilities can seize or grasp this state in which, for a moment, the scales have fallen from the mental eyes, in order to make it the vehicle of the highest realization. For those who have not gained such perfect mental control, there are various stages described in the *Bardo Thödol*, various levels down to which the mind sinks. At the same time, ways are shown for halting this descent and finding out how to rise again. It is a law of all life that where there is no effort, decay and decline set in. We can swim only as long as we are active and purposeful. As soon as we stop trying, we sink.

The *Bardo Thödol* accordingly insists that an effort must be made at every level to break through the veil of illusion and fearlessly face the facts of reality. It is therefore important in every *bardo*-state to recognize the creations of our own consciousness, and so gain control over them:

> Now when the bardo of dharmata dawns upon me,
> I will abandon all thoughts or fear and terror,
> I will recognise whatever appears as my projection
>   and know it to be a vision of the bardo;
> now that I have reached this crucial point,
> I will not fear the peaceful and wrathful one, my
>   own projections.[30]

---

[30]*The Tibetan Book of the Dead*, Fremantle & Trungpa, trs., p. 99.

If, at this decisive moment, the dying person is able to hold on to all that is noble and elevated—to the pure light of wisdom, which is embodied in his or her highest ideals and in the imagery of his or her meditations—then he or she will certainly go on a good path which leads either to total liberation from this world or to a favorable rebirth, which gives an opportunity to develop his or her best side and to realize the goal in this way. If this highest moment cannot be held firm or grasped in its full significance—that is, as the radiance of the all-embracing consciousness, the *Dharmakaya*—then there will follow the manifestations of the pure light of the *Sambhogakaya*, on the level of clarified spiritual vision:

> When the five luminous lights of wisdom shine,
> fearless may I recognise myself;
> when the forms of the peaceful and wrathful ones appear,
> fearless and confident may I recognise the bardo.[31]

These five wisdoms form the basis of the previously mentioned five orders. They are the qualities present in every Buddha, each one of which is predominant according to circumstances, and thus determines the specific character of the individual Buddha.

From the time of the earliest Pali and Sanskrit texts onward, five Buddhas of our age (*kalpa*) are mentioned, and the doctrine of the cosmic periodicity of the Buddhas is taught, according to which by the eternal law *Samyaksambuddhas* may appear in every *kalpa*. In other words, Buddhahood, or the unfolding of the perfected enlightenment-consciousness (*bodhi-citta*) is an immanent quality in the world and in every living being, just as the flower is immanent in the seed. The five Dhyāni Buddhas are, so to speak, the eternal prototypes, the spiritual proto-images, the ever-present formative principles (matrices) of these ever-arising Buddhas.

How are the five Perfectly Enlightened Ones of a particular age distinguished from one another, although the quality of enlightenment is the same? The answer is: by the path which, corresponding to the

---

[31]*The Tibetan Book of the Dead*, Fremantle & Trungpa, trs., p. 103.

conditions and needs of the time, led to this enlightenment. Tradition distinguishes the following different ways:

◇ The way of pure (universal) knowledge (*prajñā*)
◇ The way of unshakable strength (*bala*)
◇ The way of magic powers (*siddhi*)
◇ The way of mental effort, of yogic energy (*vīrya*)
◇ The way of compassionate love (maitrī-karuṇā).

Thus, Buddha Krakucandra is credited with *prajña* as his principal characteristic, Buddha Kanakamuni with *bala*, Buddha Kāśyapa with magic powers (*siddhi*), Śākyamuni, the historical Buddha, with *vīrya*, and the coming Buddha Maitreya with compassion (*karuṇā*) as an expression of selfless love (*maitrī*). Corresponding to these principal qualities or temperaments, as we may perhaps call them, we can distinguish different aspects of understanding—which are naturally all embraced in the one great enlightenment:

1) The transcendental wisdom of the highest law (*dharmadhātu-jñāna*), the recognition of the universal Dharma as the starting-point and goal of all knowledge;

2) The reflective wisdom of the Great Mirror (*mahādarśana-jñāna*), which sees things impartially, as they are (*yathābhūta*), without being moved or shaken by them;

3) The synthetic wisdom of equality (*samatā-jñāna*), the knowledge that identifies, recognizes oneself in others and makes one equal to others;

4) The analytical wisdom of distinguishing clear vision (*pratyavekṣana-jñāna*), in which the individual and general marks of all things are clearly seen;

5) The active wisdom that perfects everything through the power of love and compassion (*kṛtyānuṣṭhāna-jñāna*).

Magic depends on identification, making subject and object as one, identifying the microcosm and the macrocosm, and the parallelism of cult actions and outer events. In this way there is a close connection between *siddhi* and *samatā-jñāna*.

If we disregard the "historical" interpretation of the five *Samyak-Sambuddhas*, there are revealed here the basic features of a general type of mentality. It is this which gives this typology its value, which otherwise would only be of mythological or iconographical interest. But here we have the structure of every consciousness gifted with understanding, i.e., with the psychological basis of the above-mentioned five orders.

The *transcendental* wisdom of the supreme law belongs to the order of the Wheel of the Law, the *cakra* order of the Dhyāni Buddha Vairocana, who is the spiritual center of radiation (his name means "radiant," just as the wheel is a solar symbol) and occupies the center of the maṇḍala.

The *reflective* wisdom of the Great Mirror belongs to the *vajra* order of the Dhyāni Buddha Akṣobhya, the "Unshakable."

The *synthetic* wisdom of essential inner identity belongs to the *ratna* order of the Dhyāni Buddha Ratnasambhava. *Ratna*, the Jewel, is here the *prima materia*, the Philosophers' Stone, the spark of enlightenment potentially present in every consciousness (*bodhicitta*).

The *analytic* wisdom of clear-sighted distinction belongs to the *padma* (lotus) order of the Dhyāni Buddha Amitābha, in which is symbolized the visionary, unfolding (*śṛṣṭi-krama*) meditation. Expressions like analytical, investigating, searching, with which *pratyavekṣaṇa* is rendered, do not here refer to any kind of intellectual analysis or pulling-to-pieces, or to a logical *reductio ad absurdum* of the phenomenal world through philosophical or scientific analysis. The inadequacy of these had been seen by the Buddha, which is why he rejected the speculations of the metaphysicians and philosophers of his day. Some 19th-century Indologists concluded from this that Buddhism was a purely rational doctrine with no metaphysical background.[32] The Bud-

---

[32]"When one becomes acquainted with the scholastic literature of early Buddhism, the assertion that the Buddha held aloof from the metaphysical questions of his time becomes unthinkable. He did not reject these questions because they were metaphysical, but because—considered from the Buddha's metaphysical standpoint—they were logically

dha was no enemy of logic, in fact he made full use of it himself. But he knew its limits and therefore taught what transcends it—immediate seeing (*dhyāna*), which goes beyond mere verbal thinking (*avitarka-avicāra*). This is given expression in the form of Amitābha as the spiritual prototype of Buddha Sākyamuni. The active, *perfecting* wisdom which works through the power of compassion belongs to the *karma* order of the Dhyāni Buddha Amoghasiddhi, whose idea will find its human expression in the form of Buddha Maitreya.

◇ ◇ ◇

We compared the apparitional forms of the Dhyāni Buddhas with the rays of light broken up by a prism, in which the various qualities of the light become visible. We will now explore the symbolism of space, colors, elements and spiritual qualities. This comparison is appropriate because colors play an important part in the figures of the Dhyāni Buddhas. They are representative of certain qualities and spiritual associations, to which the initiate is just as sensitive as a musically trained person is to different notes. They give to every form of enlightenment, or every aspect of understanding or wisdom a particular vibration, which is audibly represented by the corresponding vibration of the *mantra,* and physically by the gesture (*mudrā*).

The net of relationships extends over all areas of mental and sensual perception and ideation so that out of the chaos of the world-orientated consciousness a well-ordered, clear and controllable cosmos slowly emerges. The basic element of this cosmos is space. Space is all-embrac-

---

impossible to answer. How can we explain why European authors have so emphatically denied the metaphysics of original Buddhism? This phenomenon can be partly explained through two tendencies. On the one hand, Christian missionaries unconsciously, and occasionally perhaps deliberately, stressed in their works the unmetaphysical character of Buddhism in order to prove its inadequacy as a religious system, owing to the lack of the most important elements of a religious character. On the other hand, some pointed to the absence of metaphysics in Buddhism as an advantage, thereby presenting Buddhism as a system that might replace religion without contradicting the modern scientific outlook. We must not forget that the beginnings of the study of Buddhism in Europe coincided with the decline of metaphysical philosophy and the rise of materialist systems of thought."—Otto Rosenberg, *Die Probleme der Buddhistischen Philosophie* (Heidelberg, W. Germany, 1924), p. 59. The translation is mine. *Tr.*

ing, the principles of unity. Its nature is emptiness, and because it is empty it can embrace and contain everything. In contrast to space is the principle of substance, of differentiation, of "thingness." But nothing can exist without space. Space is the precondition of all existence and everything that exists—whether material or immaterial—for we cannot imagine any object and any existence without space. Therefore space is not only the *conditio sine qua non* of all existence, it is also a fundamental feature of our consciousness.

Our consciousness determines the nature of the space we live in. The infinity of space and the infinity of consciousness are identical. The moment a being becomes aware of its consciousness, it becomes aware of space. The moment it becomes aware of the infinity of space, it recognizes the infinity of consciousness. Thus, if space is a quality of our consciousness, then we can say with equal right that the experience of space is the criterion of mental activity and higher consciousness. The manner of experiencing or perceiving space is characteristic of the dimensions of our consciousness.

If people look up to the sky and call upon heaven, or on some power that is believed to dwell there, then in reality they awaken the powers of their own interior which are projected outward and represented and made visible as space, heaven or cosmos. If we consider the mysterious depth and blue of the firmament, we are really contemplating the depth of our own nature, our own mysterious, all-embracing consciousness in its original unstained purity—unstained by thoughts and ideas, undivided by distinctions, desires, or rejections. It is in this that the indescribable and inexplicable joy lies that fills us at such a contemplation.

It is from this kind of experience that we can understand the meaning of the deep blue which is the center and starting point of meditative symbolism and visions. It is the light of the transcendent wisdom of the *Dharmadhātu,* the origin of all consciousness and understanding, undifferentiated, potential, all-embracing, like endless space, which shines forth as a brilliant blue from the heart of Vairocana, the primordial Buddha. This light, which in the *Bardo Thödol* is regarded as the prototype or the pure element of consciousness in its complete-

ness, at the same time symbolizes the potentiality of the Great Emptiness, of *śūnyatā,* which forms the central concept of all Mahāyāna
doctrines.

The philosophical and epistemological interpretations of this concept would fill a whole book. Let us therefore content ourselves with
the language of symbolism, which gives even the philosophically or
meditatively untrained a starting-point for their own thought and experience, as expressed in the simple and beautiful words of the Sixth
Patriarch of Zen (Ch'an) in China:

> Learned Audience, when you hear me talk about the Void,
> do not at once fall into the idea of vacuity (because this
> involves the heresy of the doctrine of annihilation). It is of
> the utmost importance that we should not fall into this idea,
> because when a man sits quietly and keeps his mind blank he
> will abide in a state of "Voidness of Indifference."

> Learned Audience, the illimitable Void of the universe is
> capable of holding myriads of things of various shape and
> form, such as the sun, the moon, stars, mountains, rivers,
> worlds, springs, rivulets, bushes, woods, good men, bad men,
> Dharmas pertaining to goodness or badness, Deva planes,
> hells, great oceans, and all the mountains of the Mahameru.
> Space takes in all these, and so does the voidness of our
> nature. We say that the Essence of Mind is great because it
> embraces all things, since all things are within our nature.[33]

But just as space—although we obviously live in it, are filled with it,
surrounded by it, and carry its entire infinite extent in our hearts—
cannot be described, explained, or defined as a whole, but only in its
partial aspects and in relation to the individual, so, too, the nature of
consciousness (and Buddhahood) can only be brought closer to our
understanding by separating their qualities and individualizing their
various aspects. Just as we orient ourselves in space by speaking of an

---

[33]*The Sutra of Wei Lang (or Hue Neng),* translated from Chinese by Wong Mou-Lam,
1944, revised by Christmas Humphreys (London: Luzac & Co., 1953), p. 28.

eastern, southern, western or northern direction, connecting a phase of the sun's course with each of these directions, and without calling into question the unity of the space or the source of light, so too we make distinctions in the space of our mental experiences, corresponding to the aspect of their unfolding—an eastern, southern, western or northern direction, viewpoint, attitude, or form of expression—without denying the unity and the corresponding existence in and with one another of all phases and aspects of space. In the seed are the root, trunk, leaves, flowers and fruit—and potentially present in undifferentiated unity. But only when they are separated in time and space do they become a reality for us.

Therefore there emerges from the deep blue of space (that is, out of the depths of undifferentiated consciousness) the forms and brilliant rays of the Dhyāni Buddhas. In the east the space-colored (blue) Akṣobhya stands, from whose heart radiates the still unseparated colorless (like Vairocana) white light of the mirror-wisdom, in which the forms (rūpa) of all things for the first time (to stay within a "temporal" image) stand forth and are reflected with the clarity, imperturbability and impartiality of a mirror that is itself untouched by objects. This is the impartiality of the impartial observer, the pure spontaneous becoming-aware (the immediacy of satori in Zen Buddhism), when our habitual (i.e., prejudiced) thinking is cut out, as well as that apparently objective but usually arbitrary isolation or dissection of living events or organic data which goes under the name of "analysis."

This is the attitude of the Buddha in the night of his enlightenment. His gesture of touching the earth (bhūmisparśa-mudrā) symbolizes an unshakable certainty, the basis of a solid foundation of "fact," that is, the dispassionate understanding of reality which sees the world as it is (yathā-bhūta). Akṣobhya is therefore the principle of form that underlies all appearance and all materiality (Sanskrit rūpa), in its purest condition. At the level of the elements his correspondence is water, which, itself colorless and formless, reflects all colors and forms, without being changed or touched by them.

In the Tibetan manuscript used by Lama Kazi Dawa Samdup, which forms the basis of his translation of the Bardo Thödol, edited by W. Y. Evans-Wentz, the principle of form is ascribed to Vairocana, and the blue light emanating from him is explained as "the aggregate of matter resolved into its primordial state," whereas Akṣobhya's white light is described as "the aggregate of the consciousness-principle in its pure form." Although Vairocana and Akṣobhya have much in common and can, in certain meditation systems, be interchanged (both can be shown either blue or white, according to whether the stress is on the active or the passive side of their nature, or according to their relation to certain aspects of consciousness or space), there is no reason to prefer the version of a single manuscript to the version of the authorized woodblock edition that is recognized in the whole of Tibet, the more especially when the latter takes the more logical point of view which ascribes the aggregate of pure consciousness to the central Buddha Vairocana, since out of this proceed the pure principles of form, feeling, perception, and volition.

The Dhyāni Buddha of the South is, like the sun at midday, the symbol of giving from the fullness of spiritual power. Ratnasambhava, whose color yellow corresponds to the warm light of the sun, appears in the gesture of giving (dāna-mudrā) of the Three Jewels (triratna). From his heart breaks forth the golden light of the Wisdom of the Essential Equality of All Beings. The pure principle of feeling[34] is associated with him, for the unity of all beings is nowhere more deeply felt than in sympathy, in the sharing of the joy and sorrow, happiness and pain of others, from whence proceeds the urge to give, to share, and finally to sacrifice oneself for all beings.

At the elemental level, Ratnasambhava corresponds to the earth, which bears and nourishes all beings and whose traditional color is yellow. In its purest form this is represented in gold, the noble metal, or in the precious stone (ratna), and in the mysticism of alchemy as the prima materia or the Philosopher's Stone.

Amitābha, the Dhyāni Buddha of the West, appears in the color of the setting sun, red, and—in accordance with the contemplative time of day—his hands rest in the meditation gesture. The deep-red

[34]Lama Kazi Dawa Samdup translates: "the aggregate of touch in its primal form," which is neither correct nor appropriate in the context.

light of clear distinction bursts forth from his heart, and the open red lotus of unfolding creative meditation blossoms in his hands. The capacity for intuitive vision proceeds from the sublimated principle of perception, which is associated with Amitābha. At the elemental level he is represented by fire, which in traditional symbolism is ascribed to the eye and the function of sight.

The Dhyāni Buddha of the North represents, so to speak, "the sun at midnight," the mysterious activity of spiritual powers which, far from the senses, invisibly and secretly work to bring beings to the maturity of understanding and liberation. The yellow light of an inner sun that is hidden from view (bodhi), combines with the deep blue of the night-space of the universe to form the peaceful, mystical green of Amoghasiddhi. The green light of active, all-perfecting wisdom that radiates from his heart combines the universality of Vairocana's blue light with the emotional warmth of the light of equality that flows from Ratnasambhava.

Thus, the knowledge of the unity of all beings is transformed into the universal, spiritualized activity for the benefit of all beings through self-sacrifice—through the power of all-embracing love (maitrī) and unlimited sympathy (karunā). These two powers form, when anchored in the above-mentioned wisdoms, the indestructible double scepter (viṣva-vajra) of Amoghasiddhi, which in this sense is an intensification of the vajra borne by Akṣobhya, and here represents the principle of volition when freed from all selfishness, which is the magic spiritual power (siddhi) of a Buddha. To this all-penetrating power there corresponds at the elemental level air, which expands, is moved and moves— the principle of life and of the breath of life (prāṇa).

◇   ◇   ◇

Now we discuss sublimation of the skandhas and the symbolism of the lights. When we establish a relationship between the spiritual qualities, principles of consciousness, elements of existence, and the symbolic figures, gestures, colors and spatial positions that accompany them, this is no idle play of fancy or arbitrary speculation. It is rather a matter of the clear presentation of the collective experience confirmed by many generations, of a certain "symphonic" or multidimensional way of experiencing reality in the sense of all the various cooperating powers at the material, sensorial, psychic and spiritual levels. This cooperation is only a harmonious one when undisturbed by any impure (i.e., self-centered) vibrations, and it requires clear understanding and purposeful effort to maintain the inner "harmony." The instrument of human consciousness is like a musical instrument. It has to be continually tuned, and to tune it properly depends on knowledge of the right vibration, on being able to hear the correct harmony, and on the devotion and empathy of the performer.

It is this knowledge that the *Bardo Thödol,* like every tantric method of visualization, seeks to convey at various levels. The actual simultaneous existence (often interpenetration) of these levels and the simultaneity of their functions is observed by the thinking mind as a succession or contiguity, and can therefore only be expressed piecemeal and in separate phases.

The consequences for thought or world-view are therefore revealed only by approaching the problem from different sides and viewpoints, through, so to speak, a "concentric attack" on the central problems. The incommensurable remainder that lingers on after every partial solution can only be eliminated through a total view or through the experience of wholeness. Therefore, to pursue this principle to its final conclusion, true liberation is only possible through perfect enlightenment, and not merely through denying the world and its problems which can only lead to spiritual death, to pure nihilism.

We must be aware of the inadequacy of all words and attempts at intellectual explanation, realizing that these only provide us with approximations to prepare us for the deeper experience, just as the theory of harmony and counterpoint is only a preparation and can never replace the actual musical experience. We will confine ourselves to a few brief indications which illuminate the philosophical background of tantric thought.

The links between the five *skandhas* (*rūpa, vedanā, saṁjñā, saṁskāra, vijñāna*) to the five qualities of the enlightened consciousness, and the corresponding five wisdoms, indicate an essential principle of this world-view—that the highest qualities are contained in embryo in the lower ones, and that evil and good, profane and sacred, sensual and spiritual, mundane and supramundane, ignorance and enlightenment, *saṁsāra* and *nirvāṇa*, are not absolutely opposite concepts, totally separate from each other, but are two sides of the same reality. Thus the world is neither condemned out of hand nor split up into irreconcilable opposites. Rather, a bridge is shown that leads from the everyday world of temporal sense-impressions to the realm of timeless knowledge—a way that leads not through denial and rejection, but through ennobling and sublimation of existing conditions and qualities to that which is beyond them.

From the standpoint of the five groups or substrates of individual existence (the *skandhas*) this means that the principles of corporeality (*rūpa*), sensation (*vedanā*), perception (*saṁjñā*), mental formations or volitional formative powers (*saṁskāra*), and consciouness (*vijñāna*) are transformed in the state of Buddhahood into the corresponding qualities of enlightened consciousness. The limited, ego-bound, individual consciousness becomes cosmic consciousness as we see it symbolized in the figure of Vairocana, and the principle of corporeality becomes the total body, the latent principle of all form, as it is symbolized in the *ālaya-vijñāna*, the "store-consciousness" which, like a great mirror, reflects and preserves the shapes of all formations, and is personified in Akṣobhya.

Similarly, out of egocentric feeling and sensation grows empathy, the inner fellow-feeling and sharing with all that lives that we find embodied in the figure of Ratnasambhava. From sense-perception comes the suprasensual function of perception and distinction of visions in meditation, which is the special function of Amitābha. From the ego-bound karma-producing volition and the powers created by this is produced the karma-free activity of the saints, that is, the realization of the holy path in the Bodhisattva career, in the life of a saint or a Buddha—a life whose effective cause is no longer in the thirst for life, in clinging and attachment, but in compassion and love of one's neighbor. If these higher qualities have once taken root within us, then we are attracted by the vibrations of pure light from the Dhyāni Buddhas, and we are then able to enter into harmony with them and their specific color-vibrations and vibrate with them. If, however, we are not capable of this, we feel the purity of these vibrations to be incompatible with the vibrations of our being. And just as a too bright light blinds our eyes used to earthly conditions and frightens us, so too we draw back in fright before the clarity and purity of the Buddha's radiance that overcomes our senses, preferring instead the impure but milder colors of the dull radiances that correspond to our instincts and our mundane inclinations.

That is why it says in the *Bardo Thödol* that for those whose minds are not prepared the visions of light and radiations experienced in the *bardo* of reality are frightening and confusing. Whoever can interpret them, or still more, whoever has previously created the forms within himself into which can be poured the fullness of light, color and sound that wells up from the depth of his original consciousness will experience neither fear nor fright, but only the lofty vision of supramundane harmony which carries him away and enables him to become one with everything that is brilliant, clear and pure, liberating and emancipating—that, in fact, leads to liberation.

If we have cultivated the highest in ourselves we are attracted by the highest. But if we are attached to lower things we will be drawn to lower things. And if we have not devoted ourselves during life to the practice of meditation we are not capable of remaining for long in this realm of pure light. We will feel drawn to the dull but more familiar radiations and reflexes of lower impulses, such as greed, attachment, envy, pride, anger, self-complacency, laziness, dullness, and other such results of ignorance and egoism.

These impulses are like the vibrations of impure colors and notes. That is why, beside the pure emanations of the Dhyāni Buddhas, the opposite radiations of the other realms are found, realms of qualities directly opposed to those embodied by the Dhyāni Buddhas, and which therefore try to hinder us in the realization of those pure qualities.

Thus, opposed to the all-embracing knowledge of universal law (the *Dharmadhātu* wisdom) that is expressed in the miraculously pure radiation of Vairocana is the self-satisfied ignorance of the gods (who imagine they are eternal). Just as banks of cloud hide the deep blue of all-embracing space, so the dull white light that proceeds from the realm of happy ignorance "veils" the *Dharmadhātu* wisdom from the weak and distracts them from its radiance. "Thereupon," says the text, "because of bad karma the glorious blue light of the Wisdom of the *Dharmadhātu* will produce in you fear and terror, and you will want to flee from it. But the dull white light of the devas will seem pleasant (attractive) to you."

The imperturbability of Akṣobhya and the untouched objectivity and impartiality of the Mirrorlike Wisdom is opposed by the passionate restlessness of hatred, whose burning flames are the sign of hellish states of existence born of hatred, and whose dark, smoky outpourings will appear beside the pure white light of the Mirrorlike Wisdom. Beside the brilliant golden radiance of Ratnasambhava, who embodies the equality of all living beings, there appears the opposing dull blue light of pride[35] (which is based on inequality) as a typical emanation of the human world.

The pure, deep red rays of discriminating wisdom and meditative clear vision that proceed from the figure of Amitābha are opposed by the dull yellow rays of greed, passion and possessiveness which lead to the *preta* world, the realm of unfulfilled desires, where all is painful because it is unsatisfying. The compassion and love of Amoghasiddha, who completes all works, which is expressed in the pure deep green radiance of all-perfecting wisdom, is opposed by the dull red radiance of the ever-quarrelling *Asuras*, embodiments of envy and jealousy, the source of ambition, quarrelsomeness and war. Only when the united power of all the pure radiances combined have failed, at the end of the "*bardo* of reality," to have any effect on the dead person, there appears, as the opposite pole of Vairocana's radiance, the dull green light that comes from the animal kingdom, the realm of mental dullness and dumbness.

It is significant that the gods and the animals, although at opposite poles as forms of existence, share "ignorance" as an essential factor. The

---

[35]Tibetan: *nga-rgyal*; Sanskrit: *māna*. Lama Kazi Dawa Samdup has, in the main text, "violent egotism" for this, although when the same verse is repeated in "The Path of Good Wishes" it is correctly rendered "pride." If the text had another word in the first passage, this can only be due to an error.

ignorance (*avidyā*) of the former reposes on the absence of suffering, that of the latter on the lack of thinking capacity which is the essential precondition for responsible decision and free will. Whereas rebirth in the higher realms of existence, such as the *devalokas,* makes a return to the human world after the exhaustion of the favorable karma that led there a probability, any ascent from the animal realm is very difficult and slow on account of the mental torpor and dullness prevailing there.

Descent into an animal womb—which is probably only possible in the case of complete bestialization of the human character or through disintegration of the faculty of reason—is accordingly worse (and probably rarer) than descent into the hell-worlds, which are states of extreme suffering.

That the removal of all suffering in the *deva* worlds is a hindrance to the gaining of perfect enlightenment and liberation should give us pause and allow us to look at suffering from a different angle. We should regard suffering not as a curse, but as a teacher and a spur to higher endeavor. This thought is perfectly expressed in a poem by Christian Morgenstern.[36] A similar thought is expressed in a fine passage in the *Bardo Thödol* in which the dying person is urged to make the best even of his death, making the opportunity to strive for the well-being of all

---

[36]Christian Morgenstern (1871–1914) is best known as the author of nonsense verses, but he also wrote poems of a deeply mystical character.

Prayer

I call upon you, pain; with all your might
May this dear heart of mine be sorely stricken
Which this poor dust I call myself does quicken
And lift above the all-embracing night.

I call you, mankind's dearest, kindest friend!
Forgive me, pain, that I was so misguided
To spurn the greatest gift that you could send,
By which is man from gods and beasts divided!

I beg you, give me then your bitter flask
Regardless of my fearful hesitation;
Since joy could not equip me for my task,
Then help me, pain, achieve my consummation.

Tr.

living beings and for the perfection of Buddhahood. In the same sense we should willingly accept not only death, but every deep sorrow, every experience of suffering, and thereby turn it into a sacred sacrifice. Whoever is capable of doing this has solved the problem of suffering, and transforms the pains of *saṃsāra* into the bliss of nirvāṇa.

◇   ◇   ◇

The next stage is descent into the world. At this moment, when we leave the realm of pure light, we are caught up in the shades of unconscious drives that rise up against us in ever more confusing and threatening forms. Even the powers of light lose their peaceful and benign aspect and are transformed into fearful apparitions, as if they were making a last desperate effort to prevent the inevitable descent into darkness. Those who see through these fear-inspiring, pugnacious, and heroic forms will not flee them, but will seek their protection and aid against the twilight powers and their temptations. But those who do not penetrate their disguise will sink deeper and deeper into the abyss of darkness, where soon they will be surrounded by a pandemonium of frightful apparitions and animal-headed monsters, while the air seems to be filled with threatening voices, crazy laughter, howling and shrieks of terror.

These awesome apparitions are merely the inner forces of resistance to any total surrender to the darkness. Those who even now awaken to the consciousness of their inner reality, who recognize in all these apparitions the mirroring of their own minds, can cause them to disappear or dissolve them in the bright radiance of the higher light. "When one's own thought-forms have turned into demons, one wanders in *saṃsāra*. But whoever does not succumb to this illusion and is not afraid, will not wander in *saṃsāra*." Such words, which are repeated over and over again in the *Bardo Thödol*, show that this is not a case of some primitive demonology, but an exact description of psychological processes inside a clearly circumscribed system of traditional (and to a certain extent general human) symbolic forms.

Whereas the Christian Middle Ages and even later periods of European cultural history raised certain symbols to dogmas and considered them as "real," the Tibetans are quite clear about the nature of such manifestations. They do not fall into the extreme of denying them (as modern "enlightened" persons do) or of underestimating them, nor into the other extreme of believing in their real separate existence (as do both primitive peoples and orthodox church believers). If we can read between the lines of the *Bardo Thödol,* in which the heights and depths of the human spirit are described, we can discover vast treasures of wisdom. We will find that the human consciousness or the human soul, if we use this much abused concept in its original, undogmatic sense as "psyche," is really an image of the universe, a real microcosm— and that therefore there is from every point a way to liberation, to salvation from the terrors of self-torment—through the sudden flash of spontaneous self-knowledge.

This is the consoling and encouraging teaching of the *Bardo Thödol.* Even in the deepest hells—which in accordance with the general Buddhist view are not eternal, but temporary subjective states of consciousness—there is no reason for despair. The *Bardo* text, in the "Path of Good Wishes," protects us against the terrors of the intermediate state:

> When savage beasts of prey are roaring,
> may it become the sound of dharma, the six syllables . . . [37]

The six sacred syllables—that in Tibet greet the wanderer on every road and are engraved millions of times in stones and rocks, so as to penetrate into the very marrow of being of the inhabitants and into their innermost consciousness—are the syllables of the mantra OṂ MA-ṆI PAD-ME HŪṂ, which evoke in the heart of every believer the image of Avalokiteśvara, the ideal of all Bodhisattvahood. And just as Avalokiteśvara is the embodiment of compassionate Buddha-love that penetrates all spheres of existence in a thousand forms and stands encouraging and conforming at the side of all who desire emancipation, so too each one of the six syllables of this mantra represents a seed of effective power

---

[37]*The Tibetan Book of the Dead,* Fremantle & Trungpa, trs., p. 104.

that is related to one of the six realms of existence, thus giving the power to save oneself and, indirectly, others.

This power is not, as is continually asserted through incorrect translations or interpretations, a magic power. It is a means of awakening in our own consciousness (represented by *padma*) the slumbering powers of enlightenment (*bodhicitta*, represented by *maṇi*) to attain realization of the highest goal and to ward off lower influences. OṂ is a sound that awakens the consciousness to the infinite, whereas HŪṂ is an expression of self-sacrifice embracing the deepest ground of existence.

A mantra, therefore, is neither a "magic word" nor a "magic spell." It is an instrument of mental imagination and concentration, and a means of mental power, but not of "supernatural" powers. The root *man* means mental, and the suffix -*tra* denotes instruments or tools.[38] The effect of the mantra does not depend on its pronunciation (another widespread misunderstanding) but on the mental attitude, the conscious and subconscious associations that are created by the intuition and the associated exercises. If it were a matter of the correct pronunciation, then all mantras in Tibet would have lost their meaning and their power. In Tibet they are not pronounced according to the rules of Sanskrit, but of Tibetan, in which, for instance, *padme* becomes *péme*. This does not mean that the pronunciation and stress are of no importance. On the contrary, a pupil will always try to imitate the guru's pronunciation, because that helps to re-establish *rapport* with the guru.[39]

By associating the six sacred syllables to the six realms of existence, we liberate ourselves from the attraction which these places of rebirth exert upon us as a result of our weakness and ignorance. These realms, which we became acquainted with in the previous chapter, represent the different stages of consciousness that come into effect in the corresponding forms of material or immaterial existence, and can be experienced both in the "intermediate state" and as future forms of life.

---

[38]Heinrich Zimmer, *Myths and Symbols in Indian Art and Civilization*, edited by Joseph Campbell, Bollingen Series, Vol. 6 (New York: Pantheon, a division of Random House, 1946).

[39]For further details, see my *Foundations of Tibetan Buddhism* (York Beach, ME: Samuel Weiser, 1969; and London: Rider & Co., 1969).

Those people in whom the harmonious qualities predominate, but whose clear sight and understanding are imperfect, will be able to create for themselves (at least for a time) harmonious conditions within the six realms, and therefore feel themselves attracted by such forms of existence as provide the outward possibility of such a condition. Those who are under the sway of lower instincts will similarly feel drawn to lower and less fortunate realms or conditions of existence.

All these worlds or levels of consciousness are ultimately illusory. But the same can be said, too, of our present existence and of this, our material world. Einstein has said that reality is by no means immediately given. What is given is merely the data of our consciousness. There is only one way from the data of our consciousness to reality, namely the way of conscious or unconscious intellectual construction, which operates completely freely and arbitrarily. These facts can be expressed in a paradox, namely that reality as we know it is exclusively composed of arbitrary ideas.

It is therefore quite unimportant whether we regard this world or a "world beyond" as real, and whether we believe in gods, demons and spirits or in the forces of nature, and whether we are convinced of the truth of rebirth on earth or in the heavens and hells. All that is important is our *experience,* which conceals the fact that our consciousness is dominated by certain laws, has certain basic principles of form, and a definite structure far transcending the boundaries of our individual manifestation and our temporal existence.

We have, it seems, reached the frontiers of our material universe, if we are to believe the latest discoveries of our physicists. But we are still far from discovering the frontiers, or the true nature, of consciousness. Modern psychologists have pointed out that the unknown regions of our consciousness are far greater than the known ones, and they have found to their surprise that the latest discoveries of psychoanalysis agree with the basic types and symbolic forms (C. G. Jung calls them archetypes) as described in the *Bardo Thödol.*

Thus we are at last beginning to discover the truth that was taught by tantric philosophers and mystics, that even our illusions are the expression of a reality that we can only understand when we can read the signs of the transient. For they are nothing but letters in the book of wisdom, meaningless in themselves but in context revealing their significance. Understanding these signs is tantamount to being able to control our conscious and unconscious powers and to develop them so that we can become masters of our fate and architects of a better future.

Part Three

ART AS
CREATIVE MEDITATION

The Ancient Culture of Tibet

———

Tibet's great and ancient culture, which existed in full vigor for more than a thousand years right down to our own time, was almost totally destroyed by the armies of a power-hungry neighboring country equipped with modern weapons. Nobody came to the aid of Tibet, and so the great opportunity to save the last living link with the oldest traditions of mankind was lost. Tibet's cultural and geographical isolation had proved itself a protection for traditional cultural values and an old-fashioned way of life that lasted until just recently. But what was previously a protection became a danger. Tibet became a power-vacuum, which by its very nature attracted new lines of force, especially since its natural wealth had hitherto remained untapped. The opening up of the earth to get at these treasures seemed to the Tibetans a sacrilege, nor would it have occurred to them to desecrate the pure snowfields of their mighty mountains, whose peaks they regarded as the home of the gods, for the sake of human ambition.

Today, when we are able to review the totality of human development from the wider perspectives of modern science and psychology, we understand the importance of Tibet. We have learned to overcome the obstacles posed by nature, but not to control our own nature. In this regard we can still learn much from Tibet, especially in the field of the investigation of the human mind. The West was preoccupied with the exploration of external nature, especially the physical sciences, which are today spread throughout the world. But Tibet chose another path. Rejecting the control of the forces of nature, as it rejected the conquest of neighboring countries, especially since the introduction of Buddhism in the seventh century, it devoted itself instead to the cultivation and development of the inner powers that are the source of all human capabilities and of all perfection. If we are incapable of harmonizing these psychic powers, of concentrating them and finally integrating them, we cannot expect to be able to create a happier and more united human world. It is from this basic standpoint that the Tibetans considered the problems of the future of humanity, problems with which we are now confronted on a global scale.

Since Tibet was protected by high mountains and extreme climatic conditions, and had not built up any military defenses, it concentrated its energies first and foremost on the development of its religious life, and to the needs of its simple and self-sufficient economy. In this way it became an easy prey to armies equipped with modern weapons. And so the attempt to place spiritual values above material gains ended in a tragedy which shook the world, but which the world could not prevent. And yet the world's conscience was shaken out of its slumbers.

And so we are beginning to recognize the importance of Tibet and the part it has played in the history of mankind. This consisted in an attempt to subordinate human life to a cosmic vision, and to transform it by the power of a creative idea. It was a vision that was built on the unity and universality of consciousness, a vision that filled human existence with meaning and value and appealed to every individual to help realize it. Every important culture of the past has endeavored to explore or express a particular dimension of the human spirit. None was complete or could produce a total solution to the problems of humanity, because the circumstances and conditions of life are in a constant state of flux.

Nevertheless, each one of these cultures represented a valuable step on the way toward the solution of this problem, and thus was an enrichment for mankind. This enrichment took the form of a cultural heritage which survived the greatest and mightiest empires. Their triumphs and conquests, their wealth and splendor, as well as their ultimate failure, are today of no importance. But what has remained in the consciousness of the world and has inspired innumerable generations are the fragile works of those who possessed neither power nor worldly wealth—the artists, seers and singers, poets and thinkers who were able, in the shadow of the mighty, the kings and the wealthy, the generals and leaders, to give expression to the dreams of mankind, whether in the form of religious expectations, lofty experiences, profound feelings or great deeds of heroism. Here lies our common heritage and the guarantee of the continuity of human culture in every form of new civilization.

If, as all the signs of our times seem to indicate, we are standing on the threshold of a new world, then we have all the more reason to look back along the path we have traveled—not in order to bring the past back to life, but in order to understand our present position and the direction of our future. For this can only be understood in relation to the past that lives on in us and that has made us what we are. The past contains our source as well as our goal. Tibet was probably the last culture in which the oldest traditions of mankind were still living. The religious and intellectual culture which had ripened in India during more than a thousand years of Buddhist history had raised Tibetan culture to its highest peak of perfection and transformed it. Tibetan art, of which the Western world is only just beginning to take notice, provides more than just aesthetic pleasure. It is based not only on a pantheon of gods and deified saints, but also on the experience of meditation and on a wealth of archetypal symbols. These reveal some of the most profound mysteries of the human mind and provide the key to many problems of modern depth psychology. Most of the figures described in iconographical works are not to be regarded as deities existing separately from the meditator, but as conscious projections of meditative experiences, as they are described in the *sādhanas* (texts).

No iconography has any value without knowledge of these texts and their practical application within the living tradition, which, however, could soon be forgotten. The world has never seen anything like this sudden disappearance of a great and long-standing culture, and at the same time it has never had a greater chance to preserve its heritage and make it accessible to the whole of mankind. For at least some of the people who still today embody the living tradition of Tibetan culture are living in our midst, and we possess the technical means of reproducing all aspects of Tibetan life in art and literature, in word and picture, in audible and visible form.

Tibet's art, especially its great sculptures (in the form of temple statues and similar works) has hitherto been largely unavailable to the West, and since most of these works have in the meantime been destroyed, the two volumes of photographs from Tibet published by Li Gotami are of particular importance. These pictures were taken on a two-year expedition to Central and West Tibet from 1947 to 1949.[1]

The principal object of our expedition at that time was to explore the deserted royal city of Tsaparang, which in the 11th century was the capital of the Guge dynasty. On an earlier journey I had come across sculptures from the first great epoch of Buddhist art in Tibet. I proposed to the boards of the University and the Museum of Allahabad, who had been interested in the results of my first exploration, to equip an expedition whose object was the exploration of the ruined city of Tsaparang. This former capital of the West Tibetan Guge dynasty, deserted for hundreds of years, must, according to all the Tibetan historical sources, have been one of the earliest Tibetan cultural centers. That alone would have sufficed to awaken my interest, especially as I had good reason to suppose that in the climate of Tibet a considerable part of the earliest works of art would still be found in the ruins, and that in view of the remoteness and loneliness of the region it should be possible to examine and investigate everything that had escaped destruction.

In Lhasa, the last legitimate king of Tibet had been murdered by Langdarma. The latter tried to re-establish the power of the pre-Buddhist Bönpo religion by destroying Buddhist temples and monasteries, killing

---

[1]Some of these pictures are to be found in my *Foundations of Tibetan Mysticism* (York Beach, ME: Samuel Weiser, 1969; and London: Rider & Co., 1969).

their inhabitants and persecuting their followers. Although he himself was overthrown in 742 after years of terror and tyranny, Buddhism in Central Tibet had been almost destroyed. Even its revival by the six men of Ü and Tsang, who brought back the chief teachings of Buddhism, could not restore Lhasa to its former importance. This only occurred in the 15th century, in the time of Tsongkhapa, the founder of the Gelugpa school, who made Lhasa the main center of his reform movement and the seat of the Tibetan central government.

In the meantime, West Tibet became the center of Buddhist culture. Here Tibetan art reached its peak, and here important Buddhist scriptures were translated into classical Tibetan. From here a new wave of Buddhist learning and literature spread over Tibet. Under the guidance of great Indian and Tibetan scholars, and under the patronage of generous and pious kings, who in the tenth and 11th centuries had extended their power over the whole of western Tibet, this became an age of intellectual growth and of great works in all fields of art and science.

The re-establishment of Buddhism was for these kings worthy of the greatest sacrifices, and more important than political power. And so the 11th century became the golden age of Tibetan Buddhism, an age which originated many spiritual movements that were to give power and nourishment to subsequent Tibetan history, and thus cause religious life to radiate and penetrate into all activities of daily life. The high point of this glorious era was the great Buddhist council of Thöling, which took place in the famous Golden Temple of Thöling in the mid-11th century. This was the age of Rinchen Zangpo, Atīśa, Konchog Gyalpo, Domtön, Marpa and Milarepa, and of the schools founded by them, the Kadampa, Sakyapa, and Kargyütpa.

Atīśa, one of the greatest Indian Buddhist scholars, was invited by the reigning king to Thöling, and stayed there for several years. He came from the great Buddhist University of Vikramaśīla, and was known as the greatest religious authority on Buddhism in India. Soon he was recognized by all the schools of Tibet. His chief disciple was Domtön, who was born in 1002 and founded the Kadampa school, which was famous for its strict monastic discipline, its ritualism, and for its meditation practice. From this school there developed, at the end of the 14th century, the Gelugpa school under the leadership of Tsongkhapa (1357–1419).

Rinchen Zangpo was equally great as an artist and architect as he was as a scholar and translator of Buddhist Sanskrit texts into classical Tibetan. He founded the famous monastery and Golden Temple of Thöling, the temples of Tsaparang, and many other monasteries and religious monuments in West Tibet and Ladakh. The splendor of his statues and frescoes has never been surpassed in the history of Tibet. These works created the classical style that characterizes the best period of Tibetan art. In contrast to the more or less stereotyped Buddha-images of China and Central Asia (like that in the temple of Iwang in South Tibet), the statues of Tsaparang combine the almost abstract qualities of great sculpture with an incomparable expression of inner vitality.

That these living qualities came out in Li Gotami's photographs is mainly due to the patient and respectful attitude that she brought to these statues and frescoes during our three-month stay in the deserted ruins of the city of Tsaparang. In the course of our daily work in the presence of these awe-inspiring sculptures, we became more and more conscious of their astonishing vitality, and of an almost magical power, such as can only be given out by works that were created with limitless devotion and intensified concentration, or in a meditative vision. We felt as if we were in the presence of living beings, who surrounded us in the stillness and loneliness of this deserted city. They were like mighty friends from another world, who gave us strength and courage to continue our work even under the most difficult conditions.

Although we had no idea of the scale of the catastrophe that was so soon to overwhelm Tibet, we were well aware of the dark clouds that rose above Tibet's eastern horizon. We were simply concerned to save for posterity as much as we could of the art treasures of the decaying temples and sanctuaries. But it never occurred to us that not only the forces of nature and natural decay, but also the blind destructiveness of man would obliterate these monuments of the past. How quickly this could happen was shown by the so-called "cultural revolution" that soon engulfed the whole of China and, finally, Tibet.

As we heard, the Kumbum of Gyantse successfully survived this terrible time, although its statues and frescoes were severely damaged, but they have in part been restored. Kumbum, the pagoda-like Temple of the Hundred Thousand Buddhas, which rises in nine stories over the monastery city of Gyantse, contains not only thousands of Buddha-images and frescoes, but forms the greatest Tibetan iconography, in the works of great artists. In order to see all the wonders of the Kumbum even weeks and months would not suffice; to study them in detail would take years. There are no fewer than 80 chapels which are grouped in step-formation like the cells of a beehive round the solid core of the building. Each of these chapels contains a number of statues ranging from lifesize to giant two-storey figures of the main Buddha. Some of the most beautiful 14th century statues still show the influence of the classical period of West Tibet, although the lengthening of the lower body from this period, which gave such dignity to the Tsaparang statues (a tendency also found in Gothic figures) is no longer to be found. Further, the walls of the chapels are covered from top to bottom with finely executed frescoes.

From the architectural point of view alone, the Kumbum is one of the most remarkable buildings in Tibet. It combines the features of a *chörten* (stupa) with those of a temple, in which the innumerable forms of Buddhas, Bodhisattvas, saints and heroes, divine and demonic beings are portrayed in painting and sculpture. The whole work takes the shape of a nine-storied pagoda in the shape of an enormous *chörten*, which originally developed out of the Indian tumulus in which the relics of the Buddha or a saint were preserved.

Each one of the above mentioned chapels is dedicated to a particular aspect of Buddhahood or Bodhisattvahood, or to a special path of meditation. The latter finds its symbolic expression in the maṇḍala, which shows the concentric path to the highest realization of a divine form (a Buddha or Bodhisattva). This is surrounded by emanations of their spiritual power, corresponding to the degree to which the chosen goal has been realized. In the four great chapels of the great round central structure (*bumpa*), these maṇḍalas are especially finely represented with thousands of figures, so that every form of meditative experience is represented there.

Maṇḍalas of the highest level denote the wholeness of human consciousness, indeed a replica of the universe. The word *maṇḍala* literally means "circle," but in the religious sense it is a concentric arrangement of mutually-related symbols gained from the experiences of meditation or from general religious practice. There are purely abstract maṇḍalas consisting purely of geometrical figures or diagrams which contain either only a single character, a single syllable or a sacred formula (*mantra*). Each character, syllable or mantra represents a particular aspect of psychic or spiritual power, through which the meditator calls forth the symbols of a higher reality.

A second type of maṇḍala consists of the representation of ritual objects that serve to identify specific functions or divine beings. It should be mentioned that the beings represented here are really different states of consciousness that are latently present in every human being.

The third and most complex type of maṇḍala contains pictorial representations of enlightened beings, such as Buddhas, Bodhisattvas, divine protectors in human or superhuman form, in various positions and colors, and with distinctive gestures, accompanied by their throne-animals and surrounded by various auras or flames.

Whereas the maṇḍalas so far described are predominantly two-dimensional (i.e., take the form of frescos, *thangkas*—hanging pictures—or woodcuts), there are also three-dimensional maṇḍalas with sculptured images of Buddhas, their emanations and accompanying figures; in short the entire pantheon of beings from the spiritual worlds. And finally, there are abstract three-dimensional maṇḍalas in the shape of monumental architecture, of which the Kumbum is a particular example. In fact, not only is every chapel meant as a maṇḍala—the entire structure of the Kumbum is itself a monumental three-dimensional maṇḍala. The architectural features of the Kumbum symbolize, like all stupas, the main elements of the universe:

1) The solid condition, represented by the cubic forms of the basic structure and the square terraces;

2) The fluid condition, represented by the round drum-like central structure, which is also described as a water-pot or vase (*bumpa*);

3) The glowing or fiery condition, represented by the cone that rises above the drum;

4) The gaseous (airy) condition, represented by the umbrella-like structure above the cone;

5) The etheric or radiant condition (symbolizing unification or integration), represented by a flaming jewel over the umbrella.

In other words, the Kumbum is, like all *chörtens,* a representation of the universe in the form of the five elements—earth, water, fire, air and ether. These elements were not only regarded as varying degrees of density, or as material states of the aggregates in a universe that is continually materializing and dematerializing itself, but also as the powers of psychic centers in the human body, where they transform themselves into spiritual energy. In accordance with this, the drum- or pot-like central structure of the *chörten* denotes not only the liquid state of the aggregates, but also its spiritual counterpart, the vessel with the water of life or the elixir of immortality (Sanskrit, *amrta-kalaśa*). This is the sign of the Buddha Amitāyus, who symbolizes the infinity of life, and is the active reflex of Amitābha, the Buddha of Infinite Light, whose human manifestation is said to be Śākyamuni, the Enlightened One of our epoch.

Thus the Buddhas take the principal positions in the Kumbum, and determine the nature of the character of the maṇḍala, just as the *bumpa* (*amrta-kalaśa*) as the central structure determines the total character of the *chörten.* Whoever is treading the path of the Buddha should therefore regard this gigantic maṇḍala as a making visible of the holy path, which can only be brought to realization by one who treads it with devotion and understanding.

Just as anyone who is going on a long journey first prepares himself and studies all the relevant maps in order to plan his route, so too we must be spiritually and physically prepared when we enter the sacred area of this maṇḍala and press on from terrace to terrace into ever higher regions of experience. With every step we are reminded through the portraits of innumerable enlightened beings who have trodden this path before us, and whose spiritual presence encourages our own efforts, of the goal to be reached.

Thus, one shrine opens before us after another, and each of them forms a maṇḍala within the great maṇḍala, a world within a greater world. With every storey the pilgrim enters a higher level of intuitive vision, until in the last, all difference disappears and one stands before the great mystery, in which wisdom combines with compassion, understanding with active love in the form of Vajradhāra, the all-embracing Buddha. Here we reach the source from which all the enlightened ones draw inspiration, the source that opens up deep within us and in which all beings are mutually joined together.

The Seven Treasures of a World Ruler

Probably one of the oldest dreams of mankind is the ideal picture of an *undivided* world peopled by human beings and based on spiritual and humanitarian principles. In the earliest Buddhist scriptures, reflecting ancient Indian traditions, we can already find detailed accounts of the necessary assumptions and conditions that are supposed to have led to the realization of this ideal. Thus the Mahāsudassana Sutta of the Dīgha Nikāya of the Pali Canon tells us, in the words of the Buddha, that this ideal was once realized in a long-distant epoch, in the world-cycle before the present one.

According to this vision of Utopia ascribed to past ages, the leader of the undivided and united people of that time was the Buddha himself in one of his past births, in which, as a Bodhisattva, he was still treading the toilsome path toward full enlightenment. The memory of this episode of his past returned to him in the last days of his earthly life when, now as the Buddha Śākyamuni, he reviewed for the last time the aeons of his Bodhisattva existence.

At his last birth as Prince Siddhārtha, it has been prophesied that he would become either a world ruler or a world-delivering Buddha. But the rishi who made this declaration was not aware that the lordship over the material world was something the Bodhisattva had long since achieved—a deed of only temporal value that could no longer have any attraction for him. Now his goal could only be the gaining of the highest perfection of Buddhahood (*samyaksambodhi*). Even when he had gained this lofty goal, his love and compassion for this, our imperfect and suffering world, was greater than his satisfaction at having gained his own perfection. And so he turned his attention once more to this world, taking upon himself the responsibilities of a wandering teacher. When, after 45 years of wandering, he had established his teaching so firmly in the hearts of mankind that his pupils were capable of passing it on, he decided that the time was ripe for him to withdraw.

His disciples[2] were dismayed at this announcement, and when they realized that they could not persuade him to change his decision, they begged him at least to choose a worthier place than the Kusinārā for such a momentous event. The Buddha must have smiled at this display of human vanity. But finally he calmed his pupils by telling them that Kusinārā had once been the scene of an important event in the past, when a *cakravartin*—a world ruler—named Mahāsudassana reigned there.

The Flaming Wheel

Once, on a scared full-moon day, King Mahāsudassana sat on the roof of his palace in his favorite seat, when there appeared in the sky a flaming wheel with a thousand spokes. The King remembered that this could only be the "Sacred Wheel of the Law" (*dhammacakka*, Sanskrit, *dharmacakra*) that the wise men had told him about as being the sign of a world ruler. Rising from his seat, he paid homage to the heavenly wheel and, while pouring water from a golden bowl, he uttered the wish: "May the Noble Wheel roll victoriously to the ends of the world!" The Noble Wheel rolled to the East, and Mahāsudassana followed it with his entire army. And whenever the wheel stopped, the King stayed there and camped with his followers. All the previously hostile kings of the East approached King Mahāsudassana humbly, bade him welcome, and laid their lands at his feet. The King said: "Do not take life. Do not take what is not given. Do not commit sexual misconduct. Do not tell

---

[2]Actually Ananda, his chief disciple. *Tr.*

lies. Do not take strong drink or drugs. But enjoy all that is good and wholesome."[3] Then all the kings of the East became his followers, and likewise those of the South, the West and the North.

When the sacred Wheel of the Good Law had conquered the earth, it returned to King Mahāsudassana's capital, which was on the site of the modern Kusinārā, where the Buddha entered Parinirvāṇa. And just as at that time the grove of *sāl*-tree was filled with the radiance of the Buddha, so then the radiance of the Wheel filled King Mahāsudassana's capital with light and splendor, because he had gained the complete domination of the world—not through physical power, but by justice and non-violence.

But King Mahāsudassana's rule was based not only on the presence of the Wheel, but also on the possession of six other priceless treasures: The first of these was the most excellent of all jewels—*maṇi* or *ratna* (Tibetan, *nor-bu*), also called *cintamaṇi* or *lapis philosophorum*, the Philosopher's Stone, the embodiment of truth.[4] The second was the ideal wife (*stri*, Tibetan, *btsun-mo*), the embodiment of love and compassion, and of all feminine virtues. The third was the best of all advisers (*mantri*, Tibetan, *blon-pa*), the embodiment of active wisdom and justice. The fourth was the ideal citizen or householder (*gṛhapati*), represented in Tibet as a model warrior or general (*dMag-dPon rimpo-che*), the embodiment of energy, courage and loyalty. The fifth was the best of all elephants (*hasti*, Tibetan, *gLang-po-che*)—the embodiment of strength, steadfastness and prosperity. The sixth treasure was the ideal horse (*aśva*, Tibetan, *rTa-mchog*), the embodiment of speed and symbol of freedom—of final liberation.

King Mahāsudassana had, according to tradition, all the qualities of an ideal ruler, but none of the brutal force and harshness of a dictator. His four qualities were beauty, long life, health, and good fortune. The Mahāsudassana Sutta describes him in touchingly human terms: he loves his subjects like his own children, and his subjects look up to him

---

[3]The meaning of the last sentence is doubtful, but the translation offered here is quite likely to be correct. *Tr.*
[4]In the Pali version (*Digha Nikāya:* 17), these are given in a different order. *Tr.*

with love and respect as to a father. His physical beauty is such that when he rides abroad, the people beg him to drive slowly, so that they can enjoy the sight of him for as long as possible.

◇   ◇   ◇

In the Buddhist view, such qualities are not the result of chance, but have been gained through the long and patient exercise of the virtues. One day, in a contemplative mood, King Mahāsudassana considered the following: "What are the causes of my gaining so much wealth and power?" And he recognized: "They are derived from the triple practice of generosity, abstemiousness and renunciation." Thus considering, he suddenly saw his future path clearly before his eyes. And then there was for him no more striving for power, wealth and worthless possessions. "The more we desire, the worse it will go with us at death, whereas he who dies without attachment or greed leaves the world happily." With this thought the King calmly renounced all desires and, "just as one drops asleep easily after a good meal," he soon passed away peacefully, in order from then on to pursue his path toward the high goal of Buddhahood.

For the Buddhist, this story is not simply a tale of long ago, but a pointer to the future in accordance with the rhythmical flow of events that we call the universal law of nature, which appears partly as an evolutionary and partly as a disintegrating power. Things that have happened in a previous world cycle must essentially repeat themselves in present and future world cycles.

According to Buddhist tradition, therefore, it is assumed that before the appearance of the next Buddha on earth, the latter will, as a Bodhisattva and a Cakravartin, conquer the forces of evil that continually exert a reign of terror over mankind, and establish the rule of peace and justice. Therefore the seven treasures, or better, the seven ideals of a world ruler, have in Buddhist history and iconography a prophetic meaning, and they became ideals of the Buddhist life in general.

How decisively these symbols have influenced Buddhist art can be seen from the fact that they are the most frequent element in frescoes, reliefs, wood-carvings, printing-blocks, woodcuts and *thangkas*. They are used equally in complicated maṇḍalas and as modeled and painted altar decorations that one can find in all the lands of Northern Buddhism in public temples and private shrines, in monasteries and in homes. Often two of these symbols are combined; for instance, the horse carries the flaming jewel in his saddle, or the elephant carries the Wheel (*dharmacakra*).

The meaning of the best elephant and the best horse can only be fully understood if we know the various associations of these symbolic animals. Even in pre-Buddhist times, the elephant was associated with the raincloud that brings life and prosperity to the land. That is why he was considered as the mount of Indra, the old rain-god, the god of thunder and lightning (the latter symbolized by the *vajra* (Tibetan, *rDo-rje*). The possession of a white elephant was considered the guarantee of the nation's prosperity. This accounts for the importance that is still attached to the white elephant in Burma and Siam. It is based on an old tradition from India attested by the *Vessantara Jātaka*, according to which the prince who generously gave away the white elephant to a neighboring country is punished for this by being sent into exile.

The most important reason for this prominence attached to the white elephant in Buddhist symbols and art is this. According to the old tradition of the *jātakas* (birth-stories, tales of previous lives of the Buddha), he began his sacrificial career in the dim and distant past in the form of a six-tusked white elephant, and then appeared in the same form to Queen Māyā in a dream, when at the beginning of his last earthly life he entered her body.

So the elephant became a symbol of the birth of a Buddha and his unshakable determination and perseverance in fulfilling his noble mission. Later, the white elephant became the symbol and mount (*vāhana*) of the Dhyāni Buddha Akṣobhya, the Imperturbable, whose location is in the East. His element is water, which shows that the original symbol of the white elephant had not been forgotten. The East has a double meaning here. It denotes not only a cosmological position (or a location in space), but also a position in time, because it is in the East that the sun starts its career, just as the white elephant started the career of the Buddha. And just as the sun is daily reborn in the East, so, too, the Bodhisattva passed through innumerable lives.

The horse is originally a solar symbol. It was believed to draw the sun's chariot, and its fiery nature was also associated with the sun. But, for the Buddhist, the horse is above all a symbol of the fiery and independent spirit, the symbol of speedy liberation from the fetters of *saṁsāra*, the never-ending cycle of birth and death, just as when the Buddha, in the decisive moment when he left his home and exchanged his princely position for that of a homeless beggar in order to seek the truth, was borne into the newly-won freedom by his faithful steed Kaṇṭhaka.

Thus, whereas the elephant represents the beginning of the Buddha's earthly career, the horse denotes the end of his worldly career and the near approach of his spiritual life. Later the Dhyāni Buddha Ratnasambhava, whose position is the South, where the sun reaches its highest point, came to be associated with the symbol of the horse as well as that of the jewel, which is frequently shown lying on the horse's back. The elephant, as bearer of the *dharmacakra*, was already displayed on the stone gates (*toraṇa*) of the famous stupa in Sāñchi. It is evident that the *dharmacakra* is a further symbol of the sun. But whereas the horse represents a *secondary* characteristic of the sun, namely its fiery character, the *dharmacakra* is a *primary* solar symbol and represents its radiance. Its solar origin is attested in the description of the flaming, radiant wheel that appears with its thousand spokes in the sky when a virtuous ruler develops his rule through justice and attains to the spiritual strength that enables him to spread the rule of the "good law" (*dharma*) that serves the good of all over the entire world. Accordingly, the "Turning of the Wheel of the Law" (*dharmacakra-pravartaṇa*, Tibetan, *chos-hkhor-bskor*) is the origin of the Tibetan prayer-wheel (*ma-ni chos-hkhor*) as a synonym for the first proclamation of the Buddha's teaching, with which the thousand-spoked sun-wheel of the Dharma was set in motion so that its light should radiate through the world.

Thus the Buddha once again became a "world ruler," though not in the usual meaning of the term, but rather as one who conquered the world by self-conquest, and by realizing the highest potentialities of his being in the thousand-petalled *chakra* (*sahasrāra-cakra*) of his enlightened mind.

The *cakra* has, like every symbol, innumerable meanings according to the degree of insight and level of consciousness to which it is related. Thus it can mean universal law, or the reflection of this on the human level in the laws of ethics. It also represents both universal power and its local form in the spiritual power of human consciousness. And finally, it symbolizes the "all-sun" and the "inner light" that leads us to enlightenment or Buddhahood. Just as the legendary *cakravartin* once ruled over the physical world, so too a fully enlightened Buddha is the highest ruler in the world of the spirit. His *dharmacakra* shines over the entire universe, and the laws of this sacred wheel are not enforced by violence, but prove themselves as the essence of all that lives.

Knowledge of these laws denotes freedom and independence— failure to grasp them means being enslaved by them. Therefore the sovereignty of a Buddha depends not on world-rule, but on his under-standing of the world, through which he becomes free of it and, through this knowledge, can also liberate others. The symbolism of the wheel (*cakra*) would be incomplete if we did not also mention the significance of its parts: the rim, the spokes and the hub. The rim forms a circle, the symbol of infinity, of the world as a whole. Also, the rim is in motion, whereas the hub stays still. Thus the rim denotes not only infinity but endless motion: the eternal cycle of birth and death, eternal *saṃsāra*. And yet every point in *saṃsāra* is connected by the spokes to the motionless center, the hub.

The hub signifies liberation, enlightenment, *nirvāṇa*, where all desires come to rest. And the spokes denote the ways that lead from the restless motion of *saṃsāra* to the realization of that peace which is *nirvāṇa*. In this connection, it is important to observe that there is not only one way to realization, but many. From every point in the *saṃsāric* world there is a path that can be trodden to the center, to liberation and enlightenment. For though the goal is the same for all, the paths to it are many. This conception is the basis of Buddhist tolerance. And so the *dharmacakra* represents not only the law or sovereignty, but also tolerance. It combines both aspects of reality, the universal and the individual, rest and motion, *nirvāṇa* and *saṃsāra*.

The number of spokes in a wheel can vary. But in order to indicate the fundamental principles of Buddhism, the *dharmacakra* has either eight spokes or a multiple of eight. In this way the importance of the Noble Eightfold Path (*ārya aṣṭāngika mārga*) is stressed, for this leads to liberation: Perfect View (*samyag-dṛṣṭi*), Perfect Aspiration (or Intent: *samyak-saṁkalpa*), Perfect Speech (*samyag-vāk*), Perfect Action (*samyak-karmānta*), Perfect Livelihood (*samyag-ājīva*), Perfect Effort (*samyag-vyāyāma*), Perfect Mindfulness (*samyak-smṛti*) and Perfect Concentration (*samyak-samādhi*).[5] Finally, the Wheel also symbolizes our spiritual capabilities. In this case the spokes represent the radiations of those psychic or spiritual energies that emanate from the different centers of consciousness in the human body. These rise vertically from the base of the spine to the crown of the head, each radiation gaining in strength and power as it goes. This fact is symbolized by the continually increasing number of spokes or petals that are assigned to the individual *cakras* (here often shown as lotuses), the highest center, the *sahasrāra-cakra*, having a thousand spokes. The latent powers of these centers cannot be realized by the ordinary undeveloped consciousness, but require awakening and energizing through meditation or yoga practice.

Whoever has gained the highest center has command of the *cakras* and the related spiritual and psychic energies. He or she has become, in the truest sense of the word, a *cakravartin*. From this point of view the "seven treasures" of a world-ruler gain a deeper meaning, and point to a hidden link with the seven psychic centers. We now begin to

---

[5] The word *perfect* is not meant in a final, static or absolute sense, but in the sense of a totality of act and spiritual attitude, which must be achieved in every phase of life and every stage of spiritual development. For this reason, each one of the eight steps of the Path is designated with the word *samyak* (Pali: *samma;* Tibetan: *yang-dang*). The meaning of this word has been continually overlooked, and by being translated with the feeble and vague word *right,* it has acquired a suggestion of dogmatic moralism which is quite alien to Buddhist thought. What seems right to one person may seem wrong to another. *Samyak* has a much deeper and more definite meaning. It denotes perfection, completeness, wholeness in an action or attitude. It is thus the opposite of what is half-hearted, and therefore incomplete or one-sided. A *Samyak-Sambuddha* is a "perfectly, fully, completely Enlightened One" and not a "Rightly Enlightened One."

appreciate the profound meaning of the Buddha's words when he said that the whole world was included in our six-foot long body.

Anyone who succeeds in bringing under conscious control those hidden powers of body and mind, in which all the powers of the universe are reflected, has the ability to become either a ruler of mankind or a world teacher—a fully enlightened one, like the Buddha Śākyamuni.

The relation between the essential characteristics of the psychophysical centers (*cakras*) of the human body and the "seven treasures" of a *cakravartin* can be expressed as follows:

1) The best of all elephants, as the embodiment of imperturbability and strength, is the symbol of the root-center (*mūlādhāra-cakra*).

2) The best of all citizens (conceived either as one who is concerned for the welfare of others: *grhapati* = householder, or as the protector of others: *senapati* = general) corresponds to the *svādhiṣṭhana-cakra* in the *plexus hypogastricus*. It represents the functions basic to the economy of our organism: assimilation (i.e., preparing and processing the materials necessary for the preservation of the body) and elimination (i.e., excretion of all that is harmful).

3) The precious gem or the "flaming jewel," also called *maṇi* (Tibetan, *nor-bu*) or *cintamaṇi* (Tibetan, *nor-bu dgob-hdod dpungs-hjom*), corresponds to the *Maṇipura-cakra*, the solar plexus or navel center, in which the "inner fire" (*tapas*, Tibetan, *gTum-mo*) of yogic integration is aroused.

4) The ideal wife (*strī*), the embodiment of love and sympathy, corresponds to the *anāhata-cakra*, the *plexus cardialis* or heart-center.

5) The best of all advisers corresponds to the *viśuddhi-cakra*, the seat of language, the *plexus cervicus* or throat center.

6) The best of all horses, symbol of freedom and quick liberation, corresponds to the *ājñā-cakra*, the seat of spiritual vision, represented as the "third eye."

7) The thousand-spoked wheel, finally, corresponds to the sahasrāra-padma-cakra, the crown center, or the seat of the thousand-petalled lotus.

The seven treasures of a *cakravartin* represent not only the ideal Buddhist way of life, but also the possibilities of the human mind and its related psychic qualities on all levels of both conscious and unconscious life, which can be realized by spiritual training (*sādhana*), yoga and creative meditation (*bhāvanā*), which in turn lead to liberation and enlightenment.

Rainbow—Halo—Aura

The rainbow, although quite obviously not a material phenomenon, can in no sense be dismissed as a hallucination, but is an objective fact. It can be observed by all with sight, can be photographed, and its occurrence—through the bending and breaking of the drops of water in a raincloud—can be calculated. The millions and millions of continually changing drops of water produce a phenomenon which persists, as if in tangible form, before us for an appreciable space of time. It is just the same with our psycho-physical organism, which, although it consists of an innumerable quantity of continually changing particles, seems to be material and lasting for a considerable period of time.

But if we are quite accurate we must admit that we can no more seize hold of matter than we can of the rainbow. What we call matter is merely a concept that comes to be in our brain, as an abstraction, through a combination of sense-impressions; it is called forth by the appearance (perceived by sight) of a connected surface possessed of resistance (hardness or softness), temporal duration, and so on. Through the coordination and abstraction of these sense-impressions we think we have perceived matter. This perception of material existence would have no existence for powers that could work through it without meeting any resistance. And yet, matter is not just an invention of our minds, it is just as real as the mind that perceives it and that knows the laws of dependent origination which make it perceptible.

The rainbow is a symbol of the fleeting beauty of the human world, in whose transience are manifested eternal laws that ever afresh create the wonder of existence. In other words, the rainbow becomes the symbol of the ungraspable essence of reality, which eludes us in our world of seemingly firm objects and hard facts. It is a phenomenon which always arouses deep feelings in us, even if we have seen it a thousand times before. It astonishes us and fills us with joy and admiration, if not with religious awe, or else it becomes for us an omen of profound importance.

At the same time, the rainbow is a bridge between the real and the unreal, the tangible and the intangible, the visible and the invisible, as well as a door that leads to the world of the mysteries—a gateway into the world of imagination and fairy-tale. The rainbow is one of the most important archetypal symbols, as old as humanity itself—a symbol that appears and is treasured everywhere human beings seek to find expression in thought, speech, art, religion, song or poetry.

In the Old Testament the rainbow is the symbol of a covenant between God and mankind, between heaven and earth, between the infinite and the finite, between universal law and the moral law of humanity. It is the symbol of the constancy of the law that reveals itself in a world of incessant change. But with its beauty and colorful radiance it also makes clear that this law is a law not of compulsion, but of harmony, that transfigures our workaday world so that even its most ordinary aspects gain a profound meaning.

In the field of religious—particularly meditative—experience, the colors of the rainbow became emanations of the spiritual activity of the individual. This was the original conception of the halo, which is a common feature in the art of Christianity and various other religions. But whereas in Christianity the halo usually only surrounds the head of a saint, Buddhism assigns a similar manifestation to the whole body in the form of an aura, which is distinguished from the halo round the head. The reason is obvious: the consciousness or the psyche is not localized only in the head, but in the entire body. Whereas the West one-sidedly stresses the brain as the sole center of consciousness and mental activity, the East knows of at least seven major psychic centers and many subsidiary centers which are distributed all over the body. They are called *cakras* (wheels), because their energies radiate in all directions from the center, just as the spokes of a wheel radiate from the hub. Each one of these centers represents a particular level of consciousness with its specific activity, in such a way that in ascending order first physiological, then emotional, and finally intellectual functions prevail in turn.

In awakened or spiritually advanced human beings all these centers are activated and their energies transformed into spiritual, that is, integrated and harmonized conscious forces, whose field of activity is no longer confined to the narrow bounds of the physical body, but—according to their degree of intensity—radiate in a continually expanding circle. Therefore it is said that the aura of a perfectly enlightened one, a Buddha, embraces the entire universe, or, put differently, that the entire universe has become the body (*dharma-kāya*) of the Buddha.

Buddhaghosa[6] describes in the introductory treatise to his *Aṭṭhasālinī*[7] (which, next to the *Visuddhimagga*,[8] is one of the most important non-canonical works of the Theravāda school) the many-colored radiance that flows from the body of the Buddha in the following words:

> Rays of six colors—indigo, golden, red, white, tawny and dazzling—issued from the Teacher's body, as he was contemplating the subtle and abstruse Law by his omniscience which had found such opportunity.

---

[6]The famous Indian scholar-monk who worked for many years in Sri Lanka and wrote the principal commentaries on the Pali Canon (5th century C.E.).

[7]*Aṭṭhasālinī* or *Atthasālinī* (translated into English as *The Expositor*, Pali Text Society 1920–21, reprinted 1976) is the commentary on the *Dhammasangaṇī* ("Enumeration of Phenomena," translated by Mrs. Rhys Davids as *A Buddhist Handbook of Psychological Ethics*, 1900, reprinted 1974), which is the first book of the Pali Abhidhamma Piṭaka. *Tr.*

[8]*Visuddhimagga*, translated as *The Path of Purification* by Ven. Nanamoli, Buddhist Publication Society, 1956 and later. *Tr.*

The indigo rays issued from his hair and the blue portions of his eyes. Owing to them the surface of the sky appeared as though besprinkled with collyrium powder, or like a jewelled fan swaying to and fro, or a piece of dark cloth fully spread out.

The golden rays issued from his skin and the golden portions of his eyes. Owing to them the different quarters of the globe shone as though besprinkled with some golden liquid, or overlaid with sheets of gold, or bestrewn with saffron powder and bauhinia flowers.

The red rays issued from his flesh and blood and the red portions of his eyes. Owing to them the quarters of the globe were colored as though painted with red-lead powder. . .

The white rays issued from his bones, teeth, and the white portions of his eyes. Owing to them the quarters of the globe were bright as though overflowing with streams of milk poured out of silver pots, or overspread with a canopy of silver plates, or like a silver fan swaying to and fro . . .

The tawny and dazzling rays issued from the different parts of his body. Thus the six-colored rays came forth and caught the great mass of earth.

Then there follows a wonderful description of how the earth, the water, the air and the space beyond, as well as all the heavenly regions, were penetrated with the golden light of the Buddha-like millions of Milky Way systems. The description ends with these impressive words (which hint at the transformation or the sublimation of the physical body):

But the blood of the Lord of the world became clear as he contemplated such a subtle and abstruse Law. Likewise the physical basis of his thought, and his complexion. The element of color, produced by the calorific order, born of the mind, steadily established itself with a radius of eighty cubits.

Apart from the somewhat scholastic language of the famous commentator, the fundamental idea of the radiant being of an enlightened one—and its far-reaching influence—is clearly expressed and shows that the transcendental qualities of a Buddha were recognized by the followers of the *Hīnayāna* (or early) schools as much as by those of the *Mahāyāna.*

In the *Mahāyāna,* and especially in the *Vajrayāna* and its Tantric *sādhanas,* the visualization techniques of meditation were specially stressed, and in these, colors and mantric vibrations played a prominent part. The observation and representation of the various colors and qualities of the bodily auras and halos were here considered especially important. These were clearly defined, as we can see in the case of Tibetan *thangkas* and temple frescoes. Here, coloring is no longer bound to skin color or the material qualities of the human body, but reproduces the entire scale of elemental and spiritual qualities. This is reinforced by the rainbow which frequently appears on the outer edge of the auras of saints and Buddhas and the innumerable forms of their transcendental emanations (i.e., Bodhisattvas, and other divine or semi-divine beings).

Gladys Meyer, in her *Color and the Human Soul,* said that color is the true garment of spiritual beings whose outer clothing is the physical human body. *Color is the visible element through which the invisible reveals itself.* This is valid all over the physical world—mind, radiating through matter, employs color as its most subtle and intimate revelation. Color is to the spiritual life what food, air and water are for physical life; just as these nourish the body, so color nourishes soul and spirit.[9]

When a religion becomes old and dies, it loses color in both the literal and the metaphorical sense. It becomes gloomy and increasingly abstract and intellectual. Finally it expires in the arms of cold reason, scholastic research, and scientific argument, through which the voice of creative imagination is stifled. The mysteries have been explained away, and the rainbow has vanished.

---

[9]Gladys Meyer, *Colour and the Human Soul* (London: Knowledge Books, 1954). *Tr.*

Vajrayāna for Beginners[10]

————

The Tenfold Powerful Mantra (*namchuwangdan*) is an image of both the individual and the cosmos. In six colors ten mantric signs are arranged in such a skilled intertwining that, if we read the compact block upward from below, the human body is represented from the soles of the feet to the crown. In their cosmic significance, the same signs stand for the principles or conditions of the aggregates (*skandas*), which are referred to as wind, fire, water and earth, in addition to which there is the world-mountain Meru in the center, and also the world of form and the formless world. Above these hover the signs for moon, sun and a flame. These, when referring to the individual, are known as the three "veins of the life-force." The mantra symbolizes the penetration and the identity of the elements of body and universe, whereby the parallelism between individual and universe is clearly seen.

Of course we are not referring to the elements in the scientific sense, but of the elements in the sense of "units." These elements of earth, water, fire, air and ether are not elements in the sense of physics

————

[10]Introductory lecture for beginners in Vajrayana Buddhism, given Chamba Center, San Anselmo, California, on June 12, 1977.

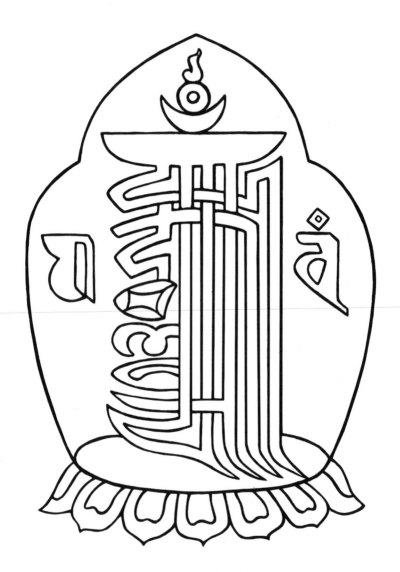

E̱—Vaṃ Oṃ Haṃsamālāvaraya

(as we often use the word), but are elements in the sense of conditions of the aggregates. They then stand for the solid, fluid, fiery, gaseous and finally the cosmic-etheric condition. All these conditions assume forms, depending on pressure, temperature and other factors, that we can see and experience. They are called, especially in Buddhism, the elements or forms of the aggregates. Each one of them is connected with a particular *cakra* in the human body. *Cakra* literally means wheel; it could also be termed a lotus. These *cakras* have different colors, and that is specially important, because the colors have been established from the earliest times. Throughout the history of Buddhism these colors have been represented in the same way in maṇḍalas and mantras. Without knowing these we would not know where we were.

The lowest *cakra* is the *mūlādhāra-cakra*. It lies at the base of the spine. Then comes the *svādhiṣṭhāna-cakra*, which represents the function of digestion. Above this lies the solar plexus, which we all know, then comes the heart-center, the laryngeal center, and finally the cranial center or the *sahasrāra-padma*, the thousand-petalled lotus. If we think of the *cakras* as lotuses, then the first lotus has four petals, the next six, and the third twelve petals, and so on. The number of petals increases the higher the *cakra*, till finally the chief one appears as a lotus with a thousand petals. What we have called petals are really the characteristics of the *cakras*. The lowest is the simplest: it has only four petals and corresponds to our organic, material base. The succeeding *cakras* become progressively more subtle with the increasing number of functions, which are represented as petals. So these petals are not just poetic fantasy: the greater their number, the more the functions associated with that particular *cakra*.

The *sahasrāra-cakra* is not at all identical with the brain, rather it is something transcending the brain. For instance, people who are clairvoyant obviously have a sense that goes beyond the functioning of the brain. However, the brain is in general the *cakra* by which the Western world lives. We generally associate our thinking function with the brain, but in the East they do not. Neither in Japan nor in China, nor in India or in Tibet would anyone believe that we think with the brain—we think with the heart. In the West, we regard the heart far more as the seat of our feelings than of our thoughts. Of course we don't really mean the heart itself, but the center or *cakra* that is associated with the heart. The East thinks more with its feelings, it's more intuitive. That is to say, we think, but it is not mere thought. It is in contrast to brain-thinking, which only has the capacity to think in terms of words and concepts. The Western attitude is based on conceptual thinking, whereas the Eastern way is more intuitive. That is the difference between the two cultures. East and West do not understand each other. Why? Because they live in different centers, and that is an important point.

In the West we are so onesided that we have, to a certain extent, only developed our thinking apparatus, our brains. What we really need is to become conscious of all our different centers: only when we are conscious of them all can we become complete human beings. If we live in only one center we cut out the others, or do not even know they exist. And we cannot attain to any sort of realization if we have only developed one special faculty, which really should not predominate in the human body.

In the Buddhist view, the body is really the temple of the mind. We should not despise the body or regard it as something provisional, something to be got rid of. The body is the home of the mind; it gives lodging to our moods and it should be respected for its needs and its capabilities. Accordingly, the basic idea of the Tantra is much wider in regard to the contemplation of the body, since it regards the body not only in the material sense as the bearer of organs of perception and emotions, but also as a totality, as a sacred place that gives refuge to our mind during our lifetime. Of course we shall have to leave this temple when it has served its purpose, but as long as it lives we must respect it and not misuse it. In this sense, the East has always rated the body higher than the West and accorded it more importance.

The various *cakras* or centers of consciousness are symbolically represented by different colors. If we look at different *maṇḍalas,* we find that each one is associated with various colors. Generally we find white, yellow, red, green, and blue. You might think this was just a pretty combination of colors to please the eye, and very decorative. And indeed most people regard a *maṇḍala* as a kind of wall-decoration. But *mandalas* are no more articles of decoration than an ordinary map. Of course you can use them as decorations, but that is not their purpose. They are to orient us, to help us find our bearings. The colors of the *mandala* are there to help the viewer understand the meaning of the *mandala*, to give him or her a profounder understanding. Most people do not know that a *mandala* that hangs on the wall as a *thangka* is not being used as was originally intended. A *mandala* is really made to lie on the ground, with the viewer sitting in front of it.

The *mandala* itself was originally laid out with different-colored sands, rather like the cultic sand-pictures of the North American Indians. But on the "map" of the *mandala* "above" does not stand for north and "below" for south. We sit at the entrance, the East, which is therefore the lowest part of the *mandala*, and we move around it with the course of the sun, to the south (left), west (top), and north (to the viewer's right). It is true we cannot see the sun at midnight (north), because it is on the other side of the earth. Thus the various sectors of the *mandala* appear in a particular spatial and temporal order, from east to south to west to north, and if we hang a *mandala* up on the wall, the entrance is at the bottom. If we do not understand the basic structure of this movement through space and time, the *mandala* will be of no more use to us as a map of our consciousness then a map would be if we did not understand its spatial arrangement and the geographical symbols.

In the lowest part of the *mandala*, turned toward us, we generally find (as in the *Bardo Thödol*) a white sector denoting the east, because even before sunrise, when the light begins to shine in the east, the earth is bathed in a white light. So white denotes the beginning. Then the sun proceeds to the midday point, and because this is its highest point, the sunlight is now shown in yellow. Sunset is red, and so the west is marked by a red sector. But the north appears in that mysterious color that lies between green and blue. It evokes a mystical feeling, because it is not just that green that we know from leaves and trees. It is composed of yellow and blue and thus includes both a positive and a negative aspect, because the night slumbers as if in an embryonic state. Here everything has its beginning. Here, everything is still hidden from our eyes, and yet contains the mysterious germs of everything to come.

But there is a fifth sector—the center. This is generally shown as blue. There is something special about this center. If there are figures in the *maṇḍala,* then we can see a blue figure in the white field of the east, and a white figure against the blue background of the center. This white and this blue always form a contrast, but they are not opposites— they stand rather in a close relationship to each other. There are various schools of Buddhism in Tibet. Some of them prefer a blue background for the east, while for others the east is white. Thus these two colors, blue and white, are interchangeable. The key to this arrangement lies in the concept of *śūnyatā,* or emptiness. The cosmic space can be represented by blue, or also by lack of color. If it is shown as white, then the positive quality of the universe is indicated in the form of light. If it is shown as dark blue, that denotes the potentiality of that which has not yet appeared, but which—although at present only embryonic or immanent in the blue—is seeking manifestation.

Let's start with the five elements, for they have a specific color. The earth element is characterized by yellow, and appears in the south of the *maṇḍala.* Earth is something we should not despise, for matter is a very, very rare thing in the universe. Matter is so rare that I would say the relationship between what we call empty space and what we call matter is this—there is infinitely more empty space and precious little matter. Matter is energy that has taken form, just as the highest point of the sun represents the highest development of all forms of existence. Matter is the totality of the five elements, which are all necessary before matter can come into contact with our senses. Therefore matter offers resistance, possesses the capacity for coherence, has a surface, can be touched, has temperature, assumes visible forms, and so on.

Without form we would never know what matter is. It calls forth a particular feeling, and yet, according to Buddhist psychology, we can never touch matter. What we really experience is the feeling of resistance from something, or we see a certain shape, feel a certain temperature. These are all sense-impressions. We combine all these sense-impressions in our minds and realize that we are dealing with matter. But in reality we cannot say that matter is here, at best it is a combination of elements. That is why I call matter the capacity for coherence.

The next element is water. Water stands for the condition in which the molecules and atoms are less coherent, so that a fluid condition of the aggregates arises. Water is a fluid element. Whenever we meet a fluid condition of the aggregates, we speak of "watery," although the liquid does not necessarily consist of H_2O. For example, if we heat metal it becomes liquid; if we heat something liquid still further, it enters a gaseous state, which applies to all metals that can be vaporized. The best-known example is the vaporization of mercury. This condition is called a gaseous condition.

The most subtle condition of the aggregates is radiation. We know various kinds of radiation, but only in the present century have we become aware of the vast quantities of radiation that surround us. Every moment we are penetrated by all sorts of rays that have an effect on us. If we have a radio or television set, we can receive all kinds of pictures, ideas, words, shapes, and so on, which are all just radiations of energy converted into sounds, colors and shapes. And so we find ourselves in the midst of a field which, even if it were empty of air, is still produced by a vast number of radiations. Our own consciousness, as well, is a kind of generator which continuously sends out energy. We understand each other not only because we speak the same language, but because each one of us intuitively shares a common field of consciousness. And so, though it is certainly important to have command of a language, linguistic knowledge alone is insufficient. Of no less importance is our capacity to react, and although it is based on the knowledge of a particular language, it combines the effect of our own thoughtwaves with the soundwaves and visible gestures—and then—in a fraction of a second, we understand each other. That is really a great miracle. Those who have learned a foreign language know how hard it is to form sentences and to understand other people who speak the language, simply because we have not yet gotten used to that language. A certain amount of attunement is needed, a kind of mutual understanding and "exchange of consciousness." Only then is it possible to communicate by means of language.

If we consider the various elements and try to allocate different colors to the different elements, we find that the earth element is yellow, the water element is white, the fire element is red, the air element is green, and the element we call ether, blue. But of course we must not identify the ether element with our scientific conception of ether. Ether means that which radiates. We do not know what radiates; although we speak of electricity, magnetism, sound waves, radio waves, but in truth we know very little about them.

We have physical theories about waves and particles, but no physicist can tell us whether there really are waves or particles, because the particles behave like waves and the waves like particles. Our logic and common sense become confused. Even using modern logic we cannot describe what really goes on. We can photograph the movements of those particles, but still we cannot say where they are; no one has ever seen them. And the more we know about such things, the more mysterious they become! All we know is that we cannot understand these things, we simply have to accept them as facts. Our imagination cannot grasp them, and we cannot explain them. The more we know, the more we know how little we know.

That is why Buddhists tried to embrace the world by means of the word *śūnyatā*. *Śūnyatā* is one of the strangest expressions ever invented in philosophy. At the superficial level, *śūnyatā* means "emptiness." Some people translate it as "nothingness." But there is nothing that one could call "nothingness," because whatever we might call "nothing" would first demand an answer to the question, "Nothing of what?" And the same applies to the concept of "emptiness." If we do not put this question, the whole thing is meaningless. We cannot say: "there is nothing there," or "there is emptiness there," but only: "there are no things there, there are no people, there is no air." We need qualifications that tell us what is to be understood by nothing or emptiness—what is lacking. We have to ask: "Empty of what?"

In Buddhism, *śūnyatā* is beyond comprehension. The word *śūnyatā* does not describe a quality, but embraces everything that could exist or appear. It is the emptiness that makes fullness possible. It is the precondition of all fullness, and is at the same time everything that cannot be seen, heard, or touched. Therefore what we call *śūnyatā* is that element of potentiality that embraces the entire world, just as without empty space neither planets nor matter nor any other functions would be possible. Therefore, the word *śūnyatā* is not a negative concept, as the Indologists thought when they first translated it.

The philosophy of *śūnyatā* became a basic conception in Buddhism, and without an understanding of this concept and its full meaning, Buddhism remains unintelligible. We can talk about everything, but in reality we only know a small part of the world. We can only speak about what is accessible to our senses. But our senses are so constituted that they only register the things that we urgently need for our life. Whatever lies beyond this is something we do not understand and have to take on trust.

If we look at a *maṇḍala*, we find symbols and colors that give us an idea of the movement of consciousness in time, and of location in interior space. Thus we come finally to a temporal sequence and a local arrangement in space. But the colors we see in a *maṇḍala* have a third meaning. We see some Buddhas shown as yellow figures, and others in white, blue, red, and green. What lies behind this idea of showing Buddhas in different colors? What does it mean when Buddhas are shown in colors that are not natural to human beings? From the color of a figure we know its place in the *maṇḍala*. Thus a yellow Buddha belongs to the yellow sector, and a red Buddha to that part of the *maṇḍala* whose background is red. Only in the case of white and blue does a blue background require a white figure, and a white background a blue figure. But in every case the colors show exactly which Buddha is represented.

When we speak here of the Buddha, we do not mean the historical Buddha. He is not alluded to in this connection, and he is represented in his natural skin-color, which has a slightly yellowish shade. Here we are concerned with the so-called Dhyāni Buddhas, Buddhas whom we picture or envisage in meditation. What we meditate about need not necessarily be the historical Buddha, but should rather be what we would *like* to be, what we wish to *become*. These possible developments for ourselves are symbolized as Dhyāni Buddhas. Incidentally, the concept of "Dhyāni Buddhas" is found neither in the Sanskrit nor in the Tibetan scriptures. There they are referred to as *Jinas* (conquerors) or by other names. However, the concept of a "Dhyāni Buddha," which was coined about one hundred years ago, gives a clear idea of what these mean: a Buddha who is experienced by ourselves in meditation.

If we were to think of the historical Buddha, there would be a feeling of something from the dim and distant past, long since vanished. We might even be surprised at the idea of calling to mind something that happened thousands of years ago. But if we experience Buddhahood in a particular aspect of ourselves, then we know that this form is really an experience in the present, and it is only this Buddha who is always with us.

Each one of the colors denotes a particular aspect of Buddhahood, and there are five different colors. If we take four (excluding white) together, or if we take the entire spectrum together, then we get white, which is not a color. Therefore the central figure is shown as white. This is the Dhyāni Buddha Vairocana, whose white color shows that he combines in his own person all the different aspects of Buddhahood that are grouped around him in the *maṇḍala*. The question then arises: why do we need all the other Buddhas? We need them, because we as human beings cannot imagine the completeness and plenitude of Buddhahood, and cannot immediately appreciate the qualities of a Buddha. We have to imagine various qualities in order to understand their meaning. Thus, we can picture the Buddha as a loving, wise, or universal human being. We can think of him as active or passive. There are many aspects, but we can only imagine one at a time. Since we are not yet Buddhas, we cannot recognize all aspects simultaneously, and that is why we have the *maṇḍala,* so that we can move through these various aspects, one after another, in time and space, until we are able to unite them all in the center. That is the final experience.

The *maṇḍala* is therefore far more than a merely aesthetic picture that we use for decoration. It is actually a map of our own consciousness. What we see in the *maṇḍala* is the human mind in its totality, with all its qualities, all its basic elements, all its strivings and yearnings. What we perceive in the *maṇḍala* is more than these basic elements, because it provides us with spiritual correspondences. The various colors appear here because these colors are related to the Buddha images that are realizable in ourselves. We cannot realize everything at once, we have to proceed in stages, just as the sun radiates its light from different positions at dawn, at midday, in the afternoon, in the evening, and finally at night.

The whole technique of the *maṇḍala* is so complicated, and at the same time so fixed, that it is impossible to invent a *maṇḍala*. It has taken thousands of years to collect all the meditative experiences, to represent them pictorially, to finally create the symbols that represent these meditative experiences. If anyone wanted to paint a picture of his or her meditative experiences, that would be something quite personal. Another person would express it quite differently. But here, in the *maṇḍala* technique, we have a canon of colors and forms that have been created through the experience of thousands of years; and many thousands of beings who have experienced the various stages have finally come to express them in symbolic forms that can be understood by everybody. When we look at the *maṇḍala*, we should know that we see the entire contents of the human consciousness in all its forms. There are thousands of details in every *maṇḍala*, and it would require a whole lifetime to study and understand them all.

Part Four

THE MEETING OF
EAST AND WEST

Teilhard de Chardin's Worldview in the Light of Eastern Thought[1]

Teilhard de Chardin is perhaps the first modern European writer to say what has been considered true for thousands of years in the East: that all life, and especially all conscious life, is not merely the product of endless combinations, permutations and transformations of blind forces and elements, but represents a meaningful evolution, a continual unfolding and becoming aware, in which differentiation and integration, individuality and universality both condition and complete each other. What the East brought forth as mythical or purely spiritual symbols of experience, or as poetic parables or metaphysical intuitions, was assumed to be scientifically-based thought by Teilhard de Chardin. A formulation based on experience must necessarily employ different modes of expression from the strictly delimited scientific method with its dependence on deduction and definition. That does not mean there is necessarily any contradiction or separation between science and experience, it simply means that we have to consider two different ways of expressing human experience.

[1]This lecture was presented at a theological seminar held at Meersburg (Germany) in 1965 under the auspices of Helmut de Terra. Used by kind permission of C.H. Beck'sche Verlagsbuchhandlung. First appeared in *Perspektiven Teilhard de Chardins*, Beck'sche Schwarze Reihe 43, Munich, 1966.

What is it that makes Teilhard de Chardin so great, so all-embracing? First of all, perhaps, that he was both a deeply religious man and a great scientist. He also raised science to a level of metaphysical understanding, and religion to a science of mankind, i.e., to an unfolding of consciousness in which not only the individual, but also that which gives motion and life to the universe becomes conscious of itself. In the language of religion, this is called the awakening of divine consciousness; in the language of science, this is called the awakening of human consciousness to a perception of the universe and to a realization of its essential universality and wholeness. Teilhard de Chardin rises above both scientific dogmatism and any single religious tradition.

For a Buddhist (as for followers of most of the religions in India and the Far East), the concept of a religion or philosophy that alone leads to salvation, or of an absolute science, is unacceptable. We believe not only that many ways lead to the understanding of reality, but also that in every epoch, in every age and culture, the same truth must find a new expression, a new form. Because different forms can express the same truth, we must not allow ourselves to be led into believing we can arbitrarily exchange the forms of expression of one cultural region or period with those of another, or equate them or mix them. This would lead to a fruitless, shallow syncretism, not to the deeper understanding that can only emerge when we strictly consider each form within the framework of its particular relationships, associations, its intellectual and organic, historical, and traditional connections.

In Teilhard de Chardin, religious experience and scientific understanding are bridged by a vast cosmic vision, an intuitive grasp of connections, such as the East has discovered by means of meditative vision and in the investigation of the human psyche. I am thinking here less of the philosophy of the modern Indian thinker Aurobindo Ghosh, in whose writing there is thought to be a similarity to that of Teilhard de Chardin, and who through his European education was familiar with the modern theory of evolution. I am thinking rather of the purely Indian, and originally Indian, idea of evolution (uninfluenced by any Western theories) as found in Buddhism, presented in mythical form already in the *jātakas* (former lives of the Buddha), and later in Hinduism with the ten incarnations of *Viṣṇu,* in which the divine rises up from the lowest forms of animal or semi-animal beings to perfect humanity as expressed in the enlightened figure of a Buddha.

For those who do not know the *jātakas,* I would briefly mention that it is a collection of hundreds of stories in which the ascent to enlightenment is portrayed through all forms of embodiment. This concept is based on the fact that spiritual evolution moves from the lowest to the highest forms of life, and that (and this is the decisive difference between Darwin's theory and the Indian interpretation of the same facts) the teleological power of consciousness seeking an immanent goal of the highest possible perfection and all-embracing universality (which we can call the realization of the divine or the state of enlightenment) already finds expression in the humblest forms of life, indeed even in the laws or behavior of so-called inorganic matter.

We may ask how we can speak of a new emergence when life first appears in organic form, since the entire cosmos is alive, and life is inherent even in so-called matter, i.e., in the inorganic world. I think we have correctly understood the situation when we say that the wholly new thing in this emergence is the emergence of a new dimension of life, the emergence of consciousness as a formative, self-perpetuating and individualizing potency.

And, just as consciousness (even in its most primitive form) represents a new dimension of life, so too consciousness marches on in the course of its development from one dimension to another, so that we can speak of different dimensions of consciousness. For example, we could suppose that the very simplest living beings belong to the first dimension, possessing only a single directional possibility (i.e., simply a kind of linear consciousness without any breadth or ("sideways extension"), and with a fixed route (thus, in the main, causally determined). The more advanced beings might belong to the second dimension, and possess a single-plane consciousness with many possible directions, and correspondingly greater freedom. In the third dimension, as we know it, the human consciousness of space might find expression; and since, finally, as we are now beginning to feel, our three-dimensional space-consciousness no longer suffices to cover the discoveries of our time, we could start from the assumption that we must already now postulate a fourth dimension, and that we cannot exclude the possibility of the existence of still higher dimensions.

It seems that always before a new dimension is made fully conscious, there is a premonition of it, for which there is no proper name. And now we are concerned with the problem of time, because we feel that there is a new dimension here that we can sense, but cannot properly define. It could be that what we call time today would present itself to a higher consciousness as something quite different, as a new kind of motion. The concept of dimension includes the ideas of extension, motion and direction. Motion in a single direction would then correspond to the lowest dimension, and with every new possibility of direction or extension, a higher dimension would be created.

When we think of a fourth dimension, or when we dimly intuit it in the strange feeling that time is, after all, something more than mere "clock-time," and that altogether there is within what we call time quite a variety of categories, then perhaps we can only say that time is a particular form of motion. And since we have exhausted the possibilities of motion in three-dimensional space, there remains for us only one other kind of motion, which is no longer motion in external space, or from the center of consciousness outward, but a motion in the opposite direction, toward the center, or from the outside *inward.* This opens up a dimension in which time becomes space, i.e., inner space. In this inner space, not only are the things of the past preserved, and the seeds of the future present, but the possibility exists of raising the past into the present, and of recognizing and guiding the seeds of the future. And, just as in external space, we can distinguish among objects of the past those which are near and those which are distant, and we can move between the surface and the depths. The more we penetrate into the depths, the more extensive our view becomes, because we have the whole universe as our basis—our center is the foundation common to all beings and all worlds in which life and consciousness have their roots.

Today we are trying—due to the desperate feeling that we are at the threshold of something new without knowing where it will lead us—to conquer outer space. I wonder if this is not a search in the wrong direction, a methodological error, since what we are really seeking lies in the interior space of our depth-consciousness, in which this whole universe is actually contained. Is it not perhaps the case that we are projecting outward an unadmitted wish, an urge arising out of inner necessity to explore the immense possibilities of that inner space? We hurl ourselves outward into endless "space," in which we shall naturally never find a real goal or center but only get lost in infinity. Nothing real will ever come of this approach.

The time is approaching when we will again start in a new direction, and it seems to me that this moment is not far away. The impossibility of conquering outer space will force us to turn to inner space in which everything we sought outside is already present. In the previously mentioned tales of the Buddha's past lives we already find the principle of divergent life and consciousness, which nevertheless, in all forms of embodiment, retains its purposive character and its tendency to create higher dimensions of consciousness, till that point of convergence is reached where the path turns inward and the already potentially present universality of the inner center becomes a reality in the consciousness of enlightenment.

In the description of the process of his enlightenment, the Buddha traces his path of development back to the cosmic origin of all life and to the realization of the universe in all its phases of arising and passing away, of blossoming and fading, in beauty and terror, in mighty evolutions and revolutions which succeed one another like systole and diastole, or like the divine breath of eternal life that finds its crowning point in that timeless moment of convergence, of conscious integration, in which the streams of all time flow into the ocean of an all-embracing present. It was out of such an experience that the Buddha drew his teaching of the Middle Way, which denied neither the value of individuality, self-responsibility and decision, freewill and effective action, nor the potential universality of a human being, and the solidarity of all life.

Whereas Orientals, especially Indians, tend to forget or deny the meaning and importance of the individual in the face of the universality

of their origins and psychic center, and so to avoid the painful consequences of personal responsibility and its problems, Westerners, on the
other extreme, are inclined to overrate individuality, and thereby to
forget the universal origins that alone gives meaning to that individuality. Both extremes are one-sided and misleading. The former leads to a
vegetable-like twilight existence and a sinking back into the unconscious—so that all suffering is eliminated, but also the whole meaning
of existence—this finds its expression in the ancient Indian ideal of the
state of deep sleep. The latter extreme leads to attachment to the
material to the extent that we identify ourselves with the body, and
thus with transience, death, and destruction.

The Buddha seems to have been the first to oppose the "deep sleep"
idea of ancient India by introducing the concept of awakening, of
becoming completely conscious within one's individual life, not to stay
in some shadowy and purely negative *nirvāṇa*—and he demonstrated
it. He recognized the necessity and meaning of rebirth—the psychic
continuity of the complete maturing of consciousness, which attains
its highest intensity and perfection in the individual's experience of
universality.

The tremendous gap between the individual and the universal, the
momentary and the eternal, the most inturned concentration and the
most all-embracing vision is bridged in that "mind-created form" which,
as Goethe says, "develops as it lives," and which no power on earth can
fragment when once it has been created and becomes a conscious reality.
From this point of view we can see the reason for the vision-development
of Tibetan Buddhism, for that which is sought takes on a mental form
in a creative symbol, and instead of a stillborn intellectual abstraction
there is the inspiration of immediate experience. The principle of effective form is an energy that can be observed on the material-organic
level of biological development: a meaningfully organizing principle
turns elementary, as yet unformed, material into self-preserving and
self-perpetuating organisms. In other words, it is a creative energy that,
despite the continually changing components of the organism it has
created, again and again re-embodies an indwelling idea (image, form,

eidos), till it finally succeeds in imparting to this such a perfect form that the latter becomes self-aware.

From this point onward, the organism has become a conscious individual—a self-acting center of consciousness that now, by virtue of its own radiance, can communicate itself to other organisms, can maintain its own continuity, and, by continual growth, reach perfect maturity. Out of a dim yearning there develops a conscious striving for perfection, for becoming whole in the experiencing mind, which concentrates this wholeness to the peak of intensity in the focal point of the individual consciousness. The change from dim yearning, unconscious drives, or instinctive action to reflective consciousness and clear thought no longer dominated by instinctive drives is, as C.G. Jung rightly says, "a second cosmogony."

Just as important as the reflective consciousness in which we become for the first time conscious of ourselves and the world (and thus, by rising above the animal, collective consciousness of inherited instincts to individuality, thus entering into the realm of responsibility and decision-making) is the creative consciousness of mental vision, which not only comes to terms with a given world, but like an artist of genius, transforms the given material in the fire of personal experience, recreating it as a meaningful cosmos, in which the individual becomes crystallized as an ever more conscious and ever clearer expression of the universal.

At the stage of complete individuation, consciousness becomes a working, self-perpetuating center; but it is only at the stage of creative vision that mental form is created that can guarantee a continuity beyond any given physical base (embodiment), and also gives it meaning and direction. Only a consciousness of this nature can be called "spirit."[2] All human beings possess the gift of consciousness, but not all have "spirit" or can be described as spiritual beings. Consciousness is the precondition and basis of spirit, but is not identical with it. Only when

---

[2]The German word *geist* can often be rendered simply by "mind," but here the rendering "spirit" seems most appropriate. *Tr.*

consciousness is creative, is it "spirit." As such it is both shaped and shaping, i.e., it is a form that, like a grain of seed, bears within itself the capacity for change and living growth.

It is interesting that the parable of the grain of seed shows how the same images, the same archetypal symbols, appear in all forms of religious expression. In fact, these forms tell us more than any purely scientific or mathematical expression that makes something precise and "fixes" it, but by so doing leaves out the essential part, which is the incommensurable factor of dynamism—of the transformation that is a feature of all that lives. It is this quality that the spirit shares with the symbol, and that is why the latter is the means that consciousness uses in order to penetrate the realm of the spirit and to become itself a living and indestructible spirit which gradually matures, through all changes and transformations, through all embodiments and disembodiments, on its path to perfection. In the act of meditative vision the spirit is symbolically formed in a way that outlives all changes, that bridges past and future, and brings the meditator into a timeless body of one all-embracing present.

Such a vision was experienced by Teilhard de Chardin in the Ordos Desert, in which the mass became for him a cosmic experience. The description of that mass was not only the first thing by Teilhard de Chardin that I read in the original, it was also what immediately convinced me that he foresaw the future of mankind like no other thinker of our time, for he clearly delineated the path that leads to the realization of that future.

It is strange but perhaps deeply significant that Teilhard had this experience in the Ordos Desert, in the Mongolian cultural region where, before the Communist advance, Tibetan Buddhism had prevailed. We are therefore concerned with a realm of consciousness in which the eucharistic idea lived in a form in which it is scarcely known in Europe, a form that is so similar to that of eucharistic Christianity that one can only be astonished to find, at two quite different points on the earth and based on quite different presuppositions, the development of an idea so similar. In fact, earlier when the history of the development of Buddhism in Tibet was unknown, it used to be imagined that there was some early Christian influence at work here, and this idea was reinforced by the impressions of the first Jesuits who reached Lhasa in 1750, for they were astonished by the similarity between certain Buddhist rites and the Christian eucharist. Nowadays, of course, we know from the literature and the entire history of Tibetan Buddhism that Christianity had no influence on its development. The idea of the transsubstantia-tion of matter and the spiritual transformation of humanity and the world in an act of religious devotion existed long before there was contact with Christianity, and was connected to a ritual that was very similar to the Christian one. This only goes to show that in the realm of the spirit there are realities that can be discovered and experienced at all times and by all who enter this realm.

I have already mentioned the mantric formula OM MAṆI PADME HŪM. It is usually interpreted in a very superficial way, such as "dewdrop in the lotus," which sounds very poetic but has very little to do with the real meaning of the mantra. What then is its more profound mean-ing, insofar as this can be expressed in simple words? It is this: that the jewel (maṇi) of divine reality may come to be in the lotus-cup (padma) of our own hearts. In a similar way Teilhard de Chardin says:

> My paten and my chalice are the depths of a soul laid widely open to all the forces which in a moment will rise up from every corner of the earth and converge upon the Spirit.[3]

What is expressed in these few words is so wonderful that, to me, they can only be said by one who has passed through an experience of profound vision and spiritual clarity. Here we have the definition that consciousness converges on the spirit when all the powers and qualities of the individual and his or her surroundings converge within to a unity. Here we see what spirit really means. Nowadays there is so much talk about the spirit and spiritual things that we have almost forgotten the

---

[3]This and subsequent quotations in this section from Pierre Teilhard de Chardin are taken from *Hymn of the Universe,* Simon Bartholomew, tr. (New York: Harper & Row, 1969; and London: Wm. Collins & Son, 1965), p. 19. Tr.

real meaning of the word. Spirit can only arise in consciousness when a creative power unites all the factors of be-ing and being-conscious to a higher unity.

What seems to me so extraordinary is that this mass goes beyond all usual theological ideas to become a hymn of praise of the Whole, and that in this mass the totality of the universe, as it appears in the experience of the celebrant, is offered up as a sacrifice:

> All the things in the world to which this day will bring increase; all those that will diminish; all those too that will die: all of them, Lord, I try to gather into my arms, so as to hold them out to you in offering. This is the material of my sacrifice, the only material you desire. . . . Receive, O Lord, this all-embracing host which your whole creation, moved by your magnetism, offers you at this dawn of a new day.[4]

Teilhard de Chardin calls this the offering of the totality of all earthly endeavor gathered up in the heart. It could not be more perfectly expressed. And now I would like to quote a parallel passage by a Buddhist poet and saint of the seventh century. His name is Śāntideva, and the passage comes from his famous work *The Path of Light* (*Bodhicaryāvatāra*). He, too, speaks of the sacrifice and of devotion, and he concludes with this beautiful prayer:

> To win this jewel of the Thought I offer perfect worship to the Blessed Ones, to the stainless gem of the Good Law, and to the sons of the enlightened, oceans of virtue. All flowers, fruits, and healing herbs, all gems and all waters clear and pleasant in the world, likewise mountains of jewels, forests sweet in their solitude, climbing plants bright with ornaments of flowers, trees whose branches are bent with goodly fruit, fragrant incenses, trees of desire, and jewel-bearing trees in the worlds of the gods and their kin, lakes bedecked with lilies

---

[4]Teilhard de Chardin, p. 20.

and wondrously pleasant with the cries of swans, harvests springing without tilth and crops of grain, and all else adorning them whom we worship, all things that are bounded by the spreading ethereal sphere and are in the possession of none, I take in spirit and offer as guerdon to the Supreme Saints and their Sons. Worthy of choicest gifts and great of compassion, may they mercifully accept this of me. I am exceedingly poor, and without righteousness; there is naught else for me to offer. So may their care for others' weal be for my weal.[5]

Let us now return to Teilhard de Chardin, who continues:

Now, Lord, through the consecration of the world the luminosity and fragrance which suffuse the universe take on for me the lineaments of a body and a face—in you.[6]

When I read these words there arises in my memory a very beautiful Japanese hanging picture (*kakemono*) showing the cosmic Buddha Amitābha rising in gigantic form above the horizon of a vast landscape. Here, too, is the cosmic representation of an inner experience. If we were to consider these only as the outpourings of a poetic fantasy, we would miss the point of the pictures. This is something that is not merely poetic or aesthetic, but which is profoundly felt and is related to the entire imagery of Oriental religiosity. And now going beyond, Śāntideva make the last and greatest sacrifice. Having opened himself up to the Enlightened Ones and offered himself to them as their instrument (as St. Francis said, "Lord, make me the instrument of your grace"), he now renounces the fruits of all the good deeds he has done and promises, instead of being concerned about his own well-being, to devote himself to the well-being of all living beings. In other words, he would rather share the suffering of his fellow beings, working sympathet-

[5]Śāntideva, *The Path of Light,* orig. pub. 1909 (New York: AMS Press; reprint not yet released). This translation is mine. *Tr.*
[6]Teilhard de Chardin, p. 25.

ically with them for their liberation, than rest on the pedestal of his own virtue in the enjoyment of his own bliss. And so he promises "in reward for all this righteousness I have won by my works I would fain become a soother of the sorrows of all creatures." Teilhard de Chardin, too, spoke, as we have heard, of an "offering to the totality of all earthly endeavor gathered up in the heart." Here we have an exact parallel to Śāntideva's words. Teilhard goes on:

> . . . what my heart craved with so little expectation of fulfillment, you now magnificently unfold for me: the fact that your creatures are not merely so linked together in solidarity that none can exist unless all the rest surround it, but that all are so dependent on a single central reality that true life, borne in common by them all, gives them ultimately their consistence and their unity.[7]

Here, too, the desire for deliverance becomes the desire for the deliverance of all.

What then is this center on which all beings depend? As is well known, the Buddha did not define God (or ultimate reality). It is sometimes thought strange that after his enlightenment the Buddha did not speak of God. I interpret it this way: that whoever has experienced the highest (in our language, has experienced God), cannot speak of it because the experience is beyond all words. As long as we still define, as long as a word denotes some distinctive idea, we are taking away something from that which transcends all concepts and can therefore only be included in what is wordless. The Buddha's silence was more eloquent than all words. It was the silence that is born of reverence for the final, ineffable mystery, a mystery that is open to all, but which each one must penetrate and experience personally. It is the mystery of that center which belongs to every human being and in which the entire universe is included.

---

[7]Teilhard de Chardin, p. 25.

This all-embracing depth-consciousness, in which the sum of all experiences and all forms of life in the beginningless and endless cycle of world history is stored, is called in Buddhist terminology the Treasury of Consciousness, or the Store-Consciousness (*ālaya-vijñāna*), and it is in this center that the solidarity of all beings is contained. It is the source of all creative powers. Without reaching this center, we cannot gain deliverance. But just because the solidarity of all beings is contained in this center, we cannot deliver ourselves without all beings sharing in that deliverance, as was demonstrated, I think, by Christ. The light of God would then be what we in Buddhism call the enlightenment-consciousness (*bodhicitta*), which consists of the individual's becoming conscious of this center. Thus universality represents at the same time the perfection of the individual. Let us again listen to what Teilhard de Chardin has to say in this connection:

> Rich with the sap of the world, I rise up towards the Spirit whose vesture is the magnificence of the material universe but who smiles at me from far beyond all victories; and, lost in the mystery of the flesh of God, I cannot tell which is the more radiant bliss: to have found the Word and so be able to achieve the mastery of matter, or to have mastered matter and so be able to attain and submit to the light of God.[8]

What he says here has again a profound parallel, especially in the tantrism of the Vajrayāna (the Diamond Vehicle) which predominates in Tibet. "The mystery of the flesh of God" is in Buddhist terminology the *Nirmāṇakāya*, the Body of Transformation. And this *Nirmāṇakāya* is, in turn, an emanation of the inspirational Spirit Body (*Sambhogakāya*) and the *Dharmakāya*, the Universal Body which is basically the body of all of us. But the creative and inspirational spiritual power of the *Sambhogakāya* is the source of the mantric word. "To have found the Word" is the same as the discovery of the mantric way, through which

---

[8]Teilhard de Chardin, p. 27.

we gain mastery over the "become" (i.e., matter) and transform and disperse it in the diverse light of the origin.

The "word" which is here mentioned is not the communicative word, it has nothing to do with cybernetics, it has nothing to do with communication or conceptualizing or what the philologist means by a "word." It is concerned with the creative word, which appears in St. John's Gospel as the *logos*, although I fear that today we mean by logos something different from what was originally intended. When we speak of the logos today, we associate this concept with operations of discursive thinking and the intellect, whereas the logos of which the New Testament speaks—if I understand it rightly—is precisely that word of power, the creative word, the, as it were, "unspeakable word." It is a word that can only be experienced within, that finds expression in pure sound-symbols and, like every symbol, has endless meanings, that gain a new significance at every level of consciousness, and that therefore cannot be defined or delimited. In short—the word as the primeval sound, out of which everything proceeds. This mantric way has unfortunately been almost lost to the West, and I believe that in this case the East could once again come to the aid of the West in order to restore the value of the mantric Word.

I have heard of the decision to translate the Catholic liturgy into the various national languages. I must confess that this idea disturbs me to some extent. How can one be so blind or deaf to the mantric significance of the liturgy in which the spirit of Christianity has been crystallized for almost two thousand years? How can one believe one can secularize it through an objective, philological translation without the slightest spiritual loss? Apart from this, the unity of Christian culture largely depends on a common sacred language, just as in India both Hinduism and Buddhism have Sanskrit as their common ritual language. Even in a country like Tibet, where Sanskrit is otherwise unknown and all the sacred scriptures have been translated into Tibetan, all the mantric formulae, especially in the liturgy, have been kept in Sanskrit—their original form.

To return to the "mystery of the flesh of God," this profound symbol called to mind a poem by Rainer Maria Rilke entitled *Buddha in der*

Glorie. In its imagery and symbolism it is not only a deeply-felt expression of the Buddhist Tantric world-view, but it also displays an astonishing closeness to Teilhard de Chardin's words. Here is Leishman's translation of the poem:

> Core's core, centre of all circulations,
> almond self-enclosed and sweetening,—
> all from here to all the constellations
> is your fruit-pulp: you I sing.
>
> How released you feel from all beginning!
> In the Infinite expands your rind,
> and within it your strong juice is thronging;
> and a radiance from without is kind,
>
> For those glowing suns of yours are spinning
> on their ways high overhead.
> But in you has had beginning
> what shall be when they are dead.[9]

I don't know if Teilhard de Chardin knew this poem. If not, the coincidence of his words is extraordinary when he says: "Rich with the

---

[9]Translator's note: the translation is from *Rainer Maria Rilke. Selected Works, Vol. II, Poetry*, J.B. Leishman, tr. (London: Hogarth Press, 1960). Leishman, a distinguished translator, seems to have been less than totally successful with this difficult poem, which in the original reads:

> Mitte aller Mitten, Kern der Kerne,
> Handel, die sich einschliesst und versüsst,
> Dieses alles bis an alle Sterne
> Ist dein Fruchtfleisch: sei gegrüsst!
>
> Sieh, du fühlst, wie nichts mehr an dir hängt;
> Im Unendlichen ist deine Schale,
> Und dort steht der starke Saft und drängt.
> Und von aussen hilft ihm ein Gestrahle.
>
> Denn ganz oben werden deine Sonnen
> Voll und glühend umgedreht.
> Doch in dir ist schon begonnen,
> Was die Sonne übersteht.

sap of the world, I rise up towards the Spirit whose vesture is the magnificence of the material universe but who smiles at me from far beyond all victories."[10] If he did know this poem, this is further confirmation of the profound parallelism between his world-view and that of Tantric Buddhism—his regarding the universe as the fruit-flesh of the divine which in our inmost center (and which outlives all suns) becomes our consciousness. This "center of all centers" is none other than the Buddhist *ālaya-vijñāna*, the cosmic and also universal depth-consciousness, which is potentially present in every being, but must first be raised into the light of full awareness before it can be realized in every individual. In this light there comes to be, as Teilhard de Chardin beautifully puts it, ". . . that marvellous 'diaphany' which causes the luminous warmth of a single life to be objectively discernible in and to shine forth from the depths of every event, every element. . . ."[11] The becoming conscious of this diaphany in the course of the last and highest experience of the universality and wholeness of the divine is also put by another thinker of our time into the center of his world-view. I mean Jean Gebser, in his monumental work, *The Ever-Present Origin*, from which I quote the following sentences:

> The undivided, ego-free person who no longer sees parts but realizes the "itself," the spiritual form of being of man and the world, perceives the whole, the diaphaneity present "before" all origin which suffuses everything.[12]

Gebser also talked about transfiguration. He said that once it was only the disciples of Christ who were able to receive Christ's transfiguration. This diaphany of the world, which happened once in the earthly realm—this once-for-all manifestation of the power of the spiritual principle—is not an event of the past.[13]

---

[10]Teilhard de Chardin, p. 27.

[11]Teilhard de Chardin, p. 28.

[12]Jean Gebser, *The Ever-Present Origin* (Athens, OH: The Ohio University Press, 1984), p. 543.

[13]Gebser, *The Ever-Present Origin*, p. 530.

In fact, this becoming conscious of and transparent to the whole is frequently mentioned in the Buddhist scriptures (especially those of the Mahāyāna and Vajrayāna), as for example the transfiguration of Milarepa (the greatest Tibetan saint and yogi) who was a contemporary of St. Francis of Assisi—or in the Śūrangama Sūtra and other well-known texts.

But more clearly than all these, the meditation descriptions of the Tantras show the universalization of consciousness and the spiritualization and sanctification of the world. In the *Demchog Tantra* it is said that one should regard oneself and everything visible as a divine maṇḍala, every audible sound as a mantra, and every thought arising in the mind as the magical unfoldment of the great divine Wisdom. In other words, the meditator should imagine himself (or herself) in the center of the maṇḍala as a divine figure of the perfect Buddhahood that he or she strives to attain. Then, all "accidentals" fall away and there is nothing that is a side-issue or arbitrary. The things of the world join together to form a sacred circle in the center of which the body becomes a temple. And the mere fact of being conscious—and of spiritual creativity—becomes an unspeakable miracle. The visible becomes the symbol of more profound realities, the audible becomes a mantra, and matter becomes the crystallization of elemental forces.

It is from a similar experience that Teilhard de Chardin blesses matter, which reveals the dimensions of the divine, and without which we would live dully, motionlessly, without knowledge of ourselves or God, because we did not encounter the necessary resistance. And so he says:

I bless you, matter, and you I acclaim: not as the pontiffs of science or the moralizing preachers depict you, debased, disfigured—a mass of brute forces and base appetites—but as you reveal yourself to me today, *in your totality and your true nature.* [14]

But in order to experience matter and the universe in their totality and in their true nature, we must descend to the origin of all consciousness,

[14]Teilhard de Chardin, p. 69.

plunge into the primal source of divine being and becoming, which can only happen in meditation, in turning inward, in the reversal of our direction of view. And so he says:

> What I want, my God, is that by a reversal of forces which you alone can bring about, my terror in face of the nameless changes destined to renew my being may be turned into an overflowing joy at being transformed into you.[15]

In a similar way it is the goal of Mahāyāna Buddhism to be transformed into an enlightened being, that is, to become a perfect, total being by oneself following in the footsteps of the historical Buddha who lived 2500 years ago, and reliving that path in oneself, instead of merely venerating him as a unique personality who lived on earth so-and-so many years ago. And strangely, this too is reflected in Teilhard de Chardin's view of Christ, when he says:

> As long as I could see—or dared to see—in you, Lord Jesus, only the man who lived two thousand years ago, the sublime moral teacher, the Friend, the Brother, my love remained timid and constrained.[16]

The Buddha who is venerated is not the historical personality of the man Siddhārtha Gautama, but rather the divine qualities that slumber in all beings, and have found and will find their expression in Gautama as in innumerable other enlightened beings. Even the Buddha of the Pali texts did not scorn to describe the practice of these high qualities, such as loving-kindness, compassion, sympathetic joy and equanimity—in a state of absorption—as a "dwelling in God," or in a divine state (brahma-vihāra). The divine is a living, directing force that manifests in the individual and becomes the form of the personality. It transcends individual consciousness, since it has its origin in universal

---

[15]Teilhard de Chardin, p. 29.
[16]Teilhard de Chardin, p. 33.

depth-consciousness. It assumes the character of personality when it is realized in a human consciousness. If it were just an abstract idea, it would have no influence on life; and if it were an unconscious life-force, it would represent no spiritual value, and thus have no formative influence on the spirit. The directing force that underlies our consciousness and, obviously, the whole development of organic life, is one of the basic conceptions of Buddhism, as of Teilhard de Chardin, according to whom everything aims at a goal, the Omega Point or, in Buddhism, the state of enlightenment and wholeness.

This directedness is distinguished, as already indicated, from Darwin's theory of evolution and the sciences that more or less follow this, all of which are based on the laws of causality. On the other side, when, owing to unforeseeable crossings of causal series not themselves related causally (the meeting of which depends on a—to us—unknown inner structure of the total world-organism, in which our conceptions of "time" and "causality" lose their meaning), a new factor appears, that the materialistic science of the last century could obviously find no better word for than "chance." Because of this, the world-process was largely (if not indeed fundamentally) branded as senseless, since according to this view even the sporadic islands of lawful development are the product of blind chance. The well-known American biologist Edmund Sinnott says in his book *The Biology of the Spirit:*

> The hardest blow that Darwin struck at faith was not the proof that man had come from beasts but the assumption that the whole evolutionary process depends finally on variations that arise by chance. A living organism, however, is not a chance creation but a well-regulated system. It draws random matter in and endows it with order and directedness. . . . The very existence of spiritual qualities in man suggests that they are manifestations of something like them in the universe outside.[17]

[17]Edmund W. Sinnott, *The Biology of the Spirit* (New York: Viking Press, 1955).

The theory of chance is certainly the weakest part of Darwin's otherwise brilliant concept. It is true that the English word "chance" means not only arbitrary happening but also opportunity. But in order to utilize an opportunity it is necessary to have a directed impulse, a creative idea, a judging mind or a continuing tendency in form and direction. This tendency seems to be inborn in everything living: it is the tendency or impulse for the complete unfoldment of all the potentialities inherent in a particular form of life. But since every form of life goes back to a beginningless past, and thus has the wholeness of the universe as its basis, the most perfect goal of all development turns out to be not progress *ad infinitum* (in which every step looks back on the previous one as inferior), but as the process of unfolding immanent capabilities, as in the growth of a plant from seed to blossom, in the course of which every stage has its own justification and its own beauty. In a conscious being, the potentially present, the universality, that lies slumbering in the darkness of the depths of consciousness becomes a reality to be experienced. In mankind the universe becomes conscious of itself. In theological terms this is the awakening of God in the individual, or else the awakening of the individual to God, or to wholeness.

To return once more to the directing force: Where do we direct ourselves to? As I already suggested, we are trying to proceed in a new direction, different from the three dimensions of outer space, and since we cannot reach or find any new dimension in outer space, the only other possibility that remains for us is the dimension of inner space, which we can only attain by reversing our direction inward toward the inner center. Western psychology, too, has recently made the discovery that human consciousness is more than what we usually term our intellect, our thought, and so on. Modern people have, most unfortunately, degraded the all-embracing depth-consciousness to the "unconscious," and thus stamped it as the enemy of all reason, the dark source of uncontrollable drives. In fact, we have committed ourselves all the more to the limited surface-consciousness of the intellect, which is confined to the fleeting interests of its momentary existence, thereby losing all connection with the living depths, the center of all centers, the source of all divine powers.

Despite all the services done through his investigation of depth-consciousness (and for which we cannot be too grateful), C.G. Jung unfortunately did not dare to change his terminology from Freud's negative formulations to the positive evaluation of the depth-consciousness, and thus to free himself from the ambiguous position in which his retention of one-sided Freudian basic concepts landed him. Although I have often mentioned this as a hindrance to modern psychology (even at lectures at the Jung Institute in Zürich), I would like to return to the subject once more, especially in the context of Teilhard de Chardin's world-view.

Some voices have already been heard in criticism, and I would just quote one or two judgments from different schools of thought that indicate how we are beginning to realize the obvious shortcomings of modern psychology. Thus Medard Boss, a Zürich psychiatrist, says that it is no secret that the venerable basic conception of modern psychology—the unconscious—is a very uncritical and vague concept. He also feels that because of this concept we quite unthinkingly and prematurely objectivize an essential partial phenomenon of human existence to a vague, foreign (*es-haft*), demonic-anonymous, stratified thing, and so proclaim a purely cerebral, hypostasized construction as a really existing object.

Equally critical is Jean Gebser, who writes:

> By its postulate of the "unconscious" as an antipode to consciousness, present-day psychology has perpetrated a falsification of primordial psychosomatic actualities. Such terminology and the consequent false structuration of phenomena is a classic example of the error which follows from a radical application of dualistic principles. *There is no so-called unconscious. There are only various modalities (or intensities) of consciousness* . . .[18]

Alan Watts once said that modern thought suffers from the strange prejudice that consciousness is merely a superficial outgrowth of reality,

---

[18]Gebser, *The Ever-Present Origin,* p. 204.

and that the more fundamental the power, principle or substance is, the more blind and unconscious it must be. He also mentioned that a modern psychology of the unconscious might really be the first faint gray before the dawn—that in the works of C.G. Jung we glimpsed a ray of sunlight and that the very use of the word "unconscious" shows how little we Westerners know about what is really our central consciousness.

For the West, Teilhard de Chardin was truly necessary to point once again to the fundamental role of consciousness (of being-conscious), and, still more, to the conscious cosmos—the idea that what we call matter is only another dimension of life, a dimension that appears as matter to us because we simply define resistance, form, and visibility as matter. For what makes matter except in our imagination? In reality we cannot touch matter, we can only feel resistance, see forms, describe tactile sensations, smell smells or taste tastes; all that is not really matter, but just a number of sense-impressions out of which we construct the concept of matter.

We speak of a material universe only in a very relative sense, as being based on our very limited sense-impressions. With this recognition, one essential difference between the data of inner and outer space has been removed, and once the "solid" ground, so to speak, of the outer world has disappeared beneath our feet, we can with the more confidence approach the inner world which is so much closer to us. Unfortunately, its contents are only regarded by modern psychology in the mirror of the unconscious as passively accepted functional effects of dreams and archetypal symbols that are regarded as an effect of compulsive drives to which the individual is subjected.

This impulse-psychology is a typical product of a science committed to causality, which finds its justification in mechanical things, but is largely a failure in the psychological field. Even from a biological point of view, this psychological drive seems to be dubious, as the following remarks of Sinnott show:

> Common experience looks on the idea that we are pushed about by such inner drives as unreal and artificial. What

meaning can it have, we say, for men whose lives are dedicated to the pursuit of knowledge or the creation of beauty or the service of their sacrifice and that endless striving for truth and human betterment which ever has distinguished man at his best? . . . Men seem not to be pushed into the finest things they do but to follow the urgent call of something that draws them on through hardship and uncertainty and discouragement to the attainment of a high desire . . . This conception has the advantage over present psychological orthodoxy in that its attitude is forward, *toward* a goal to be reached, and not back to the push and drive of circumstance and is thus in harmony with the common verdict of experience.[19]

The goal is to gain wholeness, in order that the individual consciousness develops along with his or her supra-individual depth-consciousness, where intuition and judgment combine, and turning to the concealed storehouse of universal experience is not some aimless grasping at (or being grasped by) accidentally or compulsively arising contents of experience, but is an integral experience in which each individual existence finds its universal fulfillment. Instead of being satisfied to raise fragmentary impressions of non-essential details from the depth-consciousness into sight of the intellect and exposing them to a deadly dissecting analysis, one must turn the conscious mind inward in order to turn the potential energy of the depth into active power. In other words, instead of raising archetypal symbols or visions from the depths to the surface of consciousness, only to subject them to conceptual thinking or the trivialities of temporal aims and goals, one should direct the focus of individualized consciousness onto its universal source, in order to awaken to greater life and the synthesis of the spirit.

The way to this final awakening—this perfect enlightenment—cannot be measured in life-spans; it embraces world-ages and world-embracing perspectives that a scientist of the stature of Teilhard de Chardin can visualize and conceive. From this perspective he said that

---

[19]Sinnott, *The Biology of the Spirit*, pp. 88, 90.

for people who see how the synthesis of the Spirit on earth extends beyond their short existence, every act, every event shows itself laden with meaning and promise. To this synthesis of the spirit along the axis of time is a corresponding synthesis on the axis of spatial extension; the knowledge that each individual consciousness is not totally shut off and self-contained, but penetrates other similar centers of consciousness and is in turn penetrated by the effects of other centers of consciousness.

Time and space become dimensions of consciousness. According to Teilhard de Chardin the awful power of the cosmos has nothing that can frighten us any more, because the indefinite strata of space and time are not the uninhabited desert in which we thought we were lost, but reveal themselves as the womb that collects the particles of a great consciousness which is about to emerge. We gradually become conscious of our physical relationship to all parts of the universe and this represents a real expansion of personality. Becoming conscious is really a progressive spiritualization of the totality of all the things that surround us. It means that in the realm outside of flesh our real and total body continues to take shape.

This concept corresponds exactly to the tantric idea of the universe as our spiritual body. As long as we feel the universe to be something foreign, something objectively opposed to us, we remain playthings of its powers and are helplessly driven round in the cycle of becoming and perishing. We experience the universe as *saṃsāra*. But the moment we recognize the universe as our "total body" and penetrate it spiritually, we undergo the great transformation—we have reached liberation, the state of *nirvāṇa*.

Tibetan Buddhism speaks of the three mysteries of body, psyche, and spirit. The personality of a spiritually undeveloped person is confined to his or her material manifestation, a physical body. But the personality of the spiritually developed person embraces not merely the material aspect of his or her manifestation, but also the spiritual and psychic functions, the "body of consciousness," which extends far beyond the limits of a physical body. This body of consciousness expands, in the case of people living in the ideal, beyond the sphere of individual interests and experiences into the realm of generally-valid truths, laws, and living relationships—into the realm of beauty, creative activity, aesthetic pleasure, and intuitive experience. The enlightened person, whose consciousness embraces the universe, has the universe for a body, while the physical body becomes the manifestation of the universal spirit, vision becomes the expression of the highest reality, and speech becomes the mantric word of power and sacred pronouncement. Here the mystery of body, psyche and spirit is perfected, and is revealed in its true nature as the three levels of activity on which all spiritual occurrences take place.

Teilhard de Chardin saw this process of perfection in the synthesis of these three levels of activity and in a convergence of all developmental tendencies of the cosmos in the focal point of a higher consciousness which is more than the sum of all consciousness. It is this ultimate dimension of consciousness which must be sought far beyond and high above a simple perfected human collective. To be capable of joining up the threads that extend into the world within itself, the point of the cone in which we move must be considered as superconscious, superpersonal, superreal. It must not only reach us indirectly by way of the universal net of physical syntheses, and so work on us, but also from center to center (i.e., from consciousness to consciousness) through the meeting with the finest peak in ourselves.

Seen from this level, we can understand Teilhard de Chardin's profound conviction that the purpose of modern humanity is to blaze a trail forward by crossing the threshold to a greater consciousness. Christians and non-Christians—those human beings who are filled with this conviction—form a homogeneous category. And it is with this outlook that Teilhard de Chardin is seen to embrace us all, whether we are Christians or not. For every human being who has this great goal at heart, for everyone who strives for the highest realization of the spirit, Teilhard de Chardin has performed an undying service.

Breakthrough to Transcendence[20]

W hat do we mean by transcendence? In the Christian theological sense, it is that which lies beyond all experience in the sense of an extra-mundane reality—such as a supramundane or extramundane God whose transcendent nature consists in his unattainability and "otherness." In the sense of Eastern thought as represented by both Buddhism and Taoism, transcendence is not a theological concept nor a metaphysical principle, but a psychological one. "Transcendental" in this sense means whatever goes beyond the range of ordinary sense-impressions in our physical organism, and the concepts and conclusions drawn from these by the intellect. It is thus a transcending of the normal human space-time consciousness.

We can, of course, only speak of such transcendence if we proceed from the conviction (or the experience) that consciousness has the capacity for moving in different dimensions, i.e., that it is by nature multidimensional, but has become limited to a narrow range through our imperfect or specialized employment of it.

---

[20]Originally published as *"Transzendenz als Erfahrung." Festschrift zum 70. Geburtstag von Karlfried Graf Dürckheim* (Munich: O.W. Barth Verlag, 1966). Used by permission.

The history of human development has made it clear that human consciousness is in fact not a constant factor, but is capable of extension in various directions or dimensions—indeed, is not only capable of this, but necessarily has to develop from one dimension to another in accordance with an inner law. This becomes clear in the case of mankind's gradually changing conception of space. In the earliest period, we made no distinction between psychic interior space and concrete outer space, between psychic and physical, animate and inanimate nature. For people of the mythical age, on the other hand, there was awareness of the dichotomy between the inner and outer world, of the dualism between daemonic and divine, the opposition of good and evil. For the intellectuals of the scientific, rationalist age, finally, consciousness of three-dimensional space has come to predominate to the extent that psychic inner space has become an illusion and outer space is the only reality. Under the influence of this "real space" perspective developed in art—the outward-turned direction of thought—which separated the concept of the observing subject from that of the observed object and split the world into an irreconcilable contrast between "self" and "not-self," spirit and matter, subject and object.

The "subject" turns out to be merely a situation in time, and the "object" loses its solidity with the increasing realization of its compounded, atomic, momentary and dynamic character. And so the solid-seeming world of material data fades away into a metaphysical system of transcendental forces (i.e., lying beyond the range of our sense-perceptions), which are not very different from those forces operating in the depths of our own being that we are vaguely aware of in the consciousness of self.

Therefore the distinction between the inner and outer world has become indefinable. And so it seems that we have come full circle in our development, and that the circle would close if only the intellect would stop trying to maintain its dominant position, thus preventing the breakthrough to a higher dimension. The nature of the intellect is its ability to measure, to count, to objectify, and thus to cut itself *and* the objectified world away from the living stream of deeper being. In this way the element of persistence, of ego, of holding on, comes into conflict with the living reality, and thus conjures up the illusion of transience, of death, of senseless destruction. According to Durkheim, the result of this will "to persist" is a hardening, a lack of porosity through which real life is stifled.[21] The miracle of transformation, which is the real nature of life, is thus turned into the negative concept of transience, which merely expresses the resentment of a self-asserting ego that refuses to grow out of its limitations—beyond itself.

The intellect remains the part of our consciousness that serves the interests of immediate individual existence. It is a regulating, ordering, and stabilizing principle of peripheral consciousness, which, as long as it is directed outward, produces the idea of a correspondingly regulated, law-abiding world and an unchanging ego.

When this same intellect is turned inward (or reflectively turned on itself), it recognizes the relative nature of its own functions and the illusory nature of that which it has hitherto called "I." To the extent that the intellect can free itself from this illusory I-concept, the fullness of a new consciousness can open up to its truly all-embracing, universal character—where the seemingly past once again becomes the present, where the endless interrelation of all phenomena and events, all forms and beings, is revealed.

This universal depth-consciousness is called in Buddhism the *ālaya-vijñāna*, the store-consciousness, a concept which modern psychology (through avoiding any value-judgments, or metaphysical connotations) refers to as the unconscious. Even if we are not aware of its contents, it nevertheless forms the greatest part of our faculty of consciousness—that faculty by which we are distinguished from a stone, a piece of wood, or any other thing. It is all the more a matter for rejoicing when psychologists of the standing of Karlfried Graf Dürckheim point to the divine character of depth-consciousness as the primary source of all existence, without which the intellect can act only destructively.

If we only consider one side of our intellectual surface-consciousness we end up going round in a self-created circle from which we

---

[21]Karlfried Graf Dürckheim, *Hara: The Vital Centre of Man* (York Beach, ME: Samuel Weiser, 1965; and London: Unwin Hyman, 1965), p. 167 *ff*.

cannot break free, even with the aid of discursive thought, scientific analysis, philosophical speculation, mathematical formulae or physical discoveries. In other words, the person who

> is either imprisoned in his ego or has not yet achieved one is suffering from the loss or non-existence of the right basic centre. True he strives in every way for inner oneness, but he seeks it from his I both in knowledge and action, by means of intellectually-conceived systems, or alternatively he seeks it emotionally by a resolving of all contradictions. But in either case the wholeness of life will be missed because the split dividing it into subjective and objective still remains. The growth of consciousness which truly reveals the primal oneness is made impossible. [22]

As soon as we have become aware of the limiting and strictly demarcated nature of egocentric superficial consciousness, we awaken the urge to transcend the frontiers that hem us in. This finally leads to a breakthrough to the transcendental that, in the East, is regarded as a leap into the depths of the greater, all-embracing consciousness. Whereas Western people are inclined to seek this transcendence outside of or above the self—in a realm of disembodied spirituality or pure abstraction, thus cutting themselves off even further from the source of being—the East stresses the, as it were, retrograde movement. Durkheim says:

> In the centre of all practice serving the Inner Way stands the "backward turning." For this the ego caught on the ladder of its concepts and ideas, and struggling always to maintain its foothold, is not necessary. What is necessary is a movement which leads downwards to the all-dissolving, all-absorbing depth of the source. [23]

---

[22]Dürckheim, *Hara*, p. 128.
[23]Dürckheim, *Hara*, p. 123.

Durkheim speaks here of a "downward transcendence" in contrast to the search of objective and abstract thought that looks for transcendence "above," beyond nature "regarded as purely material," which stands at the bottom of the scale of values and is despised as something low.

This general attitude is the cause of the fateful division of the world into "spirit" and "matter," where spirit is divorced from life while matter is degraded to a dead thing, devoid of spirit or soul. The result is that, on the one hand, spiritual people saw their ideals in abstract speculations or in forms of holiness dominated by negative and anti-life virtues, while the people of the world feel at the mercy of a soulless world in which there are no other values but those of utility and material well-being, and the meaning of earthly existence and the sanctity of the mundane has been lost. It is, therefore, of the highest importance for our time to once again free those who have become trapped in the hypertrophy of the rational mind, as Dürckheim so aptly puts it.

It was precisely this that was the aim of the tantric practices in the Buddhist *Vajrayāna* (the Diamond Vehicle) that was brought to Tibet in the eighth century and there reached its highest peak. The Tantras were the reaction against one-sided spiritualization and more and more remote and abstract idealism of certain Mahāyāna schools, which were once more "earthed" and given fresh blood by the *Siddhas,* the masters of the mystical path. Instead of dematerializing the spiritual, they sought to spiritualize the physical world and to transform the body into a temple of the spirit. *Saṁsāra* and *nirvāṇa* were no longer irreconcilable opposites, but aspects of one and the same reality. It was no longer the aim to flee the body or the world, but to transform both.

The means to this end is the way within, called in Tibetan Vajrayāna, the secret or direct way of the *Vajrasattva,* the Diamond-Being. Vajrasattva is the symbol of the pure, indestructible, transparent spirit-consciousness, in which all things and all beings are recognized as being in their inner nature the manifestations of an original unity and an organic process on the level of a higher reality. Here all shapes and colors and all other phenomena in which the world reveals itself to us become symbols of a supramundane order and a spiritual rule of law. And then the human body, with all its organs, becomes an image of the universe; the human spirit becomes the exponent of an all-embracing creative principle, so that even the forms of human imagination become factors creative of reality and shaping the world. Once we understand this, we realize that the world (as we experience it) is a projection of the formative power within us which, though subject to universal laws, is yet guided by individual understanding.

Just as knowledge of natural laws enables mankind to make use of the force of nature, so too the knowledge and active recognition of universal nature and the rule of the law of the spirit enables the individual to utilize the powers of the depth-consciousness. Knowledge of the natural laws can only be acquired through long observation and mental processing of what is perceived in the external world, and knowledge of spiritual laws can only be acquired through the unprejudiced observation of the inner processes of one's own consciousness. Consciousness must therefore return to its source.

But whereas the observation of external objects demands an opposition of subject and object, thus a separation of observer and observed, the perception of inner processes takes place as an interpenetration of subject and object, as an immediate experience. The difference in the manner of perception or observation necessarily requires a different method of the treatment of the data. While subject-object relationship presupposes a three-dimensional space, two-dimensional dualistic logic and a one-dimensional (irreversible) movement in time (continuity in space, continuity in time, and either/or in logic), the perception and observation of inner processes and experiences presupposes a multidimensional psychic "space" in which neither Aristotelian logic nor one-dimensional motion through time are valid.

Once we have understood this, we can see why we have no influence on the psychic processes below the threshold of peripheral waking-consciousness with logic, intellectual knowledge or discursive thought, and why the understanding of, and approach to, the forces and contents of depth-consciousness require quite different methods. These have been developed in the course of the thousands of years of experience of meditative practice, and have been set down in the tantric texts of the Vajrayāna. Owing to the inaccessibility of their contents to intellectual thought, and their symbolic language—which is incomprehensible to outsiders (and makes a further obstacle to translation into another language)—they have for the most part remained incomprehensible and so neglected, or else misunderstood and misused.

What is the method of tantric absorption—or meditation practice? It is, first, an overcoming of conceptual thinking by visualization, whereby presentation or opposition is overcome by unifying (at-one-ment) the seer with the seen in the *experience* of vision. Only that which has been experienced can transform the viewer because it enters the stream of inner life and operates further within like a seed in the earth. Second, it develops this experience through regular concentration and repeated unification with the vision. Third, one relates the archetypal symbols seen in the vision to all the functions and elements of one's own spiritual, bodily and psychic structure and the surrounding world. Finally, one completely integrates all these elements in the reverse order of their appearance, back to the timeless and spaceless zero-point of their origin—that incommensurable metaphysical emptiness (*śūnyatā*) in which is contained the plenitude of all creativity. This is the break-through to the transcendental, the breakthrough to the wholeness of the greater life and to the sovereignty of the creative spirit, in which unfolding and dissolving, fullness and emptiness, multiplicity and unity manifest like cosmic in- and out-breathing.

The perfection of the transformation of a blind world-bearing drive into the transparency of spiritual creation and understanding depends on the degree of perfection and universality of the vision. In order to attain to this, we must descend into the realm of primal images, the archetypes that slumber in the depths of our consciousness, for only they have the power of living seed. To awaken them is the task of meditation and of all religious symbolism that is anchored in a region that existed long before all doctrines and dogmas.

By becoming conscious of our vision of the world and the forces that create that world, we become master of them. As long as these primal energies are unrecognized and slumbering within us, we have no access to them. Therefore they have to be projected into the realm of the visible as visions. Visioning is not some passive and pathological process of hallucination, but a clearly conscious process of spiritual creation, which has the same reality-value as the form shaped by an artist that materializes in the visible work of art and takes on objective existence. Just as the artist shapes his work with *real*, i.e., not merely imaginary, material, so too the meditative vision must be composed of real, i.e., effectively working archetypes, which are entirely different from arbitrary wishfulfilments of individual fantasy.

People who have occupied themselves with genuinely religious art (not naturalistic portrayals of religious themes) must be clearly aware of this difference, because in genuine religious art—despite all the freedom of artistic expression—there is nothing arbitrary in the presentation of essential symbolic forms, which is what lifts the work out of the sphere of the purely natural and sensual into the realm of suprasensual reality. These symbolic forms are the products of psychic experiences of innumerable generations, and are filled with profound ideal and emotional associations.

Thus, Buddha-figures are not the representations of one unique human personality, but the ideal representation of a perfected human being reposing in his completeness, whose realization is the goal of every Buddhist, and with whom the meditator identifies in the state of absorption. The transcendental character of Buddhist art is revealed to a much higher degree in the Tibetan *thangkas* (hanging pictures), which are not only the product of meditation, but actually serve as models for the development of meditative visions. Every detail, from clouds, mountains, watercourses, trees, flowers, right down to the ornaments worn by the figures and the seemingly purely decorative elements, are in fact subjected to a strict canon of symbolic forms of expression, the archetypal profundity and subtlety of which is undreamed of by most Western observers.

The archetypal character of these pictorial projections has an immediate effect on levels of the depth-consciousness that are inaccessible to the intellect. It is this image that produces corresponding formative powers and qualities in the consciousness. With the transformation of the psyche begins the transformation of the world in which the individual lives. What is experienced as "world" is not a fixed, given quantity, or a reality existing outside and independent of the individual, but the product of sense-impressions and of the consciousness which processes and interprets them. Through the transformation of the consciousness, the experienced world is also transformed.

The way to the attainment of wholeness is shown in the Vajrayāna by mystical diagrams called *maṇḍalas*. They are representations of the graded path to the inner center, which is characterized by abstract or pictorial symbols and mantric primal sounds (seed-syllables). In order to tread this path it is necessary to be aware of, to take into oneself, and to create within oneself all the symbols found there, for these represent, so to speak, the language of the inner space. It is a language that can only be learned by way of meditative experience. It is only when we have command of this language that we can understand the true meaning of the *maṇḍala* as an image of the human psyche, and put the path into practice. Giuseppe Tucci has explained this in eloquent words:

Every shape and form that arises in the soul, every link which, in a mysterious way, joins us to the Universal Life and unites us, maybe without our being aware of it, to Man's most ancient experience, the voices which reach us from the depths of the abyss, all are welcomed with almost affectionate solicitude. Buddhism does not desire that such life of the soul should be scattered. It is of no importance if these images, visions, fears and hopes are not entirely suited to our own vision. They are a legacy which Man carries with him from his birth. They have a positive, real existence like the things we see and feel. They are an irrepressible element of our persons. If, with the rule of reason, we should desire to thrust them back down into the depths of our souls, they would burst forth, all the same, sudden and destructive. It is better, then, to assume possession of them at the first and then by degrees to transfigure them, just as one passes from the outer enclosure of the *mandala*, successively, through the others until one reaches the central point, the primordial equipoise regained after the experience of life.[24]

Transformation proceeds from the inner center, where we are aware of cosmic order and know we are united to universal life. This does not imply the destruction or negation of all individuality, but a shift of center from egocentric consciousness of the intellect to the depth-consciousness of the inner center. Intellect, reason, and logical thinking are not eliminated, but are used as necessary tools of existence in time-and-space, just as the ego has its justification for existence because it is the relative center of reference of our thinking.

In the same way, the experience of the senses are not thrust aside or devalued, but deepened and intensified so that they can become transparent in the light of complete consciousness:

> When it is a matter of rediscovering the essence and its unfolding, everything that the original still contains undiminished becomes of importance as a springboard and training-ground. This includes above all the primary experience of the senses, colour, sound, smell, tactile sensation and, above all, bodily feeling. All these things have to be rediscovered for this work on man. And it is not just a question of the rediscovery of primitive experience in the sphere of the prepersonal. Rather, the original sense-qualities possess, when experienced in meditation, in their sensory nature a suprasensory sensory depth. Thus experienced and understood, they form a root of the supersensory spirit, which opens up the fullness of life.[25]

The way to liberation is not a path of escape from the world, but a way to wholeness. Wholeness includes all mankind, the world and everything above the world, or, as it is said in the *I Ching*, "earth, man,

---

[24]Giuseppe Tucci, *The Theory and Practice of the Mandala* (York Beach, ME: Samuel Weiser, 1970; and London: Rider, 1961), p. 83.

[25]Karlfried Graf Dürckheim, *Zen and Us* (New York: Dutton, 1987).

and heaven." A human being seen as wholeness—as perfected—is not only a link between earth and heaven, between nature and spirit, but the union of both in the enlightened consciousness. According to modern research, it appears that in the universal scale, a human being is about halfway between the size of an atom and that of a fixed star like our sun.[26] If that is so, we could conclude that the highest consciousness lies in the middle between the infinitely small and infinitely large. The meaning of the humanity of individuality would then be clear. But only those people who have found their own center and achieved that inner completeness can attain to the highest state of consciousness. Being conscious—if we pursue the development of organic life from its origins—is clearly related to a certain degree of differentiation and centering. It follows that individualization is a prerequisite for the universe's becoming conscious of itself, or that the individual and the universe are the two inseparable poles of one and the same reality.

The elimination or denial of the individual would not, therefore, lead to the realization of universality, but to its elimination, while the denial of universality in favor of individuality would lead to stagnation and mental death. There is for mankind, therefore, "no access to the transcendental unless he has first clarified the structure of his own ego-centered consciousness."[27] In other words, we must make full use of *ratio*, of human reason, of the organizing capacity of logical thought, in order to reach the point where we come to the boundary of thought and can pass beyond it. Otherwise it will go with us, as with most religions based on faith, which—although they embody the most profound truths in their mythology and symbols—lose their effectiveness and power of conviction owing to the lack of an approach that satisfies the intellect. Even though the most profound is inaccessible to thought and cannot be grasped rationally, it is not in conflict with reason. A two-dimensional

---

[26]"Inside an atom the many small electrons circle round like planets round the sun, in a space which in relation to its size is no less extensive than the solar system. Approximately midway on the scale between the size of an atom and that of a fixed star is a formation no less wonderful—the human body."—Sir A.S. Eddington, *Stars and Atoms*, now out of print.

[27]Dürckheim, *Hara*, p. 76.

consciousness cannot conceive the nature of the third dimension, but that does not mean that the concepts of the second dimension are nullified in the third, any more than the cube nullifies the concept of a square. Just as a cube includes the existence of a square, so, too, transcendence does not involve the denial of the body or individual consciousness, but actually allows for the expansion and deepening of all human qualities.

This realization is also expressed in the doctrine of the psychic centers (*cakras*) of the human body; they symbolize progressively the increasing degree of awareness and differentiation of cosmic forces, and at the same time correspond to the elementary qualities or "aggregate states" of matter (solid, liquid, fiery, gaseous, etc.). According to the Tibetan Buddhist definition five such centers are distinguished:

1) The root-center (sacral plexus), which controls the regenerative and especially the reproductive powers;

2) The navel-center (solar plexus), which controls the nourishment-system, the transformative powers;

3) The heart-center (plexus cardiacus), which controls the system of blood-vessels;

4) The throat-center (plexus cervicus), which controls the breathing system;

5) The brain-center (cerebrum), which controls the cerebro-spinal nervous system.

Without going into details about these centers, let's discuss the general principles underlying this arrangement and this way of viewing. The two lowest centers represent earthbound forces, the creative and transformative forces of nature, as opposed to the two highest centers, in which cosmic and spiritual forces find expression. The heart-center is the ideal midpoint between earth and cosmos, the true center of a human being, in which heaven and earth, nature and spirit, emotion and reason establish a unity. Thus the heart-center represents the zone for the realization of all powers at the human level.

In agreement with this, the development of symbolic representation in meditative processes does not simply move upward from below by way of an ascending access of consciousness from the deepest, naturally-creative, instinctive center toward the highest organ of differentiated understanding. Instead—and here comes the parting of the ways between abstract-intellectual thought and the concrete-psychological view of the tantric approach—at this point the "return journey" sets in. After the attainment of the highest center, after becoming fully conscious in the comprehension of universal relationships and universal laws, there is a descent into the depths of the human heart, into the inner midpoint, in order—in all-embracing compassion for all that lives and breathes—to perfect the understanding that has been gained on the level of existence in space and time.

The breakthrough to transcendence is achieved by becoming fully conscious of the polar unity of the lower and upper centers, when therefore the consciousness of the depth of the origin and of the cosmogonic powers is raised up to the light of the highest understanding. This transcendence would be equivalent to a flight from the world and the dissolution of all the values of existence if did not, at the human level, become the focal point for a new and greater comprehension of life, where both poles or reality join together the living and breathing present moment of individual existence, and the supra-individual timeless which lies beyond all contrasts. Here transcendence becomes immanent reality and the world becomes a transparent *mandala* of the activity of the cosmos, reflecting outwardly what has been perfected within.

That this approach to the recognition and experience of the Vajrayana is not only accessible to "Oriental" people is demonstrated by the following deeply-felt words of Durkheim:

> To be able to fulfil his vocation, which is to prove and to bear witness to the Divine Being in his life, to ascend to the new mind, a man must first go down into the deeps of his whole and original nature. In order *to go out* to grasp the fullness

of the Primordial Unity he must first *go into* the original emptiness.

The hidden formative power of nature takes on its fullest meaning and effect for man's higher development only when he becomes conscious of its mysterious working. *Man* matures and completes himself only by becoming conscious of those great laws which, at the level of unconscious nature, are simply lived. But this is a special form of becoming unconscious.

But when man lifts himself from the earth-centre of his human nature to the heaven-centre of his spirit and when, in his heart centre he joyously accepts the obligation to actualize the Original Unity and its inherent order within his existence in this world, then will his insight and practice flow out in one stream of true creativity on earth.[28]

---

[28]Dürckheim, *Hara*, pp. 118, 119, 158, 178.

Lama Anagarika Govinda lived most of his adult life in Sri Lanka, India and Tibet. He studied and practiced several Buddhist traditions, but was viewed as a significant representative and interpreter of Tibetan Buddhism, spending over 20 years studying at the feet of masters in Tibetan hermitages and monasteries. He was committed to not only living a spiritual life but passing on his understanding to Western students exploring the spiritual path. His experiences as a pioneer in Buddhism provides a modern link between East and West.

Lama Anagarika Govinda was born Ernst Hoffman in Germany in 1898. He was both an artist and an author. He wrote the well-known *Foundations of Tibetan Mysticism* also published by Samuel Weiser, *The Inner Structure of the I Ching* published by Weatherhill, *A Living Buddhism for the West,* and *The Way of the White Clouds,* both published by Shambala. Lama Govinda died in 1985.

9897   5591